SPIRITED
PROSPECT

A PORTABLE HISTORY OF WESTERN
ART FROM THE PALEOLITHIC
TO THE MODERN ERA

D1279867

David D. Nolta and Charles A. Stigliano

Massachusetts College of Art and Design

cognella®
academic publishing

Bassim Hamadeh, CEO and Publisher
Michael Simpson, Vice President of Acquisitions
Jamie Giganti, Managing Editor
Jess Busch, Senior Graphic Designer
John Remington, Acquisitions Editor
Brian Fahey, Licensing Specialist
Sean Adams, Interior Design

ISBN: 978-1-63189-930-0 (pbk) / 978-1-63189-931-7 (br)

www.cognella.com   800-200-3908

Contents

vii...preface

1.......................................chapter one: History and Art

37..chapter two: The Greeks

61...chapter three: Rome

87..chapter four: East and West

109.............................chapter five: The High Middle Ages

135...chapter six: The Renaissance

179.......................................chapter seven: Barococo

209...........................chapter eight: The Modern World

239..Epilogue

245...Image Credits

Acknowledgments

The authors gratefully acknowledge the ongoing support and advice of their own teachers and students, without which and without whom this book would not be. Special mention must be made of our own earliest mentors, Walter Erlebacher and David Huntington. In the endless migration from comparative darkness to comparative light, from lesser to greater clarity, from the old oppressions and suppressions of culture to brighter varieties of freedom and new challenges and tyrannies and spurs, we travel together. Our families, too, have been very patient and a great help. Finally, any sacrifice this book entailed is made in thanks to the true source of any good it contains: Vincent J. Scully, Jr.

Preface

As you might suspect from its subtitle, this book was originally conceived and written to accompany a survey course in the history of Western art. The word "survey" is a rich and multivalent one, originating in the Latin "super" and "videre"—"see over" or "over view." Thus, in a scholastic context, a survey is usually a general or introductory examination of a broad topic. But the "super" in "super videre" can also mean "what is above," and as such, a survey can be thought of as looking at what stands out from or above its background, what transcends it. So, the survey of a battlefield tends to focus on the rises—the hills and bluffs that are potential obstacles to movement or easily defended elevations of the terrain. Similarly, a survey of the earth from space presents a picture of its uppermost—literally, its outstanding—features, mountain peaks, the light-filled towers of cities, and bodies of water that, however deep their beds, reflect light back up to the sky. A survey of the earth over a very long time would allow us to watch the emergence of these natural and manmade forms, which together might be taken to symbolize the ambition we have in ourselves and for what we create—the ambition to be seen.

First and foremost, then, our portable history is a concise textbook survey of Western art covering roughly five millennia of culture, focusing on, according to a tradition going back to the ancients (and sanctioned by Giorgio Vasari and his Renaissance contemporaries, as well as by writers in the eighteenth and nineteenth centuries who developed the discipline of art history), outstanding works of architecture, sculpture, and painting from the canon of art—which is our common legacy. Many books, and especially textbooks, are written in reaction to other books; that is certainly true of this book. In the first place, it was written to be read comfortably, even in bed, to which and elsewhere you may carry it without exhaustion. Unlike all other surveys of Western art, this one will not crush your rib cage or, if you are near-sighted, your collarbone, nor, should you drop it, your foot. Another of its critical aims is that it *be* a book, more precisely, a continuous prose narrative, illustrated with lovely images but not broken into bits by them or other distractions. If it sounds coot-ish, we don't care: the tendency of most survey books nowadays is to take their cues from the computer screen, with each page a collage of competing information boxes, diagrams, definitions—all in a bewildering range of shapes, styles, typefaces, and tones. Ostensibly anticipatory and comprehensive, the end result is discontinuous and distracting and invariably undermines a primary purpose of the survey to provide a cohesive view of things from a unifying perspective. And no survey is ever comprehensive; this one isn't. It is highly selective, a first view of outstanding features that enliven and help to determine the landscape of Western civilization.

That this is a Western survey is, of course, the most obvious proof of its selectivity. If, like all of our students, you are studying art and art history in New England, if you are an American embarking upon a college education anywhere in this country, if you were raised in Europe or the United States, you are inevitably, to no little degree, the product of and heir to intellectual traditions—including ways of seeing, classifying, and understanding visual phenomena—that first emerged among the ancient Greeks. Not merely traditions of classicism, these are classical traditions. Many of them you will go on to question, to benefit from, and to defy, whether or not you are aware of them. Better to be aware of them.

Finally, you will notice that our history ends with the first half of the twentieth century, a time in which many of our grandparents were alive. There are several reasons for this, all having to do with our primary motivations for writing the book, and—to use a much-used phrase—its educational mission. We have, in short (and at the risk of seeming very old-fashioned, but that is apt), accented the *history* in this history of Western art. Everybody in America is exposed, virtually from birth, to Andy Warhol's silk screen images. But, how many young people have seen a picture of the *Kritios Boy* or been taught to appreciate the curves of Borromini's little church of Saint Charles? The art of the twentieth century is a survey unto itself, and to be frank, copyright costs prohibit the inclusion of most contemporary art work. This is, after all, meant to be an affordable, as much as a portable, history of Western art.

Liber brevis, ars vita
DNC MMXIV

one

History and Art

In the beginning was the work, and the first work appeared without a written label. Of course, to say of any work of art that "it appeared" is already misleading, or at least incomplete. Never does a work of art simply "appear," though the primary proof of its existence is that it did and does appear; it is visible, accessible to what is arguably, immemorially, the most popular of the physical senses: sight.

But what makes this work—real in its visibility—art? What makes it art is that it *is* work. In short, for all that its appearance is the proof of its existence, and for all that its existence may continue for numberless generations, such that we are justified in thinking of particular works of art as not merely enduring but truly permanent, never does a work of art simply appear. To be more precise, never does a work of art appear of necessity, according to the laws and processes of nature.

The laws of nature, our versions of which are, even today, subject to serious revision (that is to say, scientists, even now, are grappling with the true nature of these laws), determine and allow us to understand

physical, including visual, phenomena. Stars appear in black space, glaciers melt, and a man and a woman procreate. But the phenomenon of art is not determined, as it cannot be explained, exclusively by natural laws. The creation of a work of art may, indeed, involve a powerful expression of energy. More often than not, it does require the transformation of materials. Impulses that lead to the creation of art have often been compared to the sexual urge, and doubtless, they have much in common with the natural impulse of most organisms to reproduce. But the "appearance" of a work of art is not necessitated by, nor subject to, the rules and processes of nature alone. There is even a time-honored tradition of thinking of art as *contra naturam*—against nature.

But that can't be the whole story—it never is. And so there are many people, scientists and philosophers included, who will say that there is nothing that humans do that is not perfectly natural, even (to an extent that varies depending upon which scientist or philosopher you are talking to) predictable, and determined by natural laws. Furthermore, neither the impulse to create nor the execution is an exclusively human function; the non-human world provides abundant proof of the natural creativity of organisms occupying different branches on the evolutionary tree, from the impressive architectural achievements of ants and bees to the domestic decorating techniques of the blue bower bird. But unlike the birds and the bees, human beings are not genetically programmed when it comes to the specific decisions that result in the visual transformation of their environment. The perfect engineering of the honeycomb is not the result of an individual bee's decision to "go with that," nor, to the extent that our experience allows us to infer a rule, is it possible that bees will suddenly switch to star-shaped cells for their combs. The impulse—the necessity—to create is there and carried

Figure 1.1 Blue Bower Bird

out; we share that instinct, that need, just as we are challenged and inspired by the result, the hive. But the appearance of what we create when we create art is determined by a complex process of decisions with an inexhaustible variety of potential results, and in this respect, we are working outside the laws of nature. In creating a pot to carry water, the creator is fulfilling a natural impulse—in effect, our "bee" side—derived, at least in part, from the necessity and convenience of finding a way to contain more liquid for a longer period of time than a pair of cupped hands, or a shell, or a gourd can hold. But, the pot we create, even if it looks just like any number of other pots, will inevitably represent the outcome of numerous decisions that are negotiated first in the mind. And the "inessential" decoration of such a pot—the decoration that is in no way required to fulfill our initial need or desire for a container—will involve still more variables and decisions, anxieties and gratifications virtually unknown to the non-human creatures with whom we share the world. And so, to adapt an oft-quoted, variously attributed saying, art really is in the details. And these details are determined primarily by the human mind reimagining the environment and drawing upon the capacity of the whole organism, often in collaboration with one or many other organisms, to realize an intangible concept in a tangible, visible form.

Art before History

So, art is natural and unnatural. With this paradox in mind, let's look at one of the oldest works of art in existence, the so-called *Venus of Willendorf*. This small (roughly four inches long) chunk of limestone is so much more than that; first and foremost, as we can all agree, it is not a natural rock formation. Our eyes tell us that it was created by human hands, and

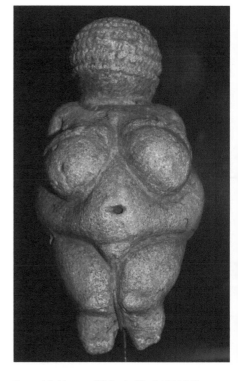

Figure 1.2 "Venus" of Willendorf (c. 26,000 BC)

our most reliable dating technology suggests that this creation occurred at least 28,000 years ago. Thus, we know that it's man-made, and it's old. Beyond that, how might we begin to classify this work, to describe it, in order to understand it better?

If there is a spectrum that includes, at either end, the natural and the man-made, there is, around that pole corresponding to the man-made, another spectrum that will prove helpful when it comes to thinking about and interpreting works of art. This spectrum has, as its poles, the representational and the abstract—or we could call them the naturalistic and the abstract.[1]

Where would we locate the "*Venus of Willendorf*" on this vast, imaginary, but very useful, spectrum? It has an overall form and many features (hips, breasts, vagina) that are recognizably those of a human female. But that general form has seemingly been altered from what many viewers might think of—justifiably or not—as the norm, and many of those features (the size of the figure, the tiny, skeletal arms, the head almost entirely covered with a thick, regular pattern—hair, perhaps, or some sort of hat or head covering?) are drastically different from any credible human features. Empathy—which is a very good thing—leads us, when encountering any representation of a human form, to an automatic comparison. We register, assess, and question the distance between the figurative object and our own experience of our physical selves. This discrepancy, which arises primarily in the consciousness of the viewer, initiates the conversation between the viewer and the maker of the work. The work is where the dialogue occurs.

In our dialogue with the so-called *Venus of Willendorf*, what does she say? Or what does the person who made her—the artist—say through or with her? Certainly nothing about being a goddess, much less about being the Roman goddess of love and beauty. The Romans didn't exist when she was made and dropped or buried near the banks of the Danube in Austria, where she was discovered in 1908. Remember, the earliest art bears no labels—and that is an open invitation to us to speculate freely, keeping in mind that our speculation is trustworthy in proportion to how closely it remains connected to the physical object. Having located the *Venus* somewhere near the middle of that spectrum between the

---

1   But we don't want to call them the "realistic" and the abstract, not yet anyway. The term "realistic" is a lightning rod for controversy; scholars come close to killing when they hear it tossed around. So, we can avoid both the controversy and the dangerous scholars by simply avoiding the term until we come to use it formally, and safely, with a capital "R," when discussing nineteenth-century French art.

naturalistic and the abstract, we can probably agree with scholars that the emphasis on her breasts, belly, buttocks, and genitals conveys an artistic priority often, if inadequately, equated with fertility. In her nudity, in the abstract exaggeration of breasts and belly relative to arms and feet, the so-called *Venus* certainly focuses our attention on the site of procreation and the avenue of birth, on the abdomen, which is the first abode of the child, and on the breasts, which sustain human life in its earliest stages outside the womb. Beyond this, it is difficult to speak with certainty as to what the *Venus* means, though it is worth adding that she feels good in the palm of the hand—in other words, with her compact, rounded forms, and her diminutive size, she appeals to the sense of touch, and for this reason and others she is sometimes, again controversially, identified as a fetish object as well as a personification of fertility. But as human history clearly shows, anything on earth can be a fetish.

From the same long prehistoric period that includes what we would be more prudent to call the *Willendorf Woman* and comparable small-scale figurative sculptures, are staggering pictures decorating the rock walls of caves in Southern France and Northern Spain. Like the little statues, but on a much larger scale, these cave paintings present a frank illustration of what art is in its primeval beginnings: the coming together of the human hand with stone, through the intermediation of manipulative tools, themselves presumably or to some extent man-made. And as with the statues, the cave paintings display combinations of naturalism and abstraction. The history of painting, which will rise to a most prestigious position as one of the finest of the fine arts, begins with these great Stone Age images of bulls, horses, bison, and rhinoceros, their silhouettes and hides in mineral pigments brushed and blown on the irregular surfaces of the subterranean passages, often to great illusionistic effect. And there are human figures and motifs as well, outlines of hands that might be interpreted as individual signatures and are, in any case, visual indications of the pivotal reality of human beings not merely among such animals—who were, of course, their prey—but also within the works representing them. In other words, the hand may function as a sort of notary's seal, testifying to the truth of the artist's experiences (real, imagined, dreamed, or all of these), as well as to the artist's role in the remaking of experience.

At times exploiting the underlying contours of the stone, many of the prehistoric cave paintings display a remarkable naturalism when it comes to the shapes and textures of animals, not to mention their movements. (We will see that the suggestion of movement in a static medium is no small artistic feat; it

Figure 1.3 Lascaux Cave Painting (c. 15,000 BC)

is, in fact, one of the great maddening goals exercising the ingenuity of artists throughout history.) It's interesting, however, that the same naturalism does not characteristically enter into the considerably rarer images of the full-length human figure. For instance, the caves at Lascaux, France, painted around 17,000 years ago, contain numerous credible evocations of running horses and shaggy bison and huge, horned aurochs.[2] But there is also a very famous painting on the wall of the pit, or well, at Lascaux, which shows a range of what we might truly call *styles* in the representation of organic forms, from the highly abstract stick figure of a male to the slightly more fleshed-out bison looming over him to the considerably more naturalistic rhinoceros facing away from both of them on the left. Possibly, but by no means necessarily, a *palimpsest*—the work of different hands over indetermi-nate time—this may be a hunting scene, according to many scholars. But if that is true, who's hunting whom? The man—if he is a man, and not a mesomorphic

---

2   Aurochs (both singular and plural): ox, massive ancestor of modern cattle; the last example died in 1627 AD.

man-bird—seems to be immobilized, lying down; his actual position relative to the beasts remains ambiguous. Similarly, it appears as though the upright bison's entrails are tumbling out. But the interaction between the two, not to mention between one or both of them and the rhinoceros, like the meaning of the bird on the stick, defies definitive explanation.

The *Venus of Willendorf* and the cave paintings of Lascaux, Altamira, Chauvet and elsewhere all belong to the Paleolithic or Early Stone Age, a phase of human evolution stretching over millions of years, characterized by the invention and improvement of rudimentary stone tools and weapons and culminating (at least from our point of view) in the very first works of art. When people began to settle into communities, farm the land and domesticate animals, and develop crafts such as cloth-making and pottery, those people entered the Neolithic or New Stone Age, which began in the Middle East by the tenth millennium BC. Here it is perhaps wise to pause before the towering challenge that involves another man-made dichotomy, the concept of the world as being divided into East and West.

What you are reading right now is an introduction to the history of Western art. The term "Western" implies a perspective, a traditional and potentially very useful, but also potentially invidious, way of seeing the world as two halves or parts, East and West. Again, this division is a human invention imposed on a continuum of spatial reality. Consequently, the attributes we associate with East and West, like the boundaries between them, have changed and shifted through-out the centuries. Although imaginary, purely relative, and ever-changing, such a division of the world has ancient roots. Even more pertinent to our exploration of the history of art, the concept of such a division was widely and enthusiasti-cally revived in the self-described West during the late eighteenth and nine-teenth centuries and played no inconsiderable role in the evolution of European, including Europeanized American, education. In fact, this is the same period in which the history of art as a formal discipline entered the curriculum. And so, sanctioned by English and German universities in the nineteenth century, and spreading to all American high schools throughout the twentieth, there is a tra-dition of scholarship that identifies itself with the West and that finds its origins in classical antiquity, specifically in the civilization that emerged in Greece by the end of the sixth century BC. And the relatively new discipline of art history is informed by, as it informs and illustrates, this conceptual identification of Western culture.

Egypt

If, as English-speaking students of art history in the opening years of the twenty-first century, we are heirs to a Western civilization that has long and often identified itself as beginning with the Greeks of the first millennium BC, we should remember that the Greeks themselves venerated the already ancient civilization of Egypt as the great font of art and creative ideals. The kingdom of Egypt, like the royal city states of Mesopotamia, emerges from the Neolithic Era or Late Stone Age with, among other innovations, the invention of writing, around the middle of the fourth millennium BC. From this point on, history will be a matter of written testimony.

Among the first works of art to combine image and text in a mutually informative and consequently historical way is the *Palette of Narmer*. With its arrow-head shape and shallow, round well, the Egyptian palette was a toiletry article used in the preparation of protective eye makeup; the larger-than-average size of the *Palette of Narmer* suggests that it was probably decorative rather than

Figure 1.4 Palette of Narmer (c. 3,000 BC)

functional. It is carved of slate, both sides covered with pictures and *hieroglyphs*, or picture-signs, which constitute the earliest Egyptian writing system. The story told on both sides of the *Palette* is of King Narmer's great military victory over an enemy, and the aftermath of that victory, seen in the gruesome images of the vanquished, decapitated dead. So much is easily deduced. Less certain, but still credible, is the common interpretation of the two reliefs as illustrating the unification of Egypt in the pre-dynastic period, for, just as surely as the Nile cleaves and sustains the whole territory from north to south, the very idea of Egypt as a unified land grows out of the notion that the country was once divided along an East–West axis into two separate and antagonistic territories, Upper (in fact, Southern Egypt, upriver), and Lower (Northern Egypt, the river's vast delta). The *Palette of Narmer*, then, would represent a mythic battle in which the Horus Narmer,[3] wearing the bowling-pin shaped "white" crown of Upper Egypt, conquers the ruler of the marshier regions of Lower Egypt. On the well-side of the *Palette*, Narmer, wearing the "red" crown of Lower Egypt, reviews the army and the enemy troops he has defeated.

Whether or not the images of the *Palette of Narmer* refer to a real battle— whether or not the horned creatures surmounting both sides are to be identified with the worship of the cow-goddess Hathor or allude simply to the bullish strength of the king; whether or not the bull bulldozing the town is also an allusion to the king; etc.—they reflect artistic tendencies and representational formulae that will last as long as the unified kingdom itself. And so, in the recurring figure of Narmer, we find an example of the composite point of view adopted more or less universally by artists of the ancient world. This viewpoint allows the artist to provide more visual information about the figure than is optically available at any one time, combining a profile of the legs and head with frontal views of the chest and eye. The hieratic scale, too, is adopted here, according to which size is a vehicle for expressing importance: on the well-side, Narmer, as king, is larger than the long-haired figure in front of him, who may be a priest, and the long-haired figure, in turn, is larger than the soldiers. Exploiting the format of the *Palette* by carving both sides reinforces the suggestion that we are viewing a sequence of events over time, an act of subjugation and the widespread repercussions of that act. In other words, this is a *diachronic* work, and thus, narrative in the truest sense.

---

3   Horus is the falcon god, whose name, in combination with the name of an individual, denotes kingship; hence, Horus Narmer, or King Narmer.

With its succinct evocation of human conflict, wrath, and vengeance, Narmer's pre-Dynastic palette packs a wallop. That impact increases proportionately with the size of Egyptian works of art. By the early Dynastic period, Egyptian rulers (generically known as "Pharaohs," though that term does not come into use until the middle of the second millennium BC) have begun to build and decorate on a scale unprecedented in human history, and monumentality has already become a byword for all things Egyptian.

For many people, of course, the word "Egypt" immediately conjures up an image of the great pyramids at Giza, built by three successive kings—Khufu, Khafre, and Menkaure—during the twenty-sixth and twenty-fifth centuries BC. The size and mass of these royal tombs looming above the desert confirms, on a vast architectural scale, what any mummy can tell you; namely, that death, proper burial, and the afterlife were preoccupations central to the existence of the ancient Egyptian people.

The first pyramid was built at Saqqara by the artist Imhotep for the Third Dynasty ruler, Zoser (or Djoser), in the twenty-seventh century BC. A limestone "step pyramid," it was originally a *mastaba*, a traditional type of tomb with four trapezoidal sides containing a *serdab* or small space for a statue of the deceased, the whole surmounting a burial chamber. Over time, several more mastabas were added above the original structure, decreasing in size toward the top, until the tomb assumed the basic pyramidal form we see today. This became the model for the true pyramids, with their unbroken triangular surfaces originally capped with a veneer of white limestone, built for the Fourth Dynasty kings at nearby Giza.

The primary purpose of the pyramids was the same as that of all Egyptian tomb-building and, on the individual level, the purpose of mummification itself: to preserve and to protect the body, in order that the deceased, king or commoner, could enjoy, via his or her *ka*, the afterlife.[4] References to and, even better, representations of the deceased helped to ensure the immortality of the ka by providing alternative houses for it; these might "stand in" for the mummified

---

4   The ka is difficult to define, though perhaps less difficult to comprehend. Egyptologists and historians of religion will often become cranky if you define the ka as "the soul." It can be thought of variously as the essence of.an individual's spirit or the larger spirit that is invested in each individual; an "other" you that is also you and potentially immortal. It may be fruitful to think of the ka in terms of the almost universal human tendency—as scientists have recently discovered, this tendency appears as early as infancy—to see ourselves dualistically, in both the first and the third persons.

Figure 1.5 Pyramids at Giza (2600 – 2450 BC)

remains, should anything cause them to deteriorate. And so, in Egypt, we find a clear, practical link between early figurative art and immortality, and, ka or no ka, that link continues to provide a primary motivation for portraiture to the present day.

Immortality was, of course, not the only purpose or message of the portraits that proliferated among the elite throughout pre-pharaonic and pharaonic Egyptian history. A sculpture in the Boston Museum of Fine Arts represents the ruler Menkaure, who built the last and smallest of the three great pyramids at Giza, with a woman, probably his queen. Though somewhat under life-size, this double portrait conveys monumentality and immutability—and strength. These qualities are the result of artistic choices, beginning with that of the material itself, greywacke, a hard and dense stone, difficult to carve. The bodies of Menkaure and his wife emerge, but only partially, from the material, as though to establish an ideal of unchanging rule; the stone is part of them, its strength is theirs to maintain this rule. The king's proportions; his rigid, rigidly symmetrical, pose; his muscular chest and upper arms; and the absolute frontality and stasis he shares with his wife are all features of a formula for aristocratic portraiture that remained standard in Egypt for thousands of years. Though the queen has an arm around her husband, and though both have one thick foot forward, there is no suggestion of movement. These figures, and hundreds of royal statues like them, in various materials on every scale, reiterate as powerfully as the pyramids the will of the dynastic rulers to survive; they personify Egypt's still-valid claim to endure.

As we have indicated, the formulaic treatment of the ruler had already been established in Egypt by the end of the fourth millennium BC. There is no great stylistic difference, therefore, between an image of Khafre and one of his immediate successor, Menkaure, nor between the latter and Ramses II, who ruled Egypt 1,200 years later and whose mortuary temple at Abu Simbel was decorated with no fewer than four colossal (more than 60 feet high) statues of the seated king. More surprising evidence of the durability of the aristocratic formulae is presented to

Figure 1.6 Menkaure and Khamerernebty (c. 2480 BC)   Figure 1.7 Ramses II at Abu Simbel (c. 1250 BC)

Figure 1.8 Mortuary Temple of Hatshepsut (after 1490 BC)   Figure 1.9 Hatshepsut (c. 1480 BC)

us in certain portraits of Hatshepsut, another builder of an impressive mortuary temple, this one at Deir el-Bahari.[5]

Hatshepsut was the principal consort of her half-brother, the Pharaoh Thutmose II. When Thutmose II died, Hatshepsut was made regent for her adolescent stepson, Thutmose III, but as the boy grew, Hatshepsut proved reluctant to relinquish power; in fact, she declared herself Pharaoh, and repeatedly had herself represented as such, that is, in the *nemes* (linen headgear like that worn by Menkaure in the Boston Museum of Fine Arts statue) and false beard of the male ruler. When at last she was dead and buried in her fantastic, cliff-side mortuary complex, her stepson took revenge by having many of her images defaced. Vandalism and iconoclasm—often politically motivated—are presumably as old as art itself.

If the standards and formulae we see repeated for royal imagery remained fairly constant in Egyptian art, it is not surprising to see something of a trickle-down effect when we consider representations of human beings occupying lower rungs of the social ladder. Near the northern boundary of the great necropolis

---

5   Notice that pyramid-building goes out of fashion by the middle of the sixteenth century BC, a casualty of changes in custom and the insurmountable fact that such large and expensive stone structures served as convenient advertisements to irreverent grave robbers.

Figure 1.10 Ti Hippopotamus Hunting (c. 2400 BC)

Figure 1.11 Nefertiti (c. 1340 BC)

at Saqqara, for example, is the lavishly decorated mastaba of Ti, a Fifth Dynasty court official whose duties included the oversight of important temples. In a famous section of painted limestone relief removed from the tomb's interior, Ti is shown standing in a boat while his servants hunt hippopotami. The artist has used the same composite viewpoint (profile head and legs, frontal chest and eye) and the same hieratic scale (Ti's size dwarfs that of his men) that we find in the *Palette of Narmer*. As in the *Palette*, such artistic clues are visual confirmations of the power and position of the main figure. But for all that Ti's proportions and posture and the serene authority suggested by his stance were clearly imitated from royal images, there's something that Ti's tiny menservants have that Ti doesn't. We might be tempted to say here that the servants "have" movement—but that would be a bit inaccurate, since in fact neither Ti nor his men, nor, for that matter, the hippopotami they are hunting among the fishes and papyri in the pond, nor the foxes and birds in the trees overhead, can truthfully be said to move. But, the servants' greater flexibility and the variety of their poses suggest movement, not to mention the sounds of rustling and splashing that would accompany a hunt through the marshes. This relaxation of the formal rules of representation for less prestigious individuals is a recurring phenomenon, and not merely in Egyptian art.

There is one fascinating moment in the history of Egypt when the old artistic formulae were tossed out completely by the royal family themselves. We are referring to the reign of Amenhotep IV, who, in a dramatic, widely unpopular, and consequently very daring, move, abandoned the many gods of his ancestors and priests and declared a new, monotheistic religion

Figure 1.12 Akhenaten and his Family (c. 1340 BC)

of the sun-disk divinity Aten. Taking the name Akhenaten, which might be translated poetically as "the right arm of Aten," the new Pharaoh also abandoned his father's capital city of Thebes and built a new capital, Akhetaten, the "horizon of Aten," now known as Amarna. Akhenaten's primary wife was Nefertiti, whose famous beauty is best known from a carved and painted, but never-completed, stone bust now in Berlin. What is astonishing is that the refined femininity of this and other portraits of the queen can also be found in images of her husband, who is invariably represented as epicene or androgynous, a pharaonic characterization altogether at odds with the longstanding type of stolid, royal masculinity established in the pre-dynastic period and accessible in thousands of works of art, including the *Palette of Narmer*, the Boston *Menkaure*, and the colossal *Ramseses* of Abu Simbel. A succinct example of the revolutionary Amarna style is the limestone relief of Akhenaten and Nefertiti "at home," enjoying the company of three of their many daughters, one of whom the king tenderly kisses. Here is a lively image of a loving family; the composite viewpoint is less noticeable among the sinuous curves of the bodies and draperies of both parents, shown blissfully, and *actively*, sharing a domestic moment under the protective beams of Aten. This loosening of ancient stylistic conventions, like the exclusive worship of the sun-disk, barely survived the reign of Akhenaten. His successor, possibly his son by a lesser wife, was the boy king, Tutankhamun, who in his turn abandoned Amarna, returned to the traditional religious practices, died at seventeen, and received a most lavish burial in the Valley of the Kings.

Mesopotamia

Mesopotamia, a vast fertile plain between and around the Tigris and Euphrates rivers where agriculture and the domestication of animals were established by 6000 BC, was home to some of the earliest known civilizations. The region never became a unified state like Egypt, but saw, instead, the development of large settlements that grew into cities and became independent city-states, each supported by what could be grown or grazed on their surrounding land and by trade established with their neighbors. It is here that we find the oldest examples of government, of organized worship, and of writing.

Sumer, a civilization in Southern Mesopotamia, was established as early as 4500 BC. In a landscape without significant resources of stone, metal, or wood,

Figure 1.13 Ziggurat at Ur (third millennium BC)

the primary building material was mud brick. The earliest Sumerian settlements comprised closely spaced homes with plastered floors and walls. These were often centered around a shrine (later a temple), in which wall paintings and baked clay or stone sculptures representing their gods have been found.

Later, in still larger cities, the central religious site became a temple complex, the focus of which was a *ziggurat*, or staged tower, a huge structure of mud brick, comparable to a stepped pyramid, with support walls and long, ramp-like staircases. The function of ziggurats is unknown, but there is some evidence that the Sumerians believed that gods dwelt in the mountains to the north and east of Mesopotamia. In the flat landscape of Sumer, these massive constructions are essentially man-made mountains with a temple on the highest level. It is therefore reasonable to assume that they represented a means of getting human beings physically closer to the gods. The ziggurat at Babylonia, said to have been the highest at over 250 feet, has been identified by some with the Biblical Tower of Babel. The remains of these structures are still visible at a number of sites, the best preserved (and most heavily renovated) being the ziggurat at Ur.

In the temple complex surrounding the ziggurat at Uruk (now Warka) an alabaster vase was found that shows nude figures bearing offerings to the Goddess Inanna, like the *Palette of Narmer*, among the oldest narrative relief sculptures ever found (3200 BC to 3000 BC). The procession moves from bottom to top with the human figures encountering the Goddess on the highest tier. Unlike the Egyptian relief, there is no schematization of the figures; one is struck by how ordinary the humans appear. Their shape, and even that of Inanna, is natural. Their proportions are a bit squat; they have a stocky, well-fed quality, and they appear to be bending slightly beneath the weight of their offerings. It is also notable that the mortals are roughly the same size as the Goddess and standing on the same floor, the only visible difference in power being that they are nude, while she is clothed.

Figure 1.14 Alabaster Vase from Uruk. Detail. (c. 3000 BC)

Figure 1.15 Goddess from Uruk (c. 3000 BC)

Figure 1.16 Sumerian Priest from Tel Asmar (c. 2700 BC)

From the same period, an alabaster head of a goddess, also from Uruk, demonstrates, again, a tendency toward naturalism in the sensitive modeling of the face and lips. The eyes and eyebrows, originally inlaid in another material, are oversized but not nearly so much as in the group of marble figures found in the temple complex at Tel-Asmar (2700 BC). These figures are highly simplified; the parts of the body and clothing are little more than cylinders and cones, yet their common gesture is human and natural, a little sag in the shoulders, a slight tilt forward. The enormous eyes may reflect an attempt to represent a momentary state of ecstasy or enlightenment brought about by communion with a deity. The posture of the figures suggests prayer, a hopeful upward gaze and clasped hands.

A wooden object heavily inlaid with shell, lapis lazuli, and red limestone was found in a grave in the Royal Cemetery at Ur. Its function is unknown, but it was once thought to have been carried on a pole during processions, and has consequently been named the *Standard of Ur* (2600 BC). Heavily restored, it appears to be a commemorative depiction of a Sumerian military victory. Some of the figures are wearing the same cone-shaped skirts as the Tel-Asmar figures, and have a similar gesture with hands clasped before their chests. All of them have a great deal in common with the worshippers from the Warka vase, the same short, dumpy proportions and rounded slouch. None of the figures can be said to inspire feelings of power or strength. Some of the seated figures in the top register of the so-called "Peace" side, including the slightly larger figure of a ruler, appear well-fed and pampered. We can see here the struggle to portray a convincing two-dimensional image of a human being without the guidance of a schematic system, such as the Egyptians had recourse to. There is something good-natured and congenial about all of the figures. They are human, though some of their positions create problems of depth and foreshortening; any attempt to deal with perspective is awkward.

Things are a little more graceful in the images on the sounding board of a lyre, one of four such lyres found in the Royal Cemetery at Ur. Using the same technique of shell inlay on wood, the image seems to be that of a preparation for some other worldly, possibly underworldly, banquet. Animals bear food and drink, an ass plays a lyre, and in the lowest tier, a human-scorpion hybrid is attended by a goat. Here, despite the subject matter (the inclusion of mesomorphs, for example), the style tends more toward naturalism; not only in the details of forms, but also in the gestures, there is less concern for finding poses that keep all limbs visible in a two dimensional plane. The top panel shows a human being between two human-headed bulls, each sporting a human beard; the man could be embracing, taming, or wrestling them. The same instrument features a beautifully rendered bull of gold leaf and lapis lazuli over a wooden form. The Bull wears a human beard identical to those pictured in the sounding board.

Around 2300 BC, King Sargon of Akkad came to be the ruler of the collected city states of Sumer. The Akkadians were a Semitic people, descended

Figure 1.17 Standard of Ur (c. 2600 BC)

Figure 1.18 Sounding Board of a Lyre. Detail. (c. 2700 BC)

Figure 1.19 Akkadian Head of a Ruler (c. 2300 BC)

from nomads who had settled in Northern Mesopotamia many generations before. Although a great deal of Sumerian influence is visible in the few Akkadian artifacts available to us, their sculpture is of a profoundly different nature.

The Akkadian *Head of a Ruler*, cast in bronze, has none of the easygoing spirit of Sumerian sculpture. While the beard, the inlaid eyes, and details of the modeling have parallels in Sumerian art, the position of the eyebrows conveys a sternness not visible in earlier work from the region. The modeling of form is sharper, with a nice balance between naturalism and stylization. The face is not as full, there is no feeling of softness or complacency, the sculpture, instead, seems to indicate power. If the nature of the artwork gives us any indication of the nature of the people who made it, this bronze is a portrait of a more disciplined and driven culture.

This is confirmed by the other major example of Akkadian art, the *Victory Stele of Naram-Sin* (2200 BC) This stone carving shows the great grandson of Sargon leading his army to victory against the Lullubi mountain dwellers. Here, the victorious soldiers are striding with great energy up a mountain path, all of them carved in the same manner and nearly the same position, face in profile, shoulders seen from the front, a narrow waist (rare in Sumerian art), and left knee raised high. The enemy is in disarray, falling, trampled beneath the feet of the conqueror or fleeing in panic. The eyes of all, victors and vanquished alike, are on Naram-Sin, the tallest figure by far, fiercely erect and marching with the same stride as his warriors. His eyes are on the two suns above, representing the gods who bless his victory, but it is clear that he alone is the star and focus of this scene.

The rule of the Akkadians ended around 2100 BC when they were conquered by a warlike people, the Guti, from the northern mountain area. The next sixty years were a period of disarray and destruction until, with the Guti unable to gain definitive control over the region, the Sumerians managed to reestablish power under the leadership of the rulers of Ur. From the City of Lagash, which maintained its independence and was spared most of the turmoil, are more than twenty statues of the king, Gudea, in various types of stone. Except for one bare arm, the figures are posed and dressed in a manner very similar to the Tel-Asmar figures, but the Gudea figures are more refined. The eyes and eyebrows, now carved in stone, mimic the contours of the shell and lapis inlays of the earlier centuries. While the face has regained some of the Sumerian roundness, there is a clarity of form similar to that of the Akkadian *Head of a Ruler*, and the wide-eyed look has been toned down to one of respect-ful dignity. Worth noting is the attention to anatomical definition in the bare arm and shoulder. The modeling of the form gives the appearance of physical strength, and this is an early instance of musculature contributing to a physical ideal.

Figure 1.20 Victory Stele of Naram-Sin (c. 2200 BC)

Figure 1.21 Gudea of Lagash (c. 2050 BC)

Figure 1.22 Stele of Hammurabi (c. 1790 BC)

The succeeding period saw the rise of Babylonia, in Southern Mesopotamia. By 1780 BC, it was the most powerful of the city-states and the latest to establish a centralized government. Hammurabi, the sixth king of Babylonia, is famous for standardizing a code of law in a land where various successive regimes had, for centuries, been generating confusing and conflicting ideas of contracts, behavior, crime, and punishment.

The best surviving example of the code of Hammurabi is engraved on a diorite *stele* over seven feet tall. At the top, in relief, is Hammurabi, receiving his authority from the god Shamash. This format (a seated god approached by a mortal) was fairly common in Mesopotamian cylinder seals and had been repeated so often as to become formulaic, but this version brings new life to the genre.

Shamash is shown seated in the composite perspective. He wears a horned helmet and in his hand he is holding, perhaps offering, the ring and the rod, symbols of power. Hammurabi faces him, one arm raised in worship. His bare right shoulder and arm appear in profile joined to a chest and left shoulder seen from the front, while his face is clearly in profile. His traditional cylindrical robe has a long concave contour interrupted by the projecting elbow of the draped arm. If the god were to stand, he would be nearly twice the height of the human. The combination is such that Shamash appears formal and solid, powerful and immovable while Hammurabi, seemingly caught in the motion of turning, seems smaller, weaker, and a little off balance.

The reign of Babylonia ended around 1600 BC. There was again a long period of turmoil and conflict, with wars, military raids from the mountain regions, and migrations of various cultures through the area. The land between the Tigris and Euphrates rivers was, as we have seen, always a high-traffic area. Without significant natural defenses, the cities in the broad flat plain of the region were always open to attack. The Hittites, an Indo-European people, controlled an area to the north so vast that it rivaled that of Egypt, and their massive stone architecture in Anatolia was said to have been made by giants. From the curving stones of an archway at Hattusa (modern Boghazkoy, Turkey; the arch was in use during the fourteenth and thirteenth centuries BC) emerge two powerful lions, seemingly imbedded in the rock, inseparable from the architecture, clearly conveying the strength and threatening power that were obviously, if

Figure 1.23 Hittite Lion Gate at Boghazkoy, Turkey (c. 1300 BC)

not exclusively, Hittite ideals. These aggressive, energetic people were, at times, involved in trade with the growing Assyrian civilization to the northeast, the Mesopotamian city-states, Egypt to the south, and numerous other cultures in various stages of development. Over centuries, through trade, diplomacy, and war, these cultures were involved in a constant exchange of aesthetic, religious, and civil ideas and influences.

Sometime after 900 BC, Mesopotamia fell under the control of the Assyrians. These fiercely warlike people had gained enormous wealth through their success in battle, and their building projects were more ambitious than any yet seen in the region. The character of Assyrian art grew out of the need to overwhelm the viewer with the might of their military and the power of their king. At Kalhu (modern Nimrud), the walls of the throne room and reception areas of the palace of Ashurnasirpal II (ruled c. 883–859 BC) were covered with limestone reliefs of battle and hunting scenes, executed with unprecedented boldness. Every panel bore the name of Ashurnasirpal and told the story of his exploits. The *cuneiform* (a writing system of wedge-shaped characters) is often directly superimposed on the sculpted relief and is both texture and text. While the themes of carnage and conquest are repetitive, the necessity of creating a historical narrative led to new ways of composing in a two dimensional space and greater possibilities for suggesting movement among figures.

The entrances and doorways at Kalhu, reminiscent of Hittite structures, were protected by enormous sculpted guardians: lions, lion-men and *lamassu* (human-headed bulls) of limestone with open, flowing wings. The faces, with

Figure 1.24 Assyrian Lamassu (ninth century BC)

long beards and wide eyes, follow a tradition as old as the Sumerian period, but the sculpture itself is bolder and more powerful than anything seen so far in Mesopotamia. The stone is beautifully carved and polished and the various textures of beard, hair, feathers, and fur serve as both representations of nature and as intricate abstract patterns.

The Assyrians continued to build; the citadel begun by Sargon II in Khorsabad (717 BC) covered more than 20 acres and included an elevated palace and a ziggurat seven levels high. The palace of Ashurbanipal (668–627 BC) in Nineveh again featured scenes of war and hunting (an Assyrian king's glory was apparently directly related to the quantity of real estate captured or life, human and animal, he had taken). The staleness of the themes was often overcome by the inventiveness of the artists. Whole armies in disarray form rhythmic patterns, and natural elements, such as trees or rivers, provide details

Figure 1.25 Dying Lioness from Nineveh (seventh century BC)

that shape landscapes. In the hunting scenes, there are variations in the composition of the panels that are almost cinematic; some feature a number of lions either charging or falling before the king's arrows, others focus on a single animal. In many cases, the flight or struggle of the lions shows a surprising empathy for the king's victims.

The Assyrian Empire began to crumble during Ashurbanipal's reign, and ended during that of his son. There was a brief resurgence of Babylonia and the Sumerian culture, and during this period, the famous ziggurat of Babylon was built. Babylon itself was, in turn, conquered by the Persians, whose empire expanded dramatically during the sixth and fifth centuries BC, such that it came to include Egypt and very nearly the entire Aegean.

The Aegean

When we consider that Western Civilization usually locates its roots in the ancient Aegean, it is surprising to realize how little civilization there was in this region at the beginning of the third millennium BC. We have seen that, by this time, the Sumerians and the Egyptians had developed vast and complex governmental and religious systems; they had invented written languages; they had created monumental architectural structures, and standardized artistic practices to reflect and enhance their respective cultures. Nothing comparable existed among their contemporaries in the Aegean, which is not to say that there was no civilization.

Figure 1.26 Cycladic Female (third millennium BC)

Throughout the third millennium, a people flourished on the large group of islands in the Southern Aegean known as the Cyclades. Though pre-historic, the Cycladic people nevertheless left behind a variety of artifacts, including pottery and, most interesting of all, marble figurative sculptures.

Ranging in size from one or two inches to over five feet, most of these sculptures are of nude females; traditionally they are associated with burial pits.

The same basic form—flat, with small breasts sometimes positioned awkwardly near the shoulders; tapering arms folded over the waist to isolate a squarish belly; a simple, incised triangle indicating the genitals; and a lozenge-shaped head with a fin-like nose—is repeated over and over, though with considerable variety in terms of proportion and detail. Given their gender, their nudity, and their usual discovery among funerary remains, scholars tend to interpret them as idols, possibly, like the much earlier *Venus of Willendorf*, as fetishes; more precisely, they interpret them as fertility idols accompanying the deceased into a death that may also be a rebirth. Likewise, the sculptures may personify death itself. In any case, they are compact and introverted figures; with their knees slightly bent, their arms drawn tightly in, and their inscrutable heads thrown back, they seem perhaps chilled, even shivering, as though they have just come into, or through, the cold.

Overlapping with, and eventually eclipsing, the Cycladic people, the Mediterranean civilization known to us as Minoan originated on the largest, southernmost island of the Aegean, Crete, and was the dominant culture throughout all the Greek islands from about the middle of the third to the middle of the second millennium BC. The name comes from the legendary King Minos, ruler of the people of Knossos, son of Europa and reluctant stepfather to the minotaur.

Minoan culture is remarkable in a number of ways. Unlike their Egyptian and Mesopotamian contemporaries, the Minoans appear to have been unconcerned with history; their enormous artistic output in numerous media includes no monuments or memorials commemorating individuals or events. Their greatest architectural efforts seem not to have been temples but rather centers of administration and luxurious living. The Minoans of Crete attained a high level of civilization that included written language, though their script, if ever translated, would probably reveal little more than lists of goods and records of contracts and deliveries.

Archeological finds on Crete show an existing population from as early as 6000 BC. During this (Neolithic) period, we find stone tools, ceramic vessels, mud brick homes, and some small clay and stone sculptures, primarily of *steatopygous* (large-buttocked) female figures, but including some animals. A wave of immigration, possibly from Anatolia or the Levant, began what is known as the Early Minoan period (2700–2000 BC). During this era, we see the development of various craft techniques, including ceramics, metalworking, jewelry-making, and the manufacture of stone vessels. We find human figurines in stone, some influenced by the earlier residents of the island and some by the Cycladic figures of their island neighbors, with whom they had established communication and trade.

The Middle Minoan period (2000 BC to 1500 BC) brings the first signs of a unique aesthetic sensibility. Kamares Ware, a type of thin-walled, wheel-thrown pottery named for the cave on Mount Ida in which the first examples were found, was decorated with a variety of organic and geometric motifs; abstract shapes move, most often in spirals that seem to flow from stylized plant forms. If any one element could be said to characterize the art of the Minoans from this point on, it would be movement, an active, curving rhythm that is first visible in Kamares Ware and later became a primary feature of representational images.

Kamares Ware was followed by the Floral Style, vase decoration that featured representational images of plant forms, usually in black on a yellow background and again demonstrating a propensity for lively movement. Still later appeared the Marine Style, in which gracefully drawn marine life seems to swim and writhe playfully on the surfaces of thrown vessels. In all of these styles, the artists demonstrate a clear awareness of the compositional demands created by the shape of the vessel itself. Rhythms established by the outer contours are picked up and

Figure 1.27 Kamares Ware (c. 1800 BC)

Figure 1.28 Octopus Vas (c. 1700 BC)

balanced by the movement of the shapes (the tentacles of an octopus, for example, or a swimming school of nautili) drawn on the surfaces of the vases.

As the Cretan population grew, large settlements emerged, and the first palaces were built. While the greatest architectural efforts in Mesopotamia and Egypt were temples and tombs, Minoan Palaces were centers for exchange, government, ceremony, and the collection and storage of grains, olives, and other crops. Details of these first palaces are difficult to determine, because they were destroyed by a massive earthquake around 1700 BC and almost immediately rebuilt on the same locations on a more elaborate scale. The newer multi-storied buildings consisted of vast collections of small rooms and corridors built around a large central courtyard. Interior staircases were illuminated by light wells, openings that allowed light and ventilation to penetrate as far as three stories. Support columns in Minoan palaces tapered toward the bottom, inverting the natural direction of the tree trunks of which they were originally made. This inversion makes the Minoan column unique among ancient architectural supports, and easily recognizable.

The largest palace, at Knossos, was faced with gypsum, a soft white or pink stone with reflective qualities. This material, native to Crete, had been put to a variety of purposes since the Neolithic period, including the creation of stone vases. The cutting and polishing of gypsum creates powder, which could be used for plastering interior walls. The walls of the first palaces had been surfaced in this way and then painted red. In the Neopalatial period, this practice led to true frescoes, a technique in which pigment is applied to wet plaster. These frescoes covered the walls with depictions of nature; ceremonies, including dances

Figure 1.29 Palace at Knossos (first half of the second millennium BC)

and processions; and scenes from daily life. There are no historical narratives, no records of war or conquest, and no hunting scenes. Movement and vitality is once again the overriding impression. The human figure, whether involved in dance, ritual, or even seated, seems animated and lively, even the brush strokes used to create the images are fluid and active. Many of the paintings have no baseline, and this, coupled with their singular ease of movement, makes most of the figures seem almost entirely free from the constraints of gravity.

Excavators looking for connections to the myth of the Minotaur were not disappointed at Knossos. Images of bulls exist in almost every art form. The sacred nature of the bull is indicated by numerous stylized bulls' horns in various sizes that adorned the palaces, and images of similar horns on small altars in natural settings. There is ample evidence of what has come to be known as the Minoan Bull-game or Bull-sport, in which figures can be seen leaping above the animals. Clay vessels in the shape of bulls from the Early Minoan period have tiny human figures clinging to the horns. In images from across the island, figures are shown either leaping lightly above a running bull or being gored in the attempt. The famous "Toreador" fresco from Knossos gives us the youthful figures, both male and female, in various stages of executing a successful jump over a running bull.

Perhaps the most prevalent motif in Minoan art is the double axe (or *labrys*). Small, non-functional double axes appear in every medium, including stone, clay, painting, bronze, and gold. A simplified version of the double axe appears as a

Figure 1.30 "Toreador" Fresco (c. 1550 BC)

Figure 1.31 Detail, Hagia Triada Sarcophagus (c. 1450 BC)

symbol or glyph in Minoan script, and its outline is found cut into the walls and columns of the palace at Knossos, leading to speculation that this was the original labyrinth of Greek mythology, the house of the double axe. Double axes on columns appear in paintings, including those on a sarcophagus from Hagia Triada, in which animals, including a bull, are being sacrificed. Numerous small clay, bronze, and gold axes have been found and are believed to be intimately connected to the Minoan religion.

The double axe can also be seen on gems and seals, often in relation to female figures, some of whom appear to be divine. These tiny engravings demonstrate the same propensity for movement, as well as the same attention to the compositional challenges arising from a pre-determined format, that we have seen in Crete since the pottery of the early Minoan period. Many of the scenes carved into these seals show what may be priestesses involved in dance or worship, often at small outdoor altars. Their efforts seem at times to be answered by the arrival of a goddess who gives the appearance of having descended from above. This goddess also appears atop a mountain in another seal, flanked by lions and facing a figure whose arm is raised in what may be a position of worship.

Frescoes of griffins appear in a small room in the palace at Knossos, facing a throne carved from gypsum. In the same chamber are benches of gypsum and a sunken rectangular space lined with the same material, which may have served some ritual purpose. While it is not known who sat on the throne, speculation points to either a ruler or some human representative of the goddess.

King Minos is credited with creating the first navy, and the Minoans were proficient sailors, active in trade with all of their Mediterranean neighbors, including people from the Cyclades, Anatolia, the Mycenaeans (a Greek-speaking people from the mainland), and the Egyptians. A number of Egyptian articles have been found on Crete, and the influence of Egyptian art can be found in Minoan images. (Egyptian paintings of the people of a mysterious "Keftiu", carrying, among other goods, a bull-shaped vessel, may represent the people of Crete.)

Figure 1.32 Snake Goddesses (c. 1600 BC)

Later frescoes, including one of a procession at the palace at Knossos, were done in relief. This appears to be a record of an actual procession from the palace to a religious shrine on nearby Mount Juktas. The figures in this procession seem less graceful than the figures in earlier paintings and on gems; they have gained a base-line and lost some of the freedom of movement that we associate with Minoan art, perhaps as a result of the demands of working in relief.

When we look at Minoan sculpture, we see still less of this fluidity. Two ceramic females found at Knossos are stiff and awkward, at odds with the lively nature of their own dress and the writhing of the snakes in their hands. Commonly identified as "Snake Goddesses," these *faience* (a type of glazed earthenware) statuettes, and the lower half of another, were found in repositories in the Palace at Knossos. Their outfits, full skirts, and tight bodices that leave the breasts bare (seen also in frescos and engravings) may be indicative of Cretan formal or ritual dress. Snakes, with the ability to shed their skins and appear reborn, were held as sacred throughout the Eastern Mediterranean, and many objects and house shrines found on the island point to a snake cult associated with a female deity.

Numerous small figures have been found on Crete in stone, clay, ivory, and bronze, some of them female figures similar in dress to the snake goddesses and some of them male figures with hands raised, presumably in worship. There are no remaining life-size or monumental figures, but there is evidence of the existence of

Figure 1.33 Lion Gate at Mycenae (c. 1300 BC)

at least a few. Several bronze locks of hair found at Knossos and a pair of clay feet from Anemospilia are believed to have belonged to large wooden figures.

Some catastrophic event, possibly another volcanic eruption, led to the destruction of the palaces by burning around 1400 BC (the beginning of the Late Minoan Period). But the palaces continued to be inhabited, functioning as centers of trade for several more decades until they were, again, destroyed by fire and largely abandoned.

Taken all together, the artistic remains of the Minoan world consistently reflect the ideal of harmony in and with nature. What a contrast, then, with the Mycenaeans, who came to dominate the entire Aegean by the fifteenth century BC. Emerging as a distinct civilization on the mainland, this warrior race displays, throughout their architecture and sculpture, a fascinating and complex relationship with the Minoans, whom, by hook and by crook, they displaced as the major

cultural force in this corner of the Mediterranean. Compare the Cyclopean[6] forti-
fications at Tiryns or Mycenae with any of the more refined palaces on Crete, and
you have some idea of the very different priorities of the two cultures. But the Lion
Gate at Mycenae reminds us of the respect, even reverence, that the Mycenaeans
must have had for the civilization they superseded. The fact that, in this archway,
the Mycenaeans have adopted the already ancient motif of the lion guardian (was
there some camp-hopping between the Hittites and the Mycenaeans?), gives us
an idea of the wideness of their circle of experience. The placement of a Minoan
column between the lions—a position that automatically confers importance, if
not divine significance—is a strong invitation to speculate on the extent to which
Minoan culture *became* Mycenaean.

Through a post-and-lintel portal very like the Lion Gate, we enter into one
of the most remarkable structures left behind by the Mycenaeans. This is the
misidentified Treasury of Atreus, which was no treasury at all, but a great, doubtless aristocratic, tomb. Here Cyclopean stonework has been refined and manipulated with striking precision. The resulting beehive building is the best surviving

Figure 1.34 "Treasury of Atreus" (c. 1300 BC)

---

6 "Cyclopean" is, in fact, the term used later by the Greeks to describe the structures
erected by the Mycenaeans. The piling up of roughly-hewn, massive stones seemed only to
have been possible by a super race of giants, such as the Cyclopes.

example of an ancient Aegean *tholos*, a round structure used (at least as far as we know) primarily for burial. It is the prototype of a category of architectural structures based on circular designs, and as such, represents an impressive legacy of the Mycenaean builders.

Their impressive tombs and grave circles inevitably lead us to question what became of the Mycenaeans. For all of their powerful fortresses, for their great wealth, which is evidenced by the famous discoveries of often surprisingly delicate gold jewelry, including foliate crowns and face-coverings for the dead, the Mycenaean civilization itself fell victim to incursions of northern and eastern predators about whom little is known. By the middle of the twelfth century BC, the prehistoric cultures of the Aegean—Cycladic, Minoan, and Mycenaean—were forgotten, as the entire area entered a long period of instability, a cultural vacuum, a chaos or dark ages, leaving few notable artifacts and providing no clues as to what was to come.

Figure 1.35 Mycenaean Gold Mask (c. 1500 BC)

two

The Greeks

G reek civilization rests like an egg in the nest of the more ancient and powerful civilizations of Egypt and Mesopotamia and the overlapping cultures of the Aegean. From inauspicious beginnings, it will rise to spread its dominion over all of these territories and beyond. And also, of course, over time: the West, as it begins to identify itself in the historical era, will forever after always be, to some extent, inherently and inescapably Greek.

What made the Greeks so great? For, from any perspective, and certainly from that of the cultural historian and the student of art, they were great, as we shall see. But first, we would be wise to ask, what made the Greeks Greek? The simplest answer is: their language. "Ελλνηιζω," "I speak Greek," was, by the middle of the first millennium BC, a proud claim to membership in a distinct race that established new standards of achievement in every sphere of human activity. This is somewhat ironic, because, except when they faced the threat of absorption or annihilation by outsiders—by people who did not speak

Greek, that is, βαρβαροι, "barbarians"—the autonomous Greek city states did not get along very well among themselves. It is even arguable that the single most significant factor in the evolution of Greekness, and of Greek greatness, was this persistent danger from the barbarian—most notably and consistently from the seemingly limitless and all-powerful Persian empire, which, under the ambitious and aggressive rulers, Cyrus, Darius, and Xerxes, came very close to annexing the entire Aegean in the late sixth and early fifth centuries BC. Mutual protection gave rise to a true Greek culture, to Greekness, and the way in which that Greekness was communicated, in language and, increasingly, through the languages of visual art, defines classicism.

As they emerged from the rubble of the so-called "Dark Ages"—the centuries following the devastation of the Mycenaean world, centuries marked by incursions of people from the north and the east who remain difficult to identify and no easier to track—the Greeks established pockets of stability around what would eventually become the centers of artistic, political, and mercantile activity. In this new environment of at least local and temporary calm, what did the Greeks make? What survives from this period, the ninth and eighth centuries BC, as a proof of this calm and the burgeoning culture it sheltered?

Among the earliest artifacts we can identify as being indigenously Greek are ceramic domestic wares. These are decorated with dark slip linear patterns—simple bands and more complex meandering motifs, rectilinear geometries and even highly abstract animal forms—against the light ground. The prevalence of these busily ornamented pots gives the period its name, the Geometric. Some vessels, without bottoms and on a scale too large for domestic use, were created as tomb markers for the Dipylon Cemetery in Athens.[1] As they were originally placed above graves, it is inevitable to assume that libations poured into such vessels represented a means of communication, honoring and perhaps sustaining the dead in the afterlife.

The most famous of these Dipylon grave markers, from the middle of the eighth century BC, is a showcase of developing artistic preoccupations. We have the profusion of geometric patterns we expect, as well as two large narrative zones that represent distinctive approaches to pictorial composition. The funerary ritual, which is the subject of the upper register, is easily recognized as such: in

---

1   Here, Dipylon refers to the fact that the entrance to the cemetery was in the form of two pylons, which is an Egyptian architectural motif.

the center rests the horizontal body of the deceased on a bier with sacrificial animals below, while to either side are balanced groups of standing mourning women, again recognizable from the traditional grieving gesture of tearing the hair. While symmetry dominates the upper zone, the lower shows a military procession moving from left to right across the visual field; chariots drawn by teams of horses are interspersed with spear- and shield-bearing soldiers whose profiles enhance the implication of ordered dynamism. While most of the decoration on the vase is done with line, it is in the figures and horses of the narrative bands that the artist uses shape, primarily geometric but to some degree based on observation.

The emergence of the organic, and especially the human, from the hard-edged, rectilinear patterns of the Geometric period led, by the seventh century, to the triumph of curvilinear form, living—including

Figure 2.1 Dipylon Cemetery Krater (c. 750 BC)

human—beings caught up in the rhythms of life. Corinth, the city associated with the invention of black-figure ceramic ware, which descended from the simple dark-hued decoration of the Geometric era, was the primary source of innovation in decoration during this period. Behind Corinth—behind most pottery-producing centers of the Aegean in the seventh century BC—loomed the strong, ever-visible influence of Middle and Near Eastern stylistic renderings of human and animal forms. The freeing up of organic forms during this "Orientalizing" (coming from the East) phase of two-dimensional decoration constituted the experimentation that led, by the end of the century, to a new and truly original elevation of the human body to the central position as subject in Greek art.

The celebration of the human form is visible in one of its earliest large-scale three-dimensional manifestations, a limestone figure of a young man, or *kouros*, created around the turn of the sixth century BC and now in the Metropolitan Museum of Art. Here is a man of many contradictions. Though the position of his left leg suggests forward movement, his pose is completely rigid and motionless. Though he is carved in the round, his bug-eyed stare insists on the primacy of the frontal view; in fact, his entire body, for all its segmented forms of chest, arms, abdomen, thighs, kneecaps, and shins, implies a shallow rectangular space with a front. He is also, of course, a man with a past, Egypt, and specifically Egyptian Pharaonic portrait sculpture, providing the obvious model for the pose of this and virtually all Archaic Greek *kouroi*. But if we compare the Metropolitan Museum of Art *kouros* with, say, one of the colossal figures of Ramses II from Abu Simbel, a dramatic difference appears in the complete liberation of the Greek figure from the stone.

The Metropolitan Museum of Art *kouros*, though it represents a potential departure from the stolid immobility of its Pharaonic forbears, nevertheless remains a highly stylized version of the male nude as found and observed in nature. While stylized to a similar degree, and even sharing such features as the so-called

Figure 2.2 Metropolitan Museum Kouros (c. 600 BC)

Figure 2.3 Peplos Kore (c. 530 BC)

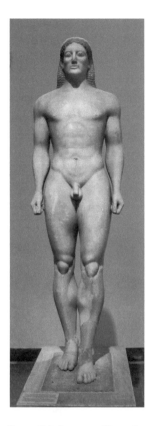 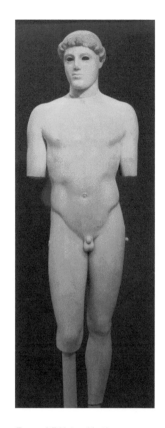

Figure 2.4 Anavysos "Kroisos" Kouros (c. 540 BC)

Figure 2.5 Kritios Youth (490-480 BC)

"Archaic smile," contemporary female sculptures such as the Peplos *kore*[2] differ decidedly from the male. Most significant, they are invariably clothed, and as a result, they appear even less capable of movement, almost columnar.

As the *kouroi* and *korai* evolve, changes in form and detail define a trajectory toward increasing naturalism. We find artists coming to terms with and mastering the interrelationship of bone, muscle, cartilage, and skin. The Anavysos "Kroisos" *kouros* of about 540BC showcases the anonymous artist's attention not only to the contours of the body, but to what they conceal, and the result includes

---

2   "Kore" is the singular noun form of "young woman" or "maiden" in Greek. "Korai" is the plural.

passages—the shoulders, for example, and the juncture of abdomen and groin—of refined modeling. The combination of sophisticated modeling and fidelity to natural form reaches spectacular heights in the so-called "Kritios Boy." A remarkable breakthrough visible in this figure is the introduction of *contrapposto*, the redistribution of the weight of the body along its various axes. The left hip rises, the torso shifts, and the head, for the first time in centuries, turns. This watershed figure ushers in the Early Classical period by its unprecedented representation of what might be called the "suspense" preceding or accompanying movement. In little more than a generation, this new kinesis gives rise to such dynamic figures as Myron's famous discus thrower (*Discobolus*) and the Artemision *Zeus*.[3]

Figure 2.6 Fallen Warrior from the West Pediment, Temple of Aphaia, Aegina (c. 500 BC)

Figure 2.7 Fallen Warrior from the East Pediment, Temple of Aphaia, Aegina (c. 490 BC)

---

3   Or is it Poseidon? The jury is still out.

The emergence of naturalism documented by the sequence of Greek figure sculptures from the early Archaic to the early Classical period is nowhere more conveniently illustrated than in the various pediment decorations produced for the temple of Aphaia at Aegina in the period 500 BC to 475 BC. There, separated by only a few years, we find two images of warriors defeated in the Trojan War, which is the subject of both east and west pediments. But the earlier warrior, with his bulging eyes and Archaic smile, falls stiffly, with no indication of torsion; he is a wooden creature of the previous century. His comrade on the opposite pediment, however, executed perhaps twenty years afterward, is no stereotypical, insensate *kouros*; he is an individual, imbued with ethos, whose entire body twists as it brooks the impact of the ground.

The Temple of Aphaia at Aegina is a transitional temple; it parallels architecturally the middle stage in that slow refinement of Greek figure sculpture from the late seventh to the early fifth century BC. An excellent opportunity to compare Archaic and Classical Greek architecture can be found in the Greek settlement at Paestum in Southern

Figure 2.8 "Hera I", Paestum (c. 550 BC)

Italy.[4] There, over a period of a hundred years, two temples were built side by side. Both are in the Doric order—with stocky, baseless columns crowned by simple, lozenge-shaped capitals—and both were, at some point, presumably dedicated to Hera. The earlier, known colloquially as Hera I, dates from the middle of the sixth century, the period of the Peplos *kore* and the Anavysos "Kroisos" *kouros*. It is a

---

4   The Greeks were great founders of colonies, and some of the best preserved Greek sites are in the south of Italy.

massive, sprawling, awe-inspiring expanse of stone, with cautiously spaced columns and a breadth that—especially in its ruined state—undermines the effect of its also impressive height. Built, like most Greek temples (and, for reasons worth speculating upon, like the earlier fortresses of the Mycenaeans), on high ground, Hera I declares its subjugation of the surrounding landscape. To the extent that nature and man are mutually antagonistic, here is a powerful statement in stone of man's mastery over the earth.

In the earlier temple to Hera the massive weight of the entablature seems to determine the bowed silhouettes of the columns that receive the force and deliver it reliably to the earth. In Hera II, not only has the entire temple form been significantly consolidated (there are six rather than nine supports along the short sides), the proportions and form of the columns have changed correspondingly; the result is a tighter and more dynamic structure. Compare the width relationship between column and capital; the distinction between them is more dramatic in the earlier building and more graceful in the later one. Or, compare the outlines of the columns themselves; at Hera I, the trajectory of the edges points to a convergence only slightly above the capital, while at Hera II that extrapolated point

Figure 2.9 "Hera II", Paestum (c. 450 BC)

is considerably further above. Such developments render the later temple a lighter and more animated sculpture in the landscape.

What is the point, or purpose, of the Greek temple? Its primary function is to house, in the interior chamber known as the *naos*, the cult figure of the god. More important in social terms, however, is the temple's function as the site of sacrifice. No Greek approaching, much less describing, a temple building could avoid references to animal slaughter; from the capital ("head," in Greek) to the *torus* (the individual base of an Ionic or Corinthian column, the Greek word for "rope") to the decorative *guttae* ("blood drops") and *dentils* ("teeth").[5] Sacrifices at these sites began in prehistoric times, before the temples themselves were constructed in stone.[6] The temple, then, came to serve the deity as house and the community as site of worship and sacrifice. It is also, for that community and everyone else who encounters it, a proclamation of civic pride and power. Nowhere are these multiple functions more spectacularly or more memorably illustrated than at the Acropolis in Athens.

Dominating the sacred area above the city ("ακροπολις" = *acropolis*) of Athens in a way that mirrors the primacy of that city state among its equals ("*primus inter pares,*" "first among equals") is the temple dedicated to Athena, virgin goddess of wisdom ("Athena Parthenos"). Built to replace an earlier Parthenon destroyed by the Persians in 480 BC, and paid for with funds stolen by the Athenians from their Greek allies—the "Delian League"—after that conflict was at least temporarily resolved by the Greek victories at Salamis and Plataea (480–479 BC), the new temple was a conscious attempt to summarize and define the ideals of Greek beauty in architecture. Here, in the world's first democracy, under the supervision of its most famous orator, Pericles, architects Iktinos and Kallikrates completed the evolution of the temple form toward perfect proportion, harmony, and what we might call architectural exhilaration. They created a monument that not only exemplifies Athenian piety and Athenian superiority, but also epitomizes the whole of Greek experience and achievement, from the collaborative defeat of the Persians to the Panhellenic movements in philosophy, literature, and the visual arts.

---

5 See George Hersey's groundbreaking study of the topic, *The Lost Meaning of Classical Architecture*.

6 Sacrifices were usually made at altars in front of the temples. Humans may have been among the original sacrificial victims, though that particular practice did not survive into the historical era.

Structural anomalies abound in the Parthenon, and they all serve a single purpose: to create the illusion of perfection. For example, let us consider the *stylobate*, or base, of the entire structure. In a perfect building, we would expect that the stylobate would be perfectly horizontal, flat. Iktinos and Kallikrates, however, understanding full well that such a surface would appear to the human eye as bowing slightly downward, have curved their stylobate upward; the calibrations are so meticulous that the surface appears perfectly flat. Similarly, if we look to the corners of the *peripteral colonnade*, we find (but only upon precise measurement) that these four columns are slightly thicker than the others, counteracting the effect of the bright sunlight so common in the Aegean, which tends to shear off the edges of forms. Among such ingenious refinements, geared to subliminally satisfy the eye, are larger, more pronounced innovations; the most meaningful has to do with the fact that, though the Parthenon, like a majority of Greek temples on the mainland, is Doric, it nevertheless incorporates Ionic features, the Ionic

Figure 2.10 Acropolis, Athens (second half of the fifth century BC)

Figure 2.11 Centauromachy, Metope from the Parthenon

Figure 2.12 Centauromachy, Metope from the Parthenon

order being more commonly associated with the islands. So, in the *opisthodomos*, or chamber behind the naos used in Athens as the temple treasury, we find four great Ionic columns. And, inside the colonnade, decorating the upper zone of the exterior wall of the temple proper, is a continuous frieze such as we are used to finding in Ionic, rather than in Doric, buildings.

If, in bringing together the two architectural orders,[7] the Parthenon reveals its ambition to represent all of Greek culture, this effort is sustained throughout the other buildings of the Acropolis. The Erechtheum, for example, is an elegant and complex, multi-level structure that sheltered, among other things, the old wooden statue of Athena rescued from the Persian conflagration. Often attributed to Mnesikles, it is Ionic and most famous for its Caryatid porch, which ultimately alludes to the fate of those who betray the Greek alliance. The diminutive temple to Athena Nike is Ionic and *amphiprostyle;*[8] its continuous frieze presents, in a rare convergence of art and what we might call journalism, scenes from the then-recent Greco-Persian wars. The large architectural complex, which would have been the

---

7   The Ionic column, slenderer than the Doric, with volutes decorating its capital and an individually carved base, was used simultaneously with the Doric. The Corinthian column, with an acanthus leaf capital, did not appear until the end of the fifth century, in the naos of the temple of Apollo at Bassae.

8   Amphiprostyle: one row of columns at each of the two short ends of the temple.

first structure encountered by anyone approaching the Acropolis, is the Propylaia, again by Mnesikles. Doric in order, the building housed an art gallery, which, in itself, says much about the reverence the Greeks maintained for the visual arts.

We have mentioned that the Athenians managed to salvage the venerable statue of their patron goddess. For the Parthenon, their new and far more ambitious temple to honor her, Pericles summoned the tried and tested sculptor Phidias to Athens to complete a colossal, chryselephantine (gold and ivory) sculpture of Athena. Phidias was, in fact, the master in charge of all sculpture at the Parthenon. This included the decoration of the East and West pediments depicting, respectively, the birth of Athena and the contest between Athena and Poseidon for supremacy over the city; the Doric metopes, which showed, along the four sides, scenes from the Trojan War, the gigantomachy, the Amazonomachy, and the battle of the Greeks and centaurs; and the Ionic frieze, picturing the Panathenaic procession, the parade to the Acropolis in which all Athenians participated.

Whether due to or in spite of the different stylistic inclinations, levels of talent, or places of origin of the many sculptors working under him, the overwhelming effect of Phidias's program is a finely, even miraculously, balanced conversation between naturalism and idealism. This balance is triumphantly embodied in a trio of goddesses from the East pediment, most often identified, from left to right,

Figure 2.13 Parthenon East Pediment: Hestia, Dione, Aphrodite(?)

as Hestia, Dione, and Aphrodite. Draped in luxuriant, naturally falling folds of fabric that do little to obscure the perfect breasts, stomachs, knees, and thighs underneath, these goddesses are both nude *and* clothed, as they are both natural and divine. Of course, there is no tradition in the fifth century BC of representing the large-scale female nude, nor will that artistic taboo be broken by the artists working on the Parthenon. In these monumental females, the Greeks indulge their love of all surfaces and forms, and display their virtuosity for suggestion, as well as representation. Their draperies are like a tidal sea; the waves at once reveal and conceal, while subtly leading the eye from the birth of Athena beyond the trio, in the center of the pediment, to the outermost corner where the chariot of the sun descends past the horizon. The positions of the female deities illustrate movement in a direction that coincides with the trajectory of the news of Athena's birth as it spreads across Olympus. Hestia has already been alerted, Dione has a dawning awareness and her daughter, Aphrodite, calmly reclining, is at this point still ignorant of the blessed event.

The representation of the passage of time as an element of a sculptural narrative is also evident in the continuous frieze depicting the Panathenaic Procession. On the western section of the relief one finds figures engaged in preparation for the procession: gathering, dressing, getting animals under control. The movement then proceeds in two directions, and the gestures of the figures, horses, and sacrificial beasts indicate, first, a gathering of speed, then a gradual slowing to a walk and, eventually, a full stop on the east wall. While the pace changes repeatedly among the figures, each individual retains something of an aura of what we might call personal space. This pageant is witnessed by the relatively stationary gods themselves, seated so that their larger figures can be accommodated in the same space as the upright mortals paying tribute to them.

Figure 2.14 Panathenaic Procession, Parthenon Frieze (detail)

Figure 2.15a Exekias, Achilles and Ajax Gaming (c. 540 BC)

Figure 2.15b Andokides Painter, Achilles and Ajax Gaming (c. 520 BC)

The fluidity of movement that characterizes so much of the sculptural ornamentation of the Parthenon was clearly a goal among Greek artists, irrespective of medium. In Greek ceramic decoration, a significant step towards attaining this goal coincides with the advent of Early Classicism.

As early as the Geometric period, as we have seen, artists decorated vessels by applying slip, most often black, to the terracotta ground. This basic process was refined by etching into the slip with a needle or stylus. Black Figure Ware, as it developed, was, on the most minute scale, subtractive, sculptural. But, at the end of the sixth century BC, this technique was eclipsed by one which was its virtual opposite. Red Figure Ware is painting, pure and simple; lines and details are brushed on, rather than scratched away. The revolutionary effects of this transition are succinctly brought home by a famous amphora in the Museum of Fine Arts in Boston, known as a "bilingual" vessel because the artist has represented the same basic scene—Ajax and Achilles playing draughts, a version of a celebrated image by the most respected of all Black Figure Ware artists, Exekias—in both the old and the new techniques. Note the increased fluidity of line and spontaneity of detail accessible to the artist working in the Red Figure technique, an artist known as the Andokides Painter, who is credited with inventing this revolutionary approach and, as such, is a significant personage in the long history of Western painting.

Creating credible forms, suggesting—in defiance of the stasis of the medium—graceful movement, imbuing those moving forms with ethos: these are the goals of the Classical artist as first articulated by the Greeks. Making of those credible forms something transcendent—*ideal* forms—is the primary pursuit of Greek artists of the fifth century BC. This is conveniently confirmed by the well-known tale of a famous painter of the period,[9] who, in an attempt to portray female perfection, requested that the most beautiful maidens appear before him so that he might select the best features to combine into his ideal. This notion of attaining the ideal through observation and what we might call "cutting and pasting" of the real is most succinctly embodied in the *Doryphoros*, or *Spearbearer*, of Polykleitos. Polykleitos is a contemporary of Phidias and an artist of equal stature. His *Spearbearer* represents a man in mid-stride, holding a spear (now usually absent) and turning his head slightly in a way that should recall the Kritios boy. One leg supports the entire weight of the spearbearer's body, and in this sense, we have a clear evolution of the principle of contrapposto. No longer is movement for its own sake the theme, as it so obviously was during the Early Classical period. Instead, a serene commingling of potential and kinetic energy is the point. The *Spearbearer* is also known to history as *The Canon*, because it was executed in conjunction with a treatise in which Polykleitos presented his personal system of proportions and anatomical perfection.[10] This double work, the statue and the text, became, for a time, a standard among Greek sculptors.

Even as we know it through later copies in stone, we can see that Polykleitos' original bronze *Doryphoros* must have demonstrated the artist's definitive ideas on beauty, harmony, and proportion. Other artists would follow his example by coming up with their own "canons." Like Polykleitos, Praxiteles, working in the middle of the next century, uses the head of the figure as a primary unit of measure in determining its overall proportions. But, the latter sculptor differs from his predecessor in the scale relation of that unit to the whole; his statue of *Hermes*

---

9   Zeuxis by name; none of his paintings survive, alas, but his successes were popular subjects of story in his own lifetime, and those stories continue to be retold to this day.
10   Long since lost, this treatise, which owes much to Pythagorean philosophy, can be partially reconstructed from ancient quotations.

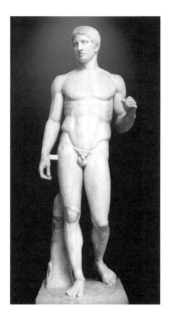

Figure 2.16 Doryphoros of Polykleitos (c. 450 BC)

Figure 2.17 Praxiteles' Hermes and the Infant Dionysus (c. 340 BC)

with the Infant Dionysus, of about 340 BC, is slimmer and more elongated than the *Spearbearer* and enjoys a far more relaxed pose. Originally dangling grapes before the baby wine god, Hermes presents a languid serpentine line. Here, the potential and kinetic energy of the solitary, idealized warrior by Polykleitos is abandoned for a luxuriant, even indolent mood of intergenerational familiarity and playfulness.

The ease that prevails in the *Hermes* group is found in another work by Praxiteles. If the sculptor had never created anything else, his *Aphrodite of Knidos* would still have guaranteed his fame. This goddess of love is, to begin with, the first life-size, freestanding, female nude in Greek art. Whereas the female form had already been displayed in great detail in monumental sculptures, such as those of the Parthenon, it was accessible only through an intervening layer of cloth; the body and its drapery were equally "subject." Now, Praxiteles takes the bold step of separating the body from its drapery and, what is more, it is the act of that separation—the disrobing—that is the true subject.

The *Aphrodite* is one of the hardest sculptures to reconstruct. Not only is the original lost, but there are—unsurprisingly—a great many copies, and rarely do they agree in any aspect, except that the goddess is invariably nude and her right hand is always ambiguously hovering before her genitals, at once concealing and indicating her sex. The *Aphrodite of Knidos* has many artistic offspring, the most famous being the *Aphrodite of Melos*, another vision of the goddess in the act of being revealed.

With the works of Praxiteles and his followers, we have entered a very different world from that of Phidias, Polykleitos, and the comparative serenity of the High Classical "moment." After successfully banding together to defeat their Persian enemies, with the new Athenian Acropolis still under construction, the Greeks turned upon each other. The conduct of the Delian League, especially the Athenian confiscation of its treasury and bullying of its less powerful members, led the Spartans to commence hostilities against their erstwhile allies, whom they had long resented for their intellectualism and refinement and for their outrageous, newfangled system of government known as "democracy." Thus began the Peloponnesian Wars. Athens was promptly deprived of its dominant status among the Aegean city states and panic led

Figure 2.18 Praxiteles' Aphrodite of Knidos (c. 340 BC)

the citizens to commit strange and questionable deeds, most notorious being the death sentence they passed on their greatest compatriot, Socrates, in 399 BC. But, Spartan hegemony lasted hardly more than a generation before it was successfully challenged by the Thebans, whose turn at the top of the Aegean heap was even shorter. A longer lasting solution to the constant conflicts and shifts of power finally came from the least likely quarter. Considered by Athenians and Spartans alike to be a negligible race of northern hill people, the Macedonians, under their brilliant and ambitious king, Philip II, succeeded in conquering and, to some extent, even unifying the Greek-speaking people. This newly-consolidated Aegean

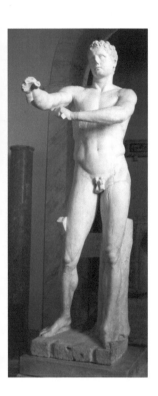

Figure 2.19 Apoxyomenos of Lysippos (c. 330 BC)

became the power base from which Philip's son (and probable assassin), Alexander the Great, would launch his bid to Hellenize the world.

Alexander's favorite artist was reportedly Lysippos, who, like Polykleitos in the previous century and Praxiteles in his own, contributed something new to the never-ending conversation about the perfect human form. Lysippos revisits the whole question of anatomical proportion in works such as his celebrated sculpture of a nude athlete. Known as the *Apoxyomenos*, or *Man Using a Strigil* (a strigil being the metal instrument with which men scraped oil, sweat, and other debris from their bodies after exertion), this figure type falls in between the comparatively stocky *Spearbearer* and the lithe *Hermes*; if Polykleitos gives us a quarter horse of a man, and Praxiteles gives us an English thoroughbred, Lysippos, clearly aware of these other canonical works, presents us with a mustang after a race. The sculptor also does something else that is dramatic. That frontal viewing plane toward which most earlier Greek figure sculptures oriented themselves is punched out, literally, by the *Apoxyomenos*, such that the body now represents a perpendicular meeting of separate planes. While all sculpture is, by definition, three dimensional, this figure demands movement by the viewer to be fully appreciated or even merely comprehended.

All discussions of Hellenistic art in some way begin with representations of the ruler who Hellenized the world, Alexander himself. Lysippos, in particular, was praised for a long-lost bronze portrait of the precocious and unscrupulous warrior king, and other artists, including Skopas, produced portraits that must have served the growing demand for images of the dazzlingly successful ruler throughout his growing empire.

A number of Alexander portrait types survive from the century following his death. One of these shows the king with his head raised on a characteristically sideward-tending neck.[11] Caught thus in mid-motion—his deep-set eyes shaded by heavy brows, his forehead furrowed under a mass of wavy hair, his pronounced lips parted—this is a man on the very brink of action. All the equanimity we associate with male imagery created during the High Classical Period is here surcharged with mental energy. Alexander is shown as being confident but also emotionally complex and capable of experiencing and reacting to any situation, including danger and pain.

One portrait of Alexander dates from around 200 BC, at the very height of the Hellenistic period. It was found at Pergamon, a Greek site in modern day Turkey, ruled, in the third and second centuries, by a series of Attalid kings. In 223, under Attalos I, the people of Pergamon scored a great victory over the barbarian Gauls. Over the next several decades, this victory was commemorated by a number of architectural and sculptural programs, including a great altar to Zeus and a temple to Athena. The most prolific artist involved in the decoration of the Pergamene Acropolis was Epigonos. His *Dying Gaul* (c. 220 BC), representing an enemy warrior succumbing to mortal wounds on the battlefield, suggests not merely a foreign type—the man's moustache, the

Figure 2.20 Alexander Bust (second century BC)

Figure 2.21 Dying Gaul of Epigonos (c. 220 BC)

---

11 Plutarch in his Moralia (335A-B) describes the original portrait by Lysippos, including what becomes the characteristic treatment of the head and neck, based, according to the author, on Alexander's own bearing.

torque he wears around his neck, etc., clearly identify him as such—but, with his unidealized physiognomy and given the less-than-ideal circumstances in which he finds himself (it is easier to look the ideal when you are gliding along with your spear than when you have fallen under the sword), he appears convincingly more individual, more specific, more *real*. From this, and, above all, from the fact that he is a powerful male figure in his prime portrayed with great dignity *in extremis*, derives the pathos of the work.

Pathos on a super-human scale characterizes the most famous and controversial of all Hellenistic sculpture groups, the *Laocoön*, which depicts, with an indulgence bordering on the sadomasochistic, the punishment of the eponymous priest of Troy for his skeptical but accurate assessment of the Greek gift of the wooden horse. In this, he contradicted the will of Athena, ally of the Greeks, who sends two serpents to silence him once and for all. They, in a famous passage of Virgil's *Aeneid*, which may in fact have been inspired by the sculpture, make for Laocoön and his sons, and then, in Dryden's equally famous translation,

> ... around the tender boys they wind,
> Then with their sharpen'd fangs their limbs and bodies grind.
> The wretched father, running to their aid
> With pious haste, but vain, they next invade;
> Twice round his waist their winding volumes roll'd;
> And twice about his gasping throat they fold.
> The priest thus doubly chok'd, their crests divide,
> And tow'ring o'er his head in triumph ride.
> With both his hands he labors at the knots;
> His holy fillets the blue venom blots;
> His roaring fills the flitting air around.
> Thus, when an ox receives a glancing wound,
> He breaks his bands, the fatal altar flies,
> And with loud bellowings breaks the yielding skies.[12]

Attributed to Hagesander, Athanadoros, and Polydoros of Rhodes, and carved from a single block of marble in the final decades of the first century BC, the *Laocoön* is, for all its explosive dynamism, a tightly knit, triangular composition,

---

12   Virgil, *Aeneid*, Book II, 214 ff., tr. John Dryden

Figure 2.22 Laocoön (first century BC)

an architecture of highly exercised human flesh constructed upon and around the diagonal of the heroic priest's immense and upward struggling form. The tangle of human figures, shown in various states of resignation to the inevitable, is fittingly controlled and even arranged or justified— literally held together—by the action of the agent of the inevitable, the snakes, whose

writhing forms seem the very essence of musculature and incontrovertible force.

A Hellenistic figure with whom it is easier, perhaps, for the viewer to identify is the bronze *Boxer* now in the Museo Nazionale Romano in Rome. Like the priest at Troy, he is aged, powerfully built, and clearly no stranger to pain. His career is written on his face and in the heavy attitude of his tired body; he seems to raise his head reluctantly, as though to avoid standing. Probably a work of the late Hellenistic period, the *Boxer* is neither a god nor an idealized warrior king, but a man beaten regularly by experience. As such, we can see in him another in the long line of heroic Greek males who project

Figure 2.23 Bronze Boxer (third century BC)

Figure 2.24 Polykleitos the Younger, Theater at Epidauros (c. 340 BC)

profound and complex human emotions, a line that began with the expressive countenance of the divine and always victorious Alexander.

The representation of human emotion is considered a hallmark of Hellenistic figure sculpture. But Greek writers had always been interested in examining and representing what we now commonly refer to as the "human condition," with all the internal convolutions and external symptoms that condition implies. The ritualistic performance of theatrical works, especially tragedies, which played as large a part in Greek life as athletics—as large a part as politics and worship, to both of which it was intimately tied—provided a public expression of such themes as the tension between individual self-definition and public responsibility, or the temptation of hubris and the inevitability of its consequences. The site of these performances was, in many communities, originally a natural depression in the landscape, to which benches and, eventually, stone seats were introduced. The shape of the theater allows sounds emanating from the orchestra to reach even the most far flung members of the audience, whose sight lines converge without interference on the proscenium. One of the best preserved fourth-century theaters was designed by Polykleitos the Younger, probably a kinsman of the great fifth-century sculptor, on the outskirts of the Peloponnesian town of Epidaurus. Most of the surviving Greek theaters have been significantly restored, and many are still in use today, allowing us some insight into what it must have been like for the lettered and the unlettered to share the experience of the tragedies of history played out against the inscrutable stage set of the mountains and the sky.

The essentially half-round plan of the theater reminds us of the Mycenaean love of circular forms, as found in the so-called Treasury of Atreus and the various grave circles nearby. The funereal associations of rounded architectural structures were, to some extent, loosened by the Greeks, though, presumably, they still apply in the Tholos at Delphi, a temple built in the middle of the fourth century BC by Theodoros of Phokaia. Dedicated to Athena, the actual purpose of the temple remains mysterious but, like all Greek temples, inevitably included references to death. Another circular Greek building was constructed in the center of Athens in 334 BC. The Choragic Monument of Lysicrates is a room-sized trophy celebrating the victory of a choir owned and operated by the wealthy impresario, Lysicrates. It marks, as well, the first usage of the Corinthian column on the exterior of a building.

Figure 2.25 Theodoros of Phokaia, Tholos at Delphi (fourth century BC)

Alexander's Hellenization of the world set an example that was reenacted by the Romans, who found, in the ambitions of the great king, the model—sometimes acknowledged, sometimes denied—for their own attempts to colonize the world. The Romans were, in fact, the self-appointed heirs to Alexander's Greece—not only territorially, in the sense that they absorbed the lands he had conquered, but also culturally, in the sense that they made Greek culture theirs. The Latinization of the West changed it forever, but also confirmed that it began with Greece and would always remain, to some extent, Greek.

What, above all, do we take with us from Greece? The deeply-felt desire of Greek artists to transform and transcend nature, to lay claim to the world and subjugate it, such that what we are born into becomes the raw material for what we make out of it: buildings that move us like beings, and carved and painted figures that act like versions of our better—or at least our more god-like, immortal—selves.

three

Rome

The rise of Rome begins with the fall of Troy. We are probably already familiar—from literature high and low, from pictures and plays, from sword and sandal cinema and tasteful British television series—with much of the story. After the Greeks set fire to his native city, Aeneas, son of Venus and prince of Troy, bows to the will of the gods and sets out with his father, Anchises, on his back and leading his little boy, Iulus, by the hand. These males also carry with them images of their ancestral gods. Aeneas has no destination, only the divine promise that his descendants will one day establish a great city whose citizens will conquer their former enemies and—fingers crossed—the world. After a long and difficult journey, which includes a protracted layover in Carthage and a day-tour of hell, Aeneas dies in Italy. Three hundred years later, his great, great, great, great grand-daughter, an independent-minded woman named Rhea Silvia, gives birth to twin boys, whom, for complex domestic reasons, she is forced to expose.[1] One of these babies, Romulus, grows up to fulfill the ancestral prophecy by founding the city of Rome in 753 BC; after killing his brother, Remus, he becomes Rome's first king. At the end of the seventh century, the kingdom falls into the hands of foreigners, who remain until they are driven out in 510 BC, at which point the Romans establish a Republic. This Republic, governed as implied by a coalition of free citizens, withstands from the outset a myriad of trials, including, at the beginning of the fourth century BC, the sack of the capital by everybody's favorite foes, the Gauls.

The Republican period is, despite significant setbacks, one of ongoing annexation for the Romans, beginning with near neighbors in Italy and extending well into the former empire of Alexander the Great. Contemporary with the expansion of Roman territory is the gradual decay of its republican form of government; the same powerful military leaders are responsible for both. So, by the first century BC, we have the notorious dictator, Sulla, who heads an unprecedentedly bloody reign of terror and is eventually devoured alive by worms. Two generations later, the nephew of another dictator, Julius Caesar, becomes the first Augustus, effectually ending the Republic and ushering in the Imperial Period. The Imperial Period, too, is initially one of conquest and expansion. In the second century AD, the Empire attains its largest perimeter under the so-called "good" emperors, extending from Egypt to Britain and from Syria to Spain. Following this so-called golden age is a century of chaos and decline, only truly stabilized at the outset of the fourth century. Finally—finally for Rome, the eternal city—the Emperor Constantine reconsolidates the fragmenting Roman world under his sole authority and transfers his capital to the old Greek town of Byzantium. As the first Christian emperor, Constantine in effect lays the groundwork for an entirely new era in Western civilization.

Given the vast time and territory associated with the rise and fall of Rome, the history of Roman art is naturally one of constant evolution and absorption, beginning with the settlement of the city in the eighth century BC. At that moment, and for the next several centuries, the Italian peninsula was inhabited by a variety of more or less mysterious peoples, most prominent being the Etruscans. Etruria was

---

1 Exposure was, sadly, a not uncommon practice among most ancient civilizations, whereby undesirable, surplus, unwanted, or expensive children were abandoned to face almost certain death at the hands of natural forces. Famous exposes include Moses, Oedipus, and our twins here.

a territory north of Rome, the central part of which corresponded roughly to modern Tuscany. Not surprisingly, given that they controlled this large region—and Rome itself—until the end of the sixth century, the Etruscans exerted the single strongest influence on the emerging Roman culture.

What we know about the Etruscans comes mainly from the works of art they left behind. Though they had already adopted the Phoenician alphabet (which they, in turn, passed on to the Romans), their surviving texts remain undecipherable to this day. Their painted tombs, their small-scale luxury objects in bronze and gold, the recurring references to them in the ancient sources we can read nevertheless give us great insight into their unique civilization. And so, in their figure sculpture, we confront evidence of the strongest influence exerted *upon them*, namely, Greek culture. As we have seen, by the sixth century BC, Greeks had colonized the southern half of Italy, including Sicily.[2] To the end of that century is dated a nearly life-size figure of Apollo, or, as the Etruscans called him, Apulu or Aplu. One glance at his face, with its bulging eyes and Archaic smile, identifies him as the provincial cousin of any number of the Greek *kouroi* we have come to know. His stance, too, with one leg forward, is superficially reminiscent of the standard Greek treatment of the male. But there are major differences, beginning with the energy expressed by the Etruscan god. Unlike any of his Greek forerunners, Apulu is striding dramatically forward, arms up and out. The rhythmic folds of his

Figure 3.1 Etruscan Statue of Apollo from Veii (c. 500 BC)

---

2   Italy, until the nineteenth century, was not a nation, nor does the term "Italian" designate a unified group of people before then. Here, it is used to refer to the land mass.

garments—and the very fact that he wears anything is another important difference between the Etruscan and Greek approach—enhance the suggestion of swift
movement. This zing or added liveliness is characteristic of Etruscan figurative
art. And the very material out of which he is made is also characteristic: terra
cotta, hollow-built on this scale, is notoriously difficult to work, but the Etruscans
specialized in exploiting it to great dynamic effect.

Found among the ruins of the Portonaccio sanctuary in the important Etruscan
town of Veii, the *Apulu* is one of a complex and somewhat controversial group of
deities that decorated the ridge beam at the top of the temple structure. In this,
we find another departure from Greek practice, since the Greeks decorated their
pediments and friezes but did not place statues on top of their temples. Because
they were originally built of mud brick and wood, and are no longer extant, most
of our information about Etruscan temples comes from Roman descriptions,
small clay models, and whatever terra cotta details survive. Again, superficially,
there are many similarities between early Greek and Etruscan temples, all of which
featured a chamber with a peaked roof on a platform for worship and some sort
of colonnade. Even Etruscan capital forms resemble the Doric and Ionic forms of
their Greek neighbors. But in the comparatively greater height of the platform or
podium upon which the temple is set; in the clear designation of an axial approach,
via a stairway at the center of one of the short ends; and in the restriction of the
freestanding colonnade toward that same end, the Etruscans created a distinctive
model that would be copied for centuries by the Romans.

As mentioned, one of our important sources of information about the
Etruscans is the painted subterranean tombs that survive in great numbers at sites
such as Cerveteri and Vulci. From their mural decorations,[3] which include details
of daily life, athletic events, banquets, and funeral practices, we can infer much,
for instance, about the greater status of Etruscan women compared to all their
contemporary and, most notably, contemporary Greek, counterparts. A number
of sarcophagi also survive from this period; many are surmounted by nearly life-
size, semi-reclining figures in poses similar to those we find in, for example, the
early fifth-century *Tomb of the Leopards* at Tarquinia. Here women and men dine
together as equals in comfort and splendor, waited upon by equally healthy- and
happy-looking servants.

---

3   Are they frescoes—true frescoes involving the application of pigment to wet plaster?
Nobody knows for sure.

Figure 3.2 Etruscan Tomb of the Leopards, Tarqunia (c. 480 BC)

Many of the early Etruscan sarcophagi, such as the most famous example, from Cerveteri, were made of terra cotta, very like the Portonaccio *Apulu*. Over time, though the Etruscans rarely worked in marble, more and more of these large scale cinerary containers came to be carved in stone. A spectacular example from Vulci is now in the Museum of Fine Arts in Boston. Created around 350 BC, long after the Romans had become the masters of the Etruscans, this work presents us with a couple in their prime, at some point after a banquet. Their bed, which is their barge into the afterlife, is the frame for the single abstract unit that the couple becomes as they embrace. The bedclothes covering their lower bodies poignantly adumbrate the dissolution of their mortal flesh, so palpable above. Their merging represents both their physical destruction and their inviolable union.

The sculpture most often associated with the Etruscans is also one of the most popular animal sculptures in the history of art. The so-called *She Wolf*, now in the Capitoline Museum in Rome, is traditionally and still widely accepted as the masterpiece of Etruscan bronze casting, probably produced around 500 BC by an

Figure 3.3 Etruscan Sarcophagus Lid (c. 350 BC)

Etruscan workshop in territory recently reclaimed by the Romans.[4] The she wolf, with or without the infant twins, is one of the primal images by which Romans referred to their origins and their tribal autonomy; just such a wolf was said to have rescued and sustained Remus and Romulus after their exposure in the wilderness. Both Romans and Etruscans would have found in this fiercely maternal creature an admirable symbol of self-preservation and familial perpetuation. Here, perhaps a hundred and fifty years before Lysippos' *Strigil-Bearer* punches out the frontal plane, the mother wolf turns her head meaningfully, expressing clearly both the intention and capacity to engage oncomers from all directions. Her stiff-legged pose, her lowering head, the suspense created by her partially open jaws (the low growl suggested is more frightening than a bark or a howl), combine with her gaunt appearance, her prominent ribs, and the sinewy muscles of her limbs to convey a powerful impression of hunger and defensiveness pushed to their limits. But for all this, her fur—what little of it is delineated around her head and front legs and

---

4   Recent scholarship has questioned the antiquity of this sculpture, based on the fact that it was cast in a single piece, which was not the practice until much later. Romulus and Remus were added during the Renaissance by Antonio del Pollaiuolo.

down her back—is the expression of a refined decorative impulse.

With the *She Wolf*, we return to the race she made possible, the Romans. Having chased out the third and last Etruscan king, Tarquinius Superbus, the Romans entered upon a long period of republican government, one which would last from the early fifth to the late first century BC. At the outset, and for most

Figure 3.4 Etruscan She-Wolf (c. 500 BC)

of this period, the most powerful element of government—the true head of the Republic—was the Senate, drawn almost exclusively from the aristocratic, or patrician, class.

A number of patrician portraits survive, and they affirm the prevalence and durability of a style known as "hyperrealism" or "verism." An example from the first century BC is the head of an elderly gentleman in the Museo Torlonia in Rome. In a society where visual signs constituted a rigid and universally recognized vocabulary of wealth and status, where the width of the stripe on your toga or whether or not your tunic was belted instantly identified you as belonging to a specific caste, the features of this man identify him as someone accustomed to leadership and respect. As in a book, every line can be read—not to mention, every furrow, indentation, and protrusion. The man's baldness confirms his age and tenacity; his deeply lined forehead and the creases above his nose portray him as perpetually immersed in thought, even preoccupied; his mouth is set with grim, if not belligerent, determination; the bags under his eyes reveal his wakeful vigilance, and the lines of his face are worn with haughty pride. Every detail of his face provides irrefutable proof that he has followed the *cursus honorum*, the path of all Roman patricians toward power, which begins with military service and ends with magistracy. The sculptor's far-from-superficial translation of this patrician's particular physiognomy into (rather

Figure 3.5 Roman Patrician (first century BC)

than onto) stone parallels the depth of the character he reveals, a character well suited to the material from which he was carved.

More obviously dependent on Greek proto-types than the *Patrician* is the architecture of the Republican period—dependent, but also different. A quick glance at the first-century BC Roman Temple of Portunus, with its pediments and Ionic colon-nade, confirms its Greek heritage. But note the high podium, high enough so that the structure can only be reached via the stairway at one of the short ends. These features—high podium, stairway—are decid-edly non-Greek, they are derived from the now lost Etruscan temples. In a notable departure from both Etruscan and Greek models, most of the Temple of Portunus' columns are *engaged*—in other words, par-tially embedded in the wall of the *cella* (the Latin term for the naos). The inevitable outcome of these Roman transpositions and innovations is a foregrounding of the architectural function of the temple at the expense of the sculptural; that is, while both Greek and Roman temples are, in essence, isolated and elevated spaces within and yet separate from their surroundings, the fact that a Greek temple has an interior is secondary to its sculptural presence in its particular scape, whereas the *room-ness* of the Roman temple—the fact of its interior, and its unique entrance—is inescapable.

The Temple of Portunus is a small building in stone, but when we think of Roman architecture, we tend to think of construction on a colossal scale. Generally speaking, the Romans build bigger than their Greek and Etruscan predecessors and, for that matter, bigger than most of their successors as well, at least until the modern era. One thing that

Figure 3.6 Temple of Portunus (first century B(

makes this possible is their development and refinement, by the second century BC, of a new building material, concrete. This, and their wholehearted adoption of the round-headed arch passed down to them by the Etruscans, allows the Romans to vie with the Egyptians in transforming the world, more and more of which (including, eventually, Egypt itself) the Romans claim as their own. The vast Sanctuary of Fortuna Primigenia at Praeneste (modern Palestrina) rivals the scale of the pyramids or the temple complexes at Luxor and Karnak, but the Roman structures are much cheaper to build. The enormous buildings of the Republican and Imperial periods also tend to combine a wide variety of materials, from brick and concrete to expensive marbles drawn from all corners of the expanding empire.

Before considering some of the great Imperial building projects, we should note the dramatic cultural changes that accompanied the shift from five hundred years of Republican government to the institution of imperial rule, which affected every aspect of Roman life and all forms of Roman art on every scale. This shift is plainly visible in the portraits of powerful individuals produced in the final decades of the first century BC. Images of Julius Caesar, for example, still paid homage to the veristic tradition of the Republican era. Images of his great nephew, Octavian, who became the first emperor (Caesar Augustus) in 27 BC, established an entirely new and revolutionary tradition. Compare our *Patrician*, above, with any of the great number of surviving portraits of Augustus. Absent from the *Patrician* is any hint of idealism of the sort we inevitably encounter in Greek sculpture from the Classical Period. This is the head of an individual with a complex personal history, a face that has been lived in. As such, it is characteristic of all Republican portraits. Augustus, however, whether we view him in his role as *Pontifex Maximus*, the highest priest, or as commander in chief of the army in the very act of addressing his troops, presents a formal, comparatively abstract, artificial image, elevating the subject to the role of personification of the state. And so we are not, perhaps, surprised to find that even when Augustus was in his seventies, he was still being portrayed as an idealized man in his prime.

The *Prima Porta Augustus*, named after the villa owned by the emperor's storied third wife, Livia, is, in its proportions, as well as in its pose (the left leg moving freely while the right leg takes the weight, the rightward tilt of his head, etc.), more than a little reminiscent of Polykleitos's *Spearbearer*. The idealism of the High Classical Period in Greece is wholeheartedly embraced by the new authoritarian government as a fitting model and vehicle for the ideals of that government and its human representatives. That these representatives do not, as we have noted,

Figure 3.7 Augustus Pontifex Maximus (after 12 BC)

Figure 3.8 Augustus Prima Porta (c. 20 BC)

age, suggests the immortality claimed for them—sometimes by them—and for Rome. This is, of course, pure propaganda. Also propaganda, in the *Prima Porta Augustus*, is the little Cupid, physically supporting the larger stone figure and also symbolically supporting Julio-Claudian claims to descent from Venus.[5]

Whereas there was great resistance to all things Greek in the earlier, conservative centuries of the Republic, the eventual annexation of important territories in the Aegean—for example, Corinth fell to the Romans in 146 BC; Pergamon was bequeathed to the Romans by the last Attalid king in 133 BC—contributed to an increasing fascination with and eventual mania for Greek culture, which

---

5   Remember Aeneas's little son, Iulus? He is the founder of the Iulian family, to which Julius Caesar and Augustus proudly belong.

Figure 3.9 Ara Pacis (13-9 BC)

rose to a climax in the first and second centuries of the new millennium and the Imperial Era.

The first Roman emperor was, by nature, a diplomat and a politician, and he took pride, above all, in what came to be known as the *Pax Augustae*, the Peace of Augustus. A great altar, the Ara Pacis, was commissioned to celebrate this universal concord and the welcoming attitude of Rome toward its growing number of subject peoples. The Altar of Peace is not, in fact, an altar, or rather, it is an altar-shaped building with an altar inside. And, despite its unusual form, it, too, reminds us that the Romans of the Imperial period looked to the Greeks for inspiration. Thus we find, in this two-story structure—a lavishly carved, multi-layered sculpture on an architectural scale—references to, for example, the Panathenaic frieze of the Parthenon, though the Roman version of a procession is a busier, more bustling, altogether less solemn and considerably "louder" affair.

Peace or no peace, the empire continued to expand throughout the first century AD, despite the growing instability and degeneracy of the imperial family itself. The Julio-Claudian successors to Augustus included some of the most notorious rulers in history, whose names and atrocities have enlivened the reading of the

Roman chronicle for centuries.[6] Thus, the new Roman practice of idealizing the ruling class went far to conceal the decadence of those individuals at the heart of government. Caligula, for instance, is always represented as a beautiful young man with features that explicitly recall those of his great grandfather, Augustus. There is no hint of the congenital illness, probably syphilis, that left him bald as a teen-ager, much less the scandals—murder, incest with all of his sisters, etc.—that marred and brought to an end his brief reign. Caligula's notoriety was eclipsed by that of his nephew, Nero, best remembered for killing his mother and performing karaoke in drag; like Caligula twenty-seven years earlier, he met a violent end. This also marked the end of the Julio-Claudian dynasty.

Not surprisingly, the new ruling family, the Flavians, took greater care than their predecessors to satisfy the wants of the Roman citizenry. The scale of their effort is made clear by the construction, beginning in the year of their accession, 69 AD, of the largest of all Roman amphitheaters,[7] the Colosseum, so called because it was erected near a colossal statue of Nero that had been reworked as a statue of the sun god, Sol. Inaugurated in 80 AD with a hundred days of games and massacres, the amphitheater held up to 50,000 people, spread over three tiers of seating, which corresponded roughly to the rank and status of the audience—nobility on the lowest level, the plebeians at the top, and the *equites* or wealthy merchant class in between. This social stratification has a parallel on the exterior, where we find engaged columns corresponding to the three basic orders, the Tuscan, or Roman version of the Doric, below; the Ionic on the second tier; and a hybrid Corinthian above that, the whole crowned by a high attic.[8] There were two stories below the main floor of the arena, containing cells and cages for the gladiators and their animal and human opponents and prey. Inside and outside, the great arches dominate and unify the structure; in fact, they are the structure. Among other achievements, the building set a new standard of luxury for entertainment venues. There were awnings that moved to block the sun and sprays of perfumed water to refresh the already bath-crazy Roman people.

---

6   There is significant overlap between the clearly biased, tabloid version of such emperors as Tiberius, Caligula, and Nero, and more trustworthy, scholarly versions of their lives by ancient and modern writers.

7   "Amphitheater", from *amphi*, meaning two, and *theater*. Thus, two theaters, facing one another.

8   A fourth tier of seating was created inside the attic story by Domitian, the son of Vespasian, who built the amphitheater. It was for women and the poorest classes.

Figure 3.10 Colosseum (finished 80 AD)

At the time the Colosseum was inaugurated, the Romans were still reeling from a cataclysm that wiped out many lives and much land in the popular resort area along the bay of Naples, the province of Campania, south of Rome. The eruption of Mount Vesuvius in 79 AD destroyed the cities of Pompeii and Herculaneum, along with numerous estates nearby, but also preserved those sites underground. Utterly forgotten for seventeen centuries, the excavated cities now provide our greatest resource when it comes to understanding Roman domestic architecture and its decoration. In addition to numerous bronze and marble sculptures, mosaics, luxury goods and glass and pottery in vast quantities, the best extant examples of Roman wall painting are to be found in this region.

Roman wall painting has traditionally been divided up into various styles, and doubtless these styles evolved from one another, though at Pompeii, all were practiced simultaneously, and there is no reason to associate any one style with a particular period. The First Style is the simplest: the wall is frescoed to represent rectangles of marble or other costly, richly patterned stone, the final effect being one of a display of expensive blocks or veneers such as would have been seen in the wealthiest houses, like Nero's Golden House (*Domus Aurea*), in the capital.

Second Style artists use paint to open up the surface of the wall, creating the illusion of space beyond: external views of other wings or rooms of the house, gardens or grottoes, or fountain-filled grounds. While the First Style exploits and reiterates the flatness of the wall, the Second Style denies and defies it, treating it as window. The Third Style, like the First, accepts the two-dimensional wall as a backdrop for pictures and other images arranged as in a gallery. And finally, in the Fourth Style, we often find elements of the other three combined in more or less logical or fantastic ways.

Figure 3.11 Still life with glass bowl of fruit and vases (early first century AD)

As we saw in the Colosseum, the arch and its various permutations are the structural and visual modules of all large- and small-scale Roman building. Arches extending across vast areas form the *barrel* vaults—and, when they intersect at right angles, the *groin* vaults—that are the basis of lavish bath structures, such as those built by Caracalla and Diocletian, capable of serving thousands of people at once. The monumental aqueducts that transported enormous quantities of water to the urban centers of the Empire constituted a network of arcuated, life-sustaining arteries, several of which are still in use today. The simple, freestanding arch was used to commemorate military victories; the Arch of Titus, for example, celebrates, in two relief panels, the Flavian conquest of Judea, and the pillaging and destruction of the Temple of Jerusalem in 70 AD.

In the Arch of Titus, as in the great baths and other public buildings, the vault is coffered; this is the standard Roman treatment of

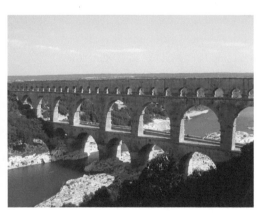

Figure 3.12 Aquaduct, Pont-du-gard (late first century BC/early first century AD)

the ceiling, and it is triply practical, because it lightens the load of the vault while strengthening and decorating it. The most perfect of all Roman buildings, in which the coffering survives in fairly good shape, is the Pantheon. Built by the architect-emperor, Hadrian, to replace an earlier, traditional rectangular structure, this temple to the planetary gods (Venus, Mercury, et al.) derives its form from the sphere. A hemispherical dome atop a cylindrical drum is illuminated by a single circular opening, the *oculus* or "eye." Here, the combination of concrete structure with costly marble veneers achieves

Figure 3.13 The Sack of Jerusalem from the Arch of Titus (after 70 AD)

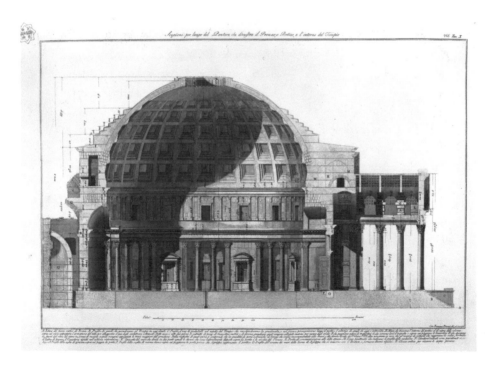

Figure 3.14 The Pantheon, Etching by Giovanni Battista Piranesi (c. 125 AD, etching eighteenth century)

Figure 3.15 Forum of Trajan (c. 110 AD)

its glorious apex and manifests the definitive marriage of Greek geometry and Roman technology.

Hadrian ruled between 117 and 138 AD, and was one of the so-called "good" emperors, whose goodness had nothing to do with personal principles. What made these emperors good was that, after a century of decadent imperial rule (the Flavian dynasty came to an end with Vespasian's son, Domitian, a sadistic creature in the mold of Nero and Caligula), these new men ended the practice of allowing family members to inherit power, opting instead to appoint and train promising younger men to succeed to the throne. Thus, Hadrian was groomed and educated to be emperor by his predecessor, Trajan. Trajan, too, had been a great builder. His temple to his patron god, Mars Ultor; his two-story brick marketplace; his Basilica Ulpia[9] all testify to a wise and generous bene-factor and doer of public good. Together, these buildings constitute the Forum of Trajan, unique in its scale and harmony and the felicitous interrelationship of its individual components. The exclamation mark in this grandiloquent public statement is the soaring Column of Trajan, around which winds a continuous carved narrative detailing the emperor's military successes against the Dacians, a barbarian tribe living along the Danube River. The style here is virtually journalistic, punctuated at regular intervals by the image of Trajan himself, who dominates the activity in every scene.

Hadrian's accession to the throne coincides with the apex of Roman territorial control: the empire was never larger. As the ruler of so unwieldy a tract, it is not

---

9   A basilica is a Roman architectural form and was used as a general tribunal or assembly hall. In its simplest version, it comprises a nave or hall and a rounded apse; the Basilica Ulpia was especially lavish and had an apse at either end, one of which was surrounded by the markets mentioned here.

surprising that Hadrian was often away from the capital. The motivation for his travels was not exclusively military, however; for example, he fell so deeply in love with Athens that he remained in the city for several years in order to oversee (always the architect) the restoration of the Acropolis. And while his wife, Sabina, attempted to divorce him in Rome, he passed his leisure time dallying with a legendarily handsome Greek boy named Antinoös, whose premature death by drowning in the Nile gave rise to suspicions of murder and suicide which still seduce novelists to this day. Hadrian's grief at the death of his beloved Antinoös led him to deify the young man, and also expressed itself in the commission of large numbers of sculptures perpetuating his beauty and the Emperor's attachment to him.

Figure 3.16 Bust of Antinoös (c .125 AD)

Ultimately Hadrian's travels were commemorated in the fantastic villa he constructed at Tiburtina, modern Tivoli, a villa made up of many separate buildings, each evoking a place the Emperor had visited and clearly considered his own. Many of the structures at the Villa Adriana are centralized and circular in plan, and incorporate curvilinear features. In this they are like the tomb of the emperor, which survives in Rome as the Castel Sant'Angelo.

Like Trajan and Hadrian, Antoninus Pius was a builder, but unfortunately few of his architectural commissions survive.[10] Like all three of them, Antoninus' successor, Marcus Aurelius, spent much of his reign on horseback. In his case, he was defending the farthest-flung territories of the empire, which had stretched to the limits the Romans' ability to maintain them. The only large-scale bronze imperial equestrian monument to survive from the Roman world represents Marcus Aurelius, the philosopher emperor, so-called because of his lifelong study and emulation of Greek, and especially Stoic, philosophers; his beard, following

---

10   For example, Antoninus Pius had a column like Trajan before him and like Marcus Aurelius after him. Unfortunately it fell down. The base survives in the Vatican Museums.

Figure 3.17 Equestrian Statue of Marcus Aurileus (c. 170 AD)

the tradition of Hadrian, indicates a love of Greek culture. The horse, hugely powerful and energetic and with a natural nobility of its own, is effortlessly held in check by the emperor, whose gesture acknowledges the respect he receives and whose perfect calm reflects his absolute control over horse and world.

In his movingly written, timeless *Meditations*, too, Marcus Aurelius expressed that same cool transcendence of mortal trials that characterizes his famous bronze portrait. The century after his death would certainly have tested the emperor's stoicism. If the second century—the century of the "good" emperors, of Trajan's Forum and Hadrian's Pantheon—is the Golden Age of Imperial Rome, the third century is the age of disaster. The usual encroachments by discontented tribes in the north and east increased in magnitude and fury, and the outcome was a straining and gradual contraction of the already overtaxed frontiers. The clearest proof of the ongoing collapse of the old Augustan Peace and the decline of imperial prestige was the capture and enslavement of the emperor Valerianus by the Persians in 260 AD.[11] The catastrophic slide into chaos continued until the reign of the brilliant, but ruthless, Diocletian, who came to power in 284 AD.

Diocletian borrowed and revised a page from the book of his "good," Golden Age predecessors; not only did he appoint and train a successor, he, in fact, appointed four of them to rule jointly as *augusti* and *caesares* over an empire now

---

11   According to widespread legend, the Emperor was forced to act as a footstool to the Sasanian King of Persia, Shapur or Sapor. When Valerian died, Shapur called in his royal taxidermists and had him preserved.

divided into East and West. Then, Diocletian retired to a spectacular fortified palace on the Dalmatian coast. His legacy, the tetrarchy, or "rule by four," is conveniently illustrated in an impressive sculpture group in porphyry. The four co-rulers are here represented as pairs of comrades in arms, literally—not only do they embrace, but each also has one hand on the hilt of his sword. After a century of internecine strife, in which an alarming number of emperors fell to ever shorter-lived successors, it would be hard to imagine a more concise and consolidated image of warily shared power. We see in these four colleagues—with their stocky proportions and their impersonal features, distinguished only in terms of their beards or lack thereof—very little of the classical tradition in the approach to the body, still less of ethos or pathos. This is a four-headed power machine. Just as dramatic events have transformed the shape of rule in Rome and Roman society, so, too, there has been a transformation of representational goals, certainly when it comes to imperial portraiture.

The face of one of the four wide-eyed porphyry *Tetrarchs* belongs to a man named Constantius, whose son, Constantine, not only succeeded to his father's position in the tetrarchy, but, after defeating several rivals, became the sole emperor of a reunified empire. His arch, celebrating the first of these great victories, over Maxentius at the Battle of the Milvian Bridge in 312 AD, is the most grandiose of all surviving triumphal arches; its decoration, however, is made up mainly of stolen goods, relief panels and roundels from earlier imperial monuments commissioned by Hadrian and others. The heads of these earlier rulers have simply been recut to resemble the new emperor. Whatever decoration is original to the arch is in the same style of streamlined characterization and simplified form that we have noted in the *Tetrarchs* group.

In those re-carved heads on his triumphal arch, Constantine is represented with another important innovation: he wears a halo. Not because he thought he was a god, as so many of his predecessors had proclaimed for themselves. Instead, the halo, like the characteristic upward rolling glance we find in most of his portraits, reminds us

Figure 3.18 Tetrarchs (c. 305 AD)

Figure 3.19 Arch of Constantine (c. 315 AD)

of the Emperor's nearness to divinity. Constantine believed that his decisive victory over Maxentius was due to the intervention of Jesus, the Christian god. And so, a year after the battle, in 313 AD, he issued the Edict of Milan, allowing freedom of worship and thereby ending centuries of persecution of the Christians.

During the first flush—or perhaps we should say blush—of imperial rule, probably at the very end of the reign of the matricide vaudevillian Nero, a man called Paul of Tarsus had been executed as a criminal in Rome. In the decade before his death, Paul had written some truly revolutionary things, nothing more so than the claim, in an epistle to the people of Galatia (in modern day Turkey), that "there is no longer Jew or Greek, no longer slave or free, no longer male and female."[12] Paul, born Saul, was a pharisaic Jew and also a Roman citizen. As such, he straddled two worlds, and he quite consciously personified the great transformation of Rome from a pagan empire to one whose citizens belong to the new cult following the teachings of the Jewish Jesus of Nazareth; these people came to be known as Christians. It was more than three hundred years before the Roman authorities came to accept this new religion, and Constantine, having had a conversionary experience very like Paul's, set out to make Christianity the religion of a new Rome.

One of the ways that Constantine began the transformation of Rome into the capital of a Christian empire was by commissioning buildings in the service of the new religion. Formerly, when Christianity was frowned upon and its adherents persecuted, its practices, from baptism to burial, including regular offering of the Mass, had been confined to hidden, especially subterranean, spaces. There are miles

---

12   Galatians 3:28

Figure 3.20 Colossal Constantine. Detail. (c. 320 AD)

and miles of catacombs beneath the City of Rome, some of them decorated with images celebrating the Judeo-Christian story. One of the most popular themes we see in the third-century catacombs—for example, those of Priscilla and those of Callixtus—is Christ as the Good Shepherd.

Among the earliest portrayals of Jesus, destined to become the primary subject of all Christian art, these paintings emphasize the gentle humanity of the God of the Gospels; in them, Jesus is seen as filial rather than paternal, serving rather than commanding, young and healthy rather than weary or suffering. Whatever images may have graced the interiors of the new churches commissioned by Constantine, we do know that the lavish decoration in precious metals and precious stones must have overwhelmed the faithful habituated to the torch lit, grave-lined passages of their former places of clandestine worship.

Not the very first, but certainly the most important and best known, of Constantine's churches was that built over what is believed to be the burial place of Saint Peter. The original St. Peter's (replaced, because it was falling down, on the exact same spot, during the Renaissance) demonstrated the wholehearted adoption by Christians of the old Roman secular basilica plan: a large hall or nave with a rounded apse at one end. Such a structure avoids any recollection of the Pagan temple form and is practical, given the importance of preaching and conversion in the new dispensation. As

Figure 3.21 Christ as the Good Shepherd, Catacomb of Saint Callixtus (mid-third century AD)

originally designed, the basilica of St. Peter's was a big meeting hall, preceded by an atrium that marked the transition from the secular world outside to the sanctified world within. On the plan, you will also notice that where the nave meets the apse area, from what, for logical reasons, is called the crossing, transept arms have emerged; the very plan of the church alludes to the central symbol of Christianity.

Not all Early Christian churches were basilicas. A small minority were built along centralized plans, that is, based on the circle, square, or octagon. One of these is the mausoleum of Constantine's daughter, Constantia. Dating to around 350 AD, Santa Costanza, as it is now known, retains its intricate mosaic decoration. It is also interesting that here, as in the earliest *tholoi* of the Aegean, the circular

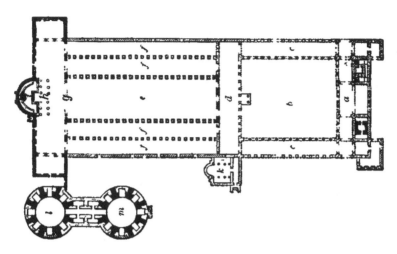

Figure 3.22 St. Peter's Basilica. Plan. (c. 325 AD)

plan is linked to burial. Constantia's actual sarcophagus, an immense porphyry vessel that originally stood in the center of the little church, is now in the Vatican museum.

It is worth noting the evolution of burial practices among Romans of the Imperial and Early Christian Periods. Until the end of the first century AD, Romans tended to be incinerated after death. One example of posthumous treatment of the body was the Column of Trajan, which was a glorified grave marker, crowned by a gilded bronze portrait of the emperor surveying his endless domain; in the room-sized base of the column was deposited the emperor's heart after the rest of his body was cremated. But, already in

Figure 3.23 Santa Costanza Detail. (begun c. 337 AD)

Figure 3.24 Sarcophagus of Junius Bassus (359 AD)

the second century, Romans, doubtless influenced by the widely propagated beliefs of certain foreign sects, including the Christians, began to adopt the practice
of burying their dead whole. Christians were against disfiguring or destroying the
corpse, instead honoring their physical bodies, which would be reanimated at the
end of time. And so the walls of the catacombs contained the *loculi,* or shelves,
the bunk beds of the dead. Many wealthier Romans, whether Christian or not,
eventually went to great pains to house their mortal remains. Elaborate sarcophagi
are among the most impressive of all artifacts surviving from the Late Roman
Period. That of Junius Bassus, a fourth-century Christian prefect and former
consul of Rome, is a masterpiece of theological and artistic syncretism. On one
side, in the center of the upper of two richly carved registers, a youthful, beardless
Jesus converses casually with Saint Peter and Saint Paul; theirs is a reunion out of
time. Below them to the left, Adam and Eve are shown trying on their fig leaves in
the first moments of shame and regret, while next door, Jesus rides into Jerusalem
on a donkey. The carving is highly detailed throughout, the depth of the spaces

creating a rich chiaroscuro, while the figural proportions recall those of the plebe-
ian style on the column of Trajan. The ideal here is to communicate not physical
refinement, but the stories, which are relatively new to Roman art.

Having reconsolidated the Empire under his sole authority, and having established, after a thousand years of paganism, Christianity as the new religion of
Rome, what was left for Constantine to do? In 324 AD, he undertook what was,
in terms of sheer boldness and energy, the crowning accomplishment of his reign.
In an effort to bring the fight to the problematic and fraying eastern boundaries,
he relocated the capital of the Empire a thousand miles away, in the old Greek city
of Byzantium. Rechristened Constantinople, the capital became the new beacon
of an old civilization, and the Roman world became the Byzantine world, though
nothing changed the legacy of Rome itself. In terms of national behavior—in
terms of the conduct of people in power, reflected in their cultural range and
achievements—Rome was the greatest model of all that is most praised and most
reviled in the history of the Western world.

four

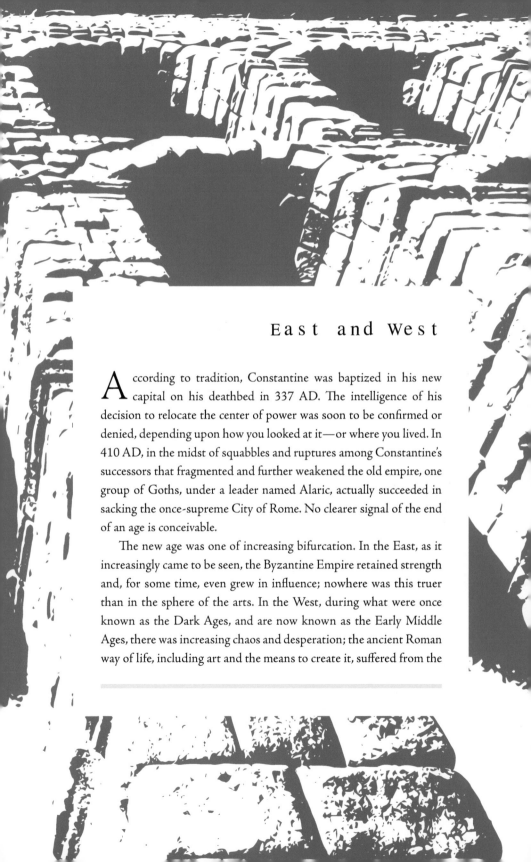

East and West

According to tradition, Constantine was baptized in his new capital on his deathbed in 337 AD. The intelligence of his decision to relocate the center of power was soon to be confirmed or denied, depending upon how you looked at it—or where you lived. In 410 AD, in the midst of squabbles and ruptures among Constantine's successors that fragmented and further weakened the old empire, one group of Goths, under a leader named Alaric, actually succeeded in sacking the once-supreme City of Rome. No clearer signal of the end of an age is conceivable.

The new age was one of increasing bifurcation. In the East, as it increasingly came to be seen, the Byzantine Empire retained strength and, for some time, even grew in influence; nowhere was this truer than in the sphere of the arts. In the West, during what were once known as the Dark Ages, and are now known as the Early Middle Ages, there was increasing chaos and desperation; the ancient Roman way of life, including art and the means to create it, suffered from the rising instability that was itself an inevitable consequence of constant foreign invasion. The very recipe for making cement was lost. No more monumental architecture, no more lavish civic entertainments, no more large-scale casting in bronze. In an era of evolving polarization between East and West—and in the West, where alienation and dissolution became the norm—the only bulwark against total collapse was the new religion. Christianity took on the role of unifier, and its spread was like the spread of Roman power in the Republican and Early Imperial Periods. Only after the slow conversion of most of the northern and eastern tribes, and the equally slow ejection or subjugation of the unconverted, did the civilization of the High Middle Ages in a newly conceived West become possible.

In the new center of the old Empire, in Constantinople, a great period of creative achievement coincided with the reign of Emperor Justinian I (527 AD to 565 AD). Like Constantine two hundred years earlier, Justinian dreamt of recreating the glory of the Roman Empire in the Golden Age. A famous ivory panel known as the *Barberini Diptych* (because it was presumably joined to another panel, now lost) shows a youthful and energetic Emperor virtually bursting out of the frame. He rides an equally exuberant and beautifully behaved horse. Horse and rider together participate in a fluid and dynamic rhythm that extends to some of the subsidiary figures, most obviously that of Earth, represented as a woman cradling her bounty while supporting the emperor's foot. Below, representatives of different subject peoples assiduously present their tribute. For all the terrestrial activity that marks the lower scenes, a celestial calm is established above by the chubby-faced and child-like Christ shown in the act of blessing and sanctioning imperial authority over the world. Framed by winged victories, the symmetry and relative stasis of this upper zone illustrate an ideal of Byzantine art.

Figure 4.1 Barberini Diptych (first half sixth century)

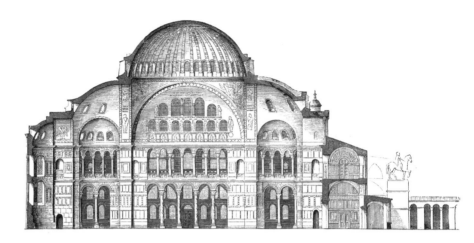

Figure 4.2 Hagia Sophia (dedicated 537)

Justinian's ambitions expressed themselves on a vast scale. Like Constantine before him, Justinian founded a number of churches and monasteries. The largest of these is the Church of Holy Wisdom, the Hagia Sophia, in Constantinople, built between 532 AD and 537 AD. Since it is an immense domed structure, it is difficult not to appreciate the allusion to Hadrian's Pantheon back in Rome. But this temple is built in a very different way. Probably the greatest Byzantine contribution to the field of engineering is the invention of a new type of dome support system. The dome of the Pantheon and all other Roman domes, such as that in the so-called Temple of Mercury at Baia near Naples, were constructed on simple, cylindrical drums. But at Hagia Sophia, the architects, Anthemius of Tralles and Isidoros of Miletos, erected enormous piers, joining above as concave triangular *pendentives*, to support a huge central dome above a rectilinear space. This innovation allowed the opening of wall surfaces, transforming them into screens of light and passages into adjacent spaces. Nowhere is the potential of the punctured surface more effectively exploited than in

Figure 4.3 Interior, Hagia Sophia

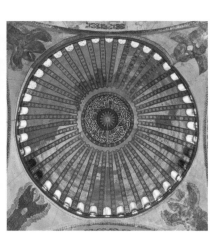

Figure 4.4 Interior, Hagia Sophia Cupola

the circle of arched lights that rings the base of the dome, which consequently seems to float or hover over all. Covering the upper story interior are sacred images worked in the decorative technique preferred by the Byzantines: gold ground mosaic.

The Romans had long practiced the art of mosaic, the technique of setting small stones or bits of glass, known as *tesserae*, into a wall or floor to create an image or pattern. But, as we know, most wall decoration in and around Rome was done in fresco. Now, in Constantinople, we are dealing with a different, considerably more humid climate, one that is less amenable to the fresco technique, for which hot, and above all dry, air is necessary. The gold ground mosaics that fill Byzantine churches are composed of glass tesserae, predominantly gilded and set irregularly into the wall in order to catch and play with light from different sources. The dynamic effect of the interiors of the Hagia Sophia and other churches in Constantinople, with their vast, glittering surfaces, became a model for builders throughout the expanding Byzantine world.

Not content with merely constructing a new Rome, Justinian wanted to reclaim the territories once ruled by his second-century predecessors. Toward this end he sent his general, Belisarius, to reconquer the Italian peninsula, which had been overrun by and parceled out among numerous contentious tribes. By the end of a brilliant campaign, Ravenna, on the north eastern coast, was reinvested as a satellite capital of the Byzantine Empire.

And it is in Ravenna that we find some of the most important and impressive Byzantine architecture. Though Justinian himself was never in Ravenna, his portrait presides over one of the greatest Byzantine buildings there or anywhere. Like the funerary church of Santa Costanza in Rome, San Vitale in Ravenna is basically an octagonal structure, though it has two unusual features for a centralized-plan church: a large porch or narthex set at a distinctive angle to the body of the edifice, and, as the altar area, a miniature, basilica-plan sanctuary complete with an apse.

And, where the little nave joins that apse, we find a glorious vision of the imperial court participating in the sacrifice of the Christian mass. To the left of the

ure 4.5 San Vitale, Ravenna (dedicated 547)

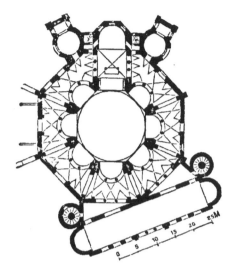

Figure 4.6 San Vitale

altar, Justinian, crowned and haloed and surrounded by priests and military attendants, invites comparison to Constantine as that emperor was represented on his triumphal Arch and, even more obviously, to Christ. Bearing a large golden dish, or paten, a vessel for the bread of the Eucharist, Justinian's simultaneous centrality in and separation from this group of (twelve) men is a visual translation of his primacy in the procession and in the world.

Like her husband moving altarward, to the east, the former circus performer-turned empress, Theodora, presenting the chalice for the sacramental wine, pauses in her procession on the facing wall. The theme of the processional, royal and sacred, is made beautifully clear on the hem of her gown, emblazoned with the three gift-bearing Magi. In both mosaics, the Byzantine figure style is summarily defined. Bodies, both male and female, are long and elegant, though far from three dimensional for all of the pleats and folds of their draperies. Faces, especially those of the emperor and his consort, are equally flat, masks of authority and prestige, wide-eyed and impassive, with arched eyebrows, long narrow noses, and little in the way of personal expression. Lavish costumes, and especially jewelry, play a major part in the composition; the haloes, crowns, and other ornaments of the royal couple are like settings for the jewels of their faces, separating them from

Figure 4.7 Justinian Mosaic San Vitale

their retinues and further communicating the timelessness and the divine sanction of their reign.

If, in the mosaics in Ravenna, the iconography of Justinian recalls that of Christ at the Last Supper, one visual model for the empress Theodora is clearly the mother of Jesus, who is, in the sixth century, well on her way to becoming the most represented woman in Western art. In the monastery of Saint Catherine, founded by Justinian at the base of Mount Sinai in Egypt, is an encaustic[1] painting depicting Mary as the *Theotokos*, or "god-bearer," with her divine child. Probably painted around the year 600 AD, Mary and Jesus are shown between saints Theodore and George with angels gazing upward behind them. In the flatness of the forms, in the standardized figures and faces, and in the symmetry of their arrangement, the style of the Ravenna mosaics recurs.

The presence of Saint George and Saint Theodore, military martyrs, made of the St. Catherine icon an object of veneration and supplication among Christians

---

1 Encaustic painting is painting with pigment suspended in wax.

Figure 4.8 Theodora Mosaic San Vitale

during the following (seventh) century, a period of mounting trouble for the Byzantine world. The death of the reluctant warrior prophet Muhammad in Medina in 632 AD marked the beginning of a dramatic expansion of the religion he founded. In general, the Christian reaction to the so-called "rise of Islam" was one of panic, and one form that panic took among the administrators of Byzantium was to re-examine longstanding practices—including religious and artistic practices—at home. After significant territorial losses to the followers of the new religion, blamed by a growing faction on the misuse of sacred images, the emperor in Constantinople, Leo III (ruled 717AD to 741 AD), called for an end to the production of icons of holy personages, thereby ushering in a period of *iconoclasm* (literally, "the breaking of images") that would last for more than a hundred years, finally ending in 843 AD.

Though diverse and often innovative in style and detail, Byzantine art of the post-iconoclastic era inevitably reflects an abiding attachment to the imperial past, to those cultural traditions associated with the reign of Justinian, and even further back, with the very origins of the Empire in the Roman world of which it claims to

Figure 4.9 Mary as Theotokos, St Catherine Monastery (sixth century)

be the sole heir. The clearest illustration of the importance of continuity and tradition—artistic, political, religious—is to be found in another Theotokos image, this time a mosaic in the vestibule of Hagia Sophia, created in the early tenth century during a major redecoration of the great church. Here again the enthroned mother and child are flanked by male figures, in this case, Justinian on the left and Constantine on the right. The now-familiar frontality and formality prevail among the group. The symmetry projects stasis and stability; the identities of the characters (all four of the characters are named in Greek, the language of the Empire since before the sixth century) validate, as it were, the ancient succession and divine sanction of Byzantine rule. Again, in the gorgeous vestments and the jeweled crowns and throne, we find an emphasis on the rich surfaces supremely suited to representation in the gold ground mosaic medium. A glowing, stately image—iconic in every

Figure 4.10 St. Catherine Monastery, Sinai (begun 548)

sense, and ahistorical, outside of time—the Hagia Sophia Theotokos represents a convergence of artistic choices that have become synonymous with Byzantine style.

Figure 4.11 Theotokos, Hagia Sofia (early tenth century)

Later Byzantine architecture, too, evinces a deep-seated reverence and nostalgia for the heady days of Justinian and Theodora, though the achievements of their reign will never be equaled; with ongoing, often violent, intrigues at court and with the perpetual threat from the Muslim east, the magnificence and triumphalism of the Hagia Sophia will never recur.[2] But, great churches and monasteries continue to be built and decorated throughout the post-iconoclastic period. Just as their mosaic decoration invariably pays tribute to longstanding tradition, the forms of many of these religious buildings continue along the path first indicated by the architects of the first Byzantine era. So, for example, the basic ground plans of the two adjacent churches, the Katholikon and the Panaghia, of the Osios Loukas (Saint Luke) monastery on the Greek mainland, constructed in the late tenth and eleventh centuries, resemble, though on a considerably smaller scale, that of Hagia Sophia, with its dome at the center of a roughly regular cross. But the elevations of the Osios Loukas churches, like that of the (perhaps slightly later) monastic church at Dafni, not far from Athens, are decidedly different, with a pronounced vertical orientation. The domes that surmount the Katholikon at Osios Loukas and the church at Dafni, crowning these much steeper edifices, are also supported on squinches[3] rather than the

---

2   We cannot know precisely or with any great certainty the details of many later imperial buildings in Constantinople, as they have not survived. See for example John Lowden, *Early Christian & Byzantine Art*, (Phaidon 1997) 229ff.

3   It is helpful and not at all inaccurate to think of squinches as representing a middle way between the drum system of dome support and the pendentive system invented by the

Figure 4.12 Dafni (monastery built c. 1100)

sort of pendentives that were used at Hagia Sofia. The overall visual effect of the later structures is a tighter, more succinct restatement of the earlier Byzantine formula.

Probably the best known of all later Byzantine churches is the one dedicated to Saint Mark, in Venice.[4] Though the origins of Venice are as murky as the marshes of the North Adriatic out of which it rises, the city was, like Ravenna, a Byzantine dependency for centuries.[5] Constructed as the private chapel of the doge, or elected leader of the city, the present basilica of San Marco was begun in 1063 AD, and its plan was based closely on that of the church of the Holy Apostles in Constantinople, a building that does not survive. Its debt to Byzantine architecture of the first period is obvious: five domes upheld by pendentives and forming a cross, the interior elevation covered with

---

Byzantines.

4   Not only dedicated to the saint, but also, according to tradition, originally built to house his body, smuggled out of Alexandria in the ninth century in a vat of pork, under the noses of the Muslims who ruled there.

5   Most scholars agree that Venice was founded by Roman citizens of the late Imperial Period as a refuge from barbarian tribes. As the wealth of Venice increased, so did its territorial ambitions and its independence. Finally, in 1204 AD, the Venetians committed the shocking act of joining the Fourth Crusade against the Muslims on the condition that they be permitted to sack the Christian city of Constantinople on the way to the Holy Land; they never made it to Jerusalem, but they did make off with huge quantities of loot from the great Byzantine capital—including the Egyptian porphyry sculptures of the *Tetrarchs* we discussed in the chapter on Rome, which serve as the cornerstone of a chapel at San Marco, and the four famous, if controversial, gilt-bronze Greek horses that long decorated the center of the façade of the basilica (they have been replaced by copies; the originals are now in the Museum of San Marco).

gold ground mosaics. And on the high altar of San Marco is one of the greatest examples of the art of metal working, the so-called *Pala d'Oro*, the "altarpiece of gold." A dazzling, monumental work, put into its present form in the middle of the fourteenth century, the *Pala d'Oro* is actually a collage of hundreds of precious stones and enameled images of saints, angels, imperial figures, and sacred stories.

Figure 4.13 Detail, Pala d'Oro, San Marco (completed 1345)

These Byzantine enamels (the original elements of the altarpiece were obtained in Constantinople in the tenth century) are, with their flattened figures set against burnished gold, the portable equivalent of the large-scale mosaics that fill Byzantine churches. The altarpiece , then, is a concise, assembled version of a Byzantine shrine.

The sad and steady decline of Byzantium finally ended in 1453 AD, with the Muslim takeover of the capital. Constantinople became Istanbul. By this time, the boundaries separating East and West had long been indelibly drawn. The origins of the division reach far back through centuries of increasing detachment reflected and magnified by differences in language (in Byzantium, Greek was standard, whereas in the West, Latin remained, at least officially, the norm), cultural practices (for example, the Romans never embraced Byzantine iconoclasm), and religious beliefs; (longstanding theological disagreements and sheer orneriness caused the Great Schism between the Eastern [Orthodox] and Western [Roman Catholic] churches, which was finally made official in the middle of the eleventh century). We have seen that, for a considerable time after its founding, the Byzantine Empire maintained control over a vast area coinciding with the eastern territories of the former Roman world, and that also, under Justinian and Theodora, the Byzantines reclaimed the Italian Peninsula. But this reclamation was short-lived. While the power and stability that made Constantinople a beacon of civilization in the East, expand and contract and eventually transfigure into myth, the West, ever more separate from that center of power and stability, faced overwhelming obstacles, and a very different fate. The long stretch of Western history between the beginning of the collapse of the Roman centers of administration in the fifth century and the phenomenal repopulation of those towns and the founding of new ones at the end of the first millennium is known as the Early Middle Ages. These centuries saw the slow and painstaking conversion of the migratory pagan tribes to settled Christian communities—communities that were the tentative prototypes for the countries, provinces, and city centers of present-day Europe.

The more we know of life in the Early Middle Ages, the grimmer the picture that emerges. During the period, a rigid and oppressive system of government, known as *feudalism*, evolved, and it lingered right up to the dawn of the Modern era in the later eighteenth century; large pockets of feudalism can still be found outside of Europe today. In Early Medieval feudal society, most people belonged to one of three classes. The feudal lords and their vassals made up the ruling, military class; they possessed the land. The professional religious sector comprised the clergy, both male and female, both secular (priests) and regular (monks and nuns, that is, who follow a *regula*, or rule, the most famous being that of the sixth-century Italian, Benedict of Nursia, founder of the Benedictines). Finally, the vast majority of people were *serfs*—"*serf*" being a somewhat easier and sunnier-sounding term than slave, which is what serfs virtually were. Tied to the land, without vocational options, serfs worked their little life spans (which were, unsurprisingly, much shorter than ours today) entirely in the service of their lords, the legal owners of whatever their agriculture produced. It's no wonder that the Early Middle Ages in Europe were traditionally known as the Dark Ages.

For all its evils, for all that it served some of the worst of human tendencies toward power and exploitation and greed, feudalism clearly developed in part as a means to combat chaos with control. And chaos *was* the primary state of affairs in the burgeoning Europe of the sixth, seventh, and eighth centuries. Like the Dark Ages of the ancient Aegean, this period was marked by large-scale migrations of tribes with widely varying laws, languages, religious beliefs, etc. Violence was the standard way of communicating territorial claims, authority (within the tribe, and among tribes), and disfavor. In the north, Norsemen—the Vikings—spread their particular, ship-borne brand of terror among the inhabitants—including long-established settlements of Saxons and Celts—of what are now Northern France and the British Isles. Further south, Franks conquered Gaul, while other Germanic tribes, among them the Goths and the Lombards, divided up Italy, and Muslims came to dominate the Iberian peninsula.[6] It is hardly surprising, given this ceaseless pinballing of heterogeneous peoples, that chaos reigned, and uncertainty was the general—really, the only possible—response.

If you live in an unstable or dangerous area, if you grow up in unpredictable economic times, what sort of art are you likely to make, or to buy? If you are on the move a lot—lucky enough to have survived the pillaging of your village, or the bloody defeat of your local lord—what sort of possessions are you likely to keep? Think small, think portable—like this book. In fact, books and small works in metal, including jewelry, constitute the primary artistic survivors of this troubled age, an age from which we have almost nothing in the way of monumental sculpture or large-scale architecture in stone.

---

6 The very fact that Muslim Spain is relegated to this footnote serves to illustrate the limitations, the inevitable fallacy inherent in any division of the world—at any period, by any people—into East and West, into native and foreigner. Between the eighth and fourteenth centuries, several Muslim dynasties rose and fell and dominated the Spanish peninsula; in fact, the East was *in* the West. The peaceful blendings of cultures that characterize various moments in this epoch remain models of globalism and tolerance. The most impressive monuments associated with Muslim Spain reflect these diverse cultural traditions and convergences. The Great Mosque at Cordoba, begun in 785 AD by Abd al Rahman, the first Muslim ruler in Spain, is itself both East and West, reusing columns and capitals from a former Christian church and incorporating design elements from Christian—including Visigothic—and Roman architecture. The topic is too large—and too important—for a survey of Western Art; this footnote humbly acknowledges that.

Figure 4.14 Interior, Great Mosque, Cordoba (begun 785)

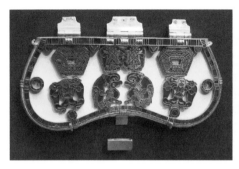

Figure 4.15 Sutton Hoo Purse Cover (c. 625)   Figure 4.15a Sutton Hoo Purse Cover, detail (c. 625)

Perhaps the most familiar horde of Early Medieval metalwork was unearthed at the site known as Sutton Hoo, in Suffolk, England. There among numerous burial mounds, is one presumed to be that of the ship-tomb of the East Anglian king, Redwald, who probably died around 625 AD. Among the celebrated artifacts from this incredibly rich find is the exquisitely wrought purse covered in gold, enamel, and semi-precious stones.[7] Though relatively small (19 cm across), it is decorated with a variety of images ranging from the naturalistic (splayed male figures flanked by wolves, eagles attacking ducks) through the mesomorphic (the mysterious creatures woven into the tracery in the upper center) to the abstract (the fantastic filigree in the hexagons on either side). Despite all the activity, much of which is difficult to decipher, an overarching symmetry stabilizes the design, and even extends into each of the individual scenes and patterns.

The specific type of enamel we see in the Sutton Hoo purse cover is *cloisonné*, so-called because of the little partitions—in French, *cloisons*—that form the cells filled with color. Lavish line work in precious metal is also prominent, and we find it again in another famous bit of Early Medieval jewelry, the Tara Brooch,[8] produced by Celtic artisans at some point during the eighth century. As in the interlaced patterns on the purse cover, several of the curling bands in and around the brooch end in animal heads; in fact, the entire piece suggests some energetic, animated creature. This same dynamism, the same playful, if unspecific, evocation

---

7   Originally the metal work was affixed to a base of ivory or bone, which is now lost.
8   Actually, a very elaborate version of a *fibula* or fastener—a glorified safety pin.

of animal forms, pervades much of the decoration of texts copied and illuminated by Celtic monks of the period. Like the anonymous artisan who created the Tara Brooch, these monastic calligraphers and painters (an illuminated manuscript is simply one decorated in color) worked in the style we call *Insular*, a term that refers to the particular traits of decoration originating with the inhabitants of *Hibernia*, that is, the island of Ireland, an area largely insulated from Roman, hence Classical, tradition, and long (but not permanently) protected by the natural barrier of the British Isles from the depredations of the piratical, sea-faring tribes.

Figure 4.16 Head of the Tara Brooch (early eighth century)

The *Book of Kells* is a *codex*,[9] profusely illuminated by artists associated with the scriptorium of the Celtic monastery at Kells in County Meath, Ireland. It probably dates to the first decade of the ninth century. The *Chi Rho* page from this manuscript gives us an elaborate variation on the first letters of the Greek word for Christ, ΧΡΙΣΤΟΣ, embedded in, but also dominating, a dense network of serpentine tracery, wheels within wheels, animal and human forms. The stylistic similarities to the *Tara Brooch* are as numerous as they are obvious.

From early on the Insular style, with its elaborate linear patterns incorporating natural and fantastic creatures, was disseminated by Celtic missionaries throughout the north, while in the south, what survived of classicism and its very different visual vocabularies constituted a diminished, but still vital, source of artistic inspiration. And so we find, in Early Medieval illuminated manuscripts, widely divergent approaches to the human figure. Compare, for example, two illuminated images of the Evangelist, Saint Matthew, one from a Celtic Gospel book, created around 700 AD at the storied island-abbey of Lindisfarne off the northeast coast of England, and the other from the so-called *Coronation Gospels*, produced at the royal scriptorium of the Italophile Carolingian court in Aachen

---

9 A codex (pl. codices) is an early form of book, developed by the Romans in the second century, comprising tablets or pages sewn or glued together, the whole often bound between covers. By the Early Middle Ages, pages are usually made from *parchment,* made of stretched and dried animal skin; *vellum* is a particularly fine kind of parchment made from calf.

Figure 4.17 Book of Kells, Chi Rho Page (c. 800)

around the year 800 AD. In the Celtic example, space—such as it is—is framed by a thin ribbon of color forming a rectangle, the corners of which resemble cloisonné. There is some suggestion of an attempt to represent depth in the relationship between the evangelist's open book, his bench, and the square of carpet at his feet. But Saint Matthew's body does not participate in that otherwise utterly undefined space. He is, in fact, a flattened form, as are the trumpeting angel above him and the disembodied head of the attendant peering from behind the curtain. The absence of real depth is some indication of the artist's true priorities, namely, color and pattern, the former of which apparently owes little to optical naturalism; note especially the orange, flame-like folds in the sitter's bright green mantle.

Similarly framed by a polychrome border, the *Coronation Gospels* Matthew exists in a comparatively naturalistic, if still somewhat tentative and ultimately illogical, space. His right foot, not to mention the legs of his chair, rests in such a way as to reaffirm that border as a true ground or baseline. And the major difference between this later Matthew and the Lindisfarne example is that this Matthew is *modeled*. The artist has used light and shade and manipulated the curving contours in order to conjure up a credible three-dimensional form. There is even the illusion of translucency in the Evangelist's garments, such that one can follow his legs beneath the fabric. All of these features are ultimately derived from the ancient Greek and Roman classical tradition of naturalistic figural representation.

The *Coronation Gospels* belonged to the greatest ruler of the Early Middle Ages, *Carolus Magnus*, Charlemagne. If the entire period seems to us like a dark

Figure 4.19 Coronation Gospel, St. Matthew (c. 810)

Figure 4.18 Lindisfarne Gospel, St. Matthew (c. 720)

and blasted forest or desert where fear and instability prevailed, the reign of Charles the Great was an oasis of cultural renewal made possible by epoch-changing successes on the battlefield and in the political and diplomatic spheres. After years of struggle, with Saxons and Vikings in the north and Lombards and Muslims in the south, Charlemagne expanded the Frankish kingdom he had inherited from his father, Pepin the Short, to encompass all of modern day France, Germany, Belgium, and the Netherlands. Like his father, who had established the temporal holdings of the papacy by presenting Pope Stephen with, among other territories, the city of Ravenna, Charlemagne also assumed the role of protector and defender of the Roman church. No one is certain whether it was Charlemagne's idea or that of Pope Leo III, but everybody agrees that the latter placed a crown on the head of the former at mass in Saint Peter's basilica on Christmas morning in the year 800 AD, thereby creating, with a gesture, the Holy Roman Empire.

However ambiguous his feelings, as first Holy Roman Emperor, Charlemagne must have been conscious of his position in the line of Roman rulers extending back

Figure 4.20 Equestrian Portrait of Charlemagne (c. 800)

through Justinian and Constantine to the First Imperial Period. In fact, so much of what we might call Charlemagne's pan-institutional project (and this project tellingly pre-dates his imperial coronation) involves a revival of classical, and specifically Roman, customs and forms. A small equestrian statue believed by many to represent the emperor shows him bearing the orb of state (the sword he presumably held in his right hand is now missing). The obvious model for this diminutive portrait is one that Charlemagne would certainly have known first hand, namely, the statue of Marcus Aurelius, the sole surviving large-scale Roman Imperial equestrian bronze. There is a stiffness and formality in the Charlemagne portrait, something a little heavy-handed in his inexpressive facial features and the way he leans backwards slightly, all of which suggests an aloofness entirely lacking from the Marcus Aurelius, who seems comparatively at ease with his great power. Unlike his second-century idol, Charlemagne seems to dominate his horse with his disproportionate size and weight; perhaps this reflects a tougher manner of ruling than was displayed by emperors of the Golden Age. [10]

A coin from the emperor's reign shows Charlemagne in profile—a profile recognizably similar to that on our statue, especially in its physical attitude—and is tellingly labeled in Latin, "KAROLUS IMP AUG," "Charles Emperor Augustus."

---

10 In the interest of full disclosure, we must point out that 1) this statue is actually composed of three separate castings, each of a different alloy; 2) the horse is believed by some scholars to predate the rider; 3) this sculpture may or may not actually represent Charlemagne. Alternately, it could be some other Carolingian monarch, such as Charlemagne's grandson, Charles the Bald.

Crowned with leaves, he is clearly the emperor of a new Rome. For his capital, he chose the town in which he had been crowned King of the Franks, Aachen, in present-day Germany. There, in true imperial fashion, he created a great palace complex combining religious, governmental, and domestic functions. What you see today at Aachen is not at all what Charlemagne built and left behind. But the palace chapel still survives as the core of a cathedral

Figure 4.21 Portrait of Charlemagne (c. 800)

that represents, in its current state, centuries of later building. In the palatine chapel, the point of Charlemagne's joint cultural and political program is clear. Not only is the octagonal ground plan clearly derived from that of San Vitale in Ravenna, but the interior elevation, replete with arcades of round-headed arches, revives, on a very impressive scale and without the use of concrete, those forms of architecture forever

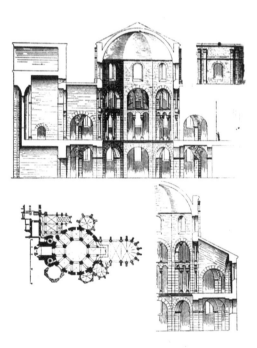

Figure 4.22 Aachen (begun 786)

Figure 4.23 Interior, Palatine Chapel, Aachen

Figure 4.24 Interior of San Vitale, Ravenna

identified with the ancient Romans and later embraced by the builders of the Byzantine East.

Though little of his original palace complex remains today, Charlemagne's Aachen was a dream of Imperial glory in the midst of the chaos that was the Early Middle Ages. Like the buildings themselves, the enormous empire Charlemagne controlled was unrecognizably altered after his death; his grandchildren fragmented their patrimony and the result was a return to the chaotic Early Medieval norm. It is interesting that at the pinnacle of his success, at the very apex of his career, Charlemagne became a suitor for the hand of the widowed Byzantine Empress, Irene. This, too, gives us some insight into his personality, his self-image and his ambitions. An embassy was sent to Constantinople to present his proposal to the court. At first, the ambassadors from the "new" Western emperor were rejected outright. Negotiations were eventually held, but they, too, like Charlemagne's dreams of an enduring empire based on the Roman model, fell apart. And yet, in the end, in his self-created role as unifier and conqueror, he perpetuated the myth of world order; what Marcus Aurelius and Constantine and Justinian were to Charlemagne, Charlemagne would become for the Ottonians of the tenth century, not to mention, in more recent times, Napoleon and Adolph Hitler.

five

The High Middle Ages

To refer to the Romanesque and Gothic periods as the High Middle Ages is to suggest that we rise into them out of the relative low point of the preceding period. We have seen that there is much to admire in the artistic achievements of the Early Middle Ages, and our admiration for the artists responsible—the metalworkers, the monastic calligraphers and illuminators, and the Carolingian builders whose job was to recreate something of the glory of Rome without recourse to Roman building techniques and materials—increases when we consider the extreme instability of the times and conditions in which they worked. But it is inevitable, when we leave the Early for the High Middle Ages, we are like a lucky serf escaping the feudal oppression of life tied to the land for the greater freedom and variety of life in town. Or, we are like theater goers moving directly from a performance of *King Lear* to one of *Romeo and Juliet.* In short, we enter a new phase of civilization, a Pan-European, now almost universally Christian, civilization of turreted castles and immense cathedrals, of sacred pilgrimages and questionable Crusades, of the founding of great universities and cults of courtly love.

If we can refer to the later Middle Ages as high at all, it is first and foremost due to the glorious achievements in architecture, out of which naturally arose the need for decoration on a great scale and in a wide variety of materials. Like the explosion of urban populations throughout Europe, the Romanesque style is widely dispersed; despite rich local contributions, it is surprisingly homogeneous. Called Romanesque because of its reliance on the round-headed Roman arch and the architectural forms that derive from it—the barrel vault and the groin vault—the style is less obviously tied to ancient Roman forms when we consider works of art on a smaller scale and in different media, including the luxury and domestic accessories that proliferate on and within the buildings of the period.

Of course, Charlemagne's architectural program was also dependent on a preference for Roman forms, but what used to be called his "Carolingian Renaissance" was exceptional and short-lived. Charlemagne's revival was itself revived, proudly and self-consciously, by the Ottonians, a dynasty of Holy Roman emperors (most of them named Otto, but a couple named

Figure 5.1 Doors of Saint Michael's, Hildesheim (c. 1015)

Figure 5.2 Detail, Doors of Saint Michael's, Hildesheim

Henry) whose rule over what is now Germany coincided with the first phase of the Romanesque.

An important member of the Ottonian Imperial court was a well-born Saxon, Bernward, who served as tutor to the young Emperor, Otto III, and who became Bishop of Hildesheim in 993. Bernward was keenly interested in the arts, was known to have learned techniques for working in bronze, and was, therefore, supposed to have played an important role in the casting of a pair of solid bronze doors for the Benedictine abbey he founded in his episcopal city. Considered by many scholars to be the first monumental cast-metal sculptures since ancient times, the doors made for St. Michael's in modern-day Hildesheim, Germany, unquestionably reflect the Bishop's first-hand experience of Roman, and more specifically Early Christian, relief decoration, such as we find on a famed pair of wooden doors at the fifth-century Roman church of Santa Sabina. The Saint Michael's doors depict, on the left, eight scenes from the Fall of Man, as described in Genesis, and on the right, eight typologically related episodes from the life of Christ, the whole sequence describing in an unbroken, downward and then upward, path, the Christian story of redemption.

In the scene of the Expulsion of Adam and Eve from the Garden of Eden, a wizened and clearly irritated old man who just happens to be God leans menacingly in the direction of the naked first couple, one of his fingers accusingly extended. The old man seems almost to levitate in his wrath, which is like a great wind, and the blame he casts is like an electrical charge, hitting first Adam, who passes it ungallantly onto Eve, his mate, who sends it downward, as best she can, into the serpent at their feet. Eve's body really seems to bear the brunt of this gathering physical force, which practically doubles her over. The stage properties—the trees and vines—frame and contextualize the drama, but also reiterate and enhance it. Though we are a long way from a classical treatment of the human figure, the individual dioramas of the Hildesheim doors are alive with actions and attitudes that are accessible to all. In fact, it is precisely in their lack of idealization, in their fragility and their ungainliness and the way in which these spindly creatures express their reaction to an overwhelming world, that they are most like us.

Though the doors survived, the church of Saint Michael's, Hildesheim, was almost entirely destroyed during World War II. Prewar photographs, which were the basis of an impressive restoration, confirm the building's seminal role in the development of German Romanesque architecture. With six towers breaking up the exterior, along with its large *westwerke*, or western apse—large in order to accommodate the imperial court—St. Michael's was clearly an important model for the great cathedrals at

Figure 5.3 Interior, Speyer Cathedral (begun 1030)

Figure 5.4 Saint Martin du Canigou (begun 1005)

Mainz, Worms, and especially, Speyer.

The cathedral of Saint Mary and Saint Stephen at Speyer was begun in 1030 and, like St. Michael's, Hildesheim, it originally had a flat, wooden ceiling over the nave. At the end of the eleventh century, during the reign of Henry IV (Holy Roman Emperor from 1084 to 1105), the ceiling at Speyer was replaced with stone groin vaults, by far the largest of their kind to date. Adding variety to the nave arcade is an alternating system of supports, every other pier marked by a slender colonette that rises unbroken to ceiling level, while those in between are broken into two smaller, but thicker, engaged columns, one atop the other. The result is a musical undulation of monumental solids and voids.

Stone-vaulted churches became standard during the eleventh century, though most Romanesque naves employed not groin vaults, but straightforward Roman barrel vaults. This preference for barrel or telescopic vaults was established in the earliest Romanesque buildings. The French abbey churches of Saint Martin du Canigou and Saint Guilhem le Désert provide excellent examples of the evolution of the taste and the tendency throughout this period toward increasing grandeur

Figure 5.5 Interior, Saint Martin du Canigou

Figure 5.7 Sainte Foy, Conques
(eleventh century)

Figure 5.6 Interior, Monastery of Saint Guilhem
(eleventh and twelfth centuries)

and refinement. Perched as proudly and defensively as any Mycenaean fortress, the complex at Saint Martin du Canigou occupies a spectacular promontory in the French Pyrenees. The abbey was begun in 1005, and the church, in its stark, even primitive, simplicity, with its undecorated walls and its tiny openings for light, again reminds us of some of the earliest structures we have seen in the West, whether Minoan or Mycenaean, though it goes without saying that the latter were completely unknown to the Romanesque builders. In comparison with the cave-like church at Saint Martin, that at the monastery of Saint Guilhem possesses greater clarity in the sense that here we have a true *clerestory* (the row of windows in the upper zone of the nave), as well as a clearer arrangement of architectural components, the barrel vault supported by the transverse arches that divide the nave into bays.

Saint Guilhem was founded early in the ninth century by a knight and cousin of Charlemagne and was rebuilt during the eleventh and twelfth centuries as a

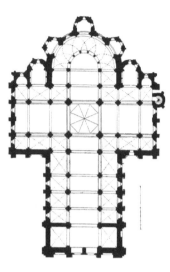

Figure 5.8 Sainte Foy, plan

Figure 5.9 Interior, Sainte Foy

popular stop en route to the most important of all pilgrimage destinations in the Middle Ages, the shrine of Santiago (Saint James) at Compostela in Northern Spain. The classic design of a pilgrimage church at the height of Romanesque style can be seen in the little town of Conques in South-Central France. Sainte Foy was a little girl who lived and was martyred in the early Christian period (c. 303) and whose remains were stolen by the monks at Conques from a nearby monastery. Her cult attracted a sufficient number of pilgrim tourists to allow a very handsome rebuilding of their church in the eleventh century. Inside and outside we see the standard features of high Romanesque religious architecture: a pronounced Latin cross plan with a distinct *narthex* (porch) at the west end; a groin-vaulted aisle on either side of the barrel-vaulted nave; substantial transept arms to the south and north; and, in the east, an apse area comprising a choir and an *ambulatory* giving access to radiating chapels that house reliquaries.

The same basic plan of Sainte Foy is amplified exponentially in the great collegiate basilica of Saint Saturninus—in French, Saint Sernin—at Toulouse, another preferred stopover on the pilgrimage route. It was presumably in the choir area—more specifically, in the ambulatory—that seven monumental marble reliefs were

Figure 5.10 Reliquary Statue, Sainte Foy

installed along with an elaborately carved altar, the latter signed and dated by the artist Bernardus Gelduinus in 1096. Though theories as to the original arrangement of the sculptural ensemble abound, there is no doubt that the *Maestà*, or *Christ in Majesty*, was central. The *mandorla*, or almond-shaped nimbus surrounding the risen Jesus, is formed by the overlap of two circles, and as such, serves as the metaphorical intersection of the heavenly and earthly spheres. In other words, the mandorla represents the dual nature of Christ, who is both human and divine. In his incarnation here, Jesus is depicted as powerful and serene; like those of the colossal Constantine, his bulging eyes signify omniscience, his bulging form represents fullness of authority and even something of what we might call comprehensiveness of capacity. But, the artistic decision to represent him as a full-figured deity is clearly based on a desire to show, even by exaggeration, a monumental, three-dimensional human form. And he is among the very first such sculptures to appear in Europe since classical times.

Though the St. Sernin *Christ in Majesty* is a static, seated figure, a profusion of curving lines swell and give rhythm to the relief, and therefore

Figure 5.11 Basilica of Saint Sernin (begun 1080)

Figure 5.12 Maestà, Bernardus Elduinus (1096)

remind us of *Saint Matthew* in the Gospel Book of Charlemagne. A much more ascetic ideal is the attenuated, impossibly proportioned figure decorating the inside of the *trumeau*, or post, separating the main doors into the church of Saint Pierre at Moissac. Probably portraying the prophet Isaiah, this figure, too, has a pronounced if very different dynamism, seen not only in the busy lines of his drapery, hair, and whiskers, but especially in the tortured, schizophrenic twistings of his torso and neck and painfully stretched and crossed legs. His face, however, is the face of someone who knows God. *Isaiah* is a completely new type for us. With him, we are as far as we can imagine from the classical conception of the human body. What *is* the body for the *Isaiah* sculptor and his audience? Only a temporary and negligible shelter or a prison for the soul. Clothed, rather than nude, hardly bursting with health, and seemingly racked rather than stepping out for exercise, *Isaiah* is the Medieval ideal of renunciation of the physical. Polykleitos, for all the perfection of his *Spearbearer*, gives us in that work only an emblem of character: the body as the physical metaphor for an inner life. But in the Middle Ages, the body is transcended, leaving the essential nature—the essence of character—exposed.

When you are nude in the Middle Ages, it's a bad thing—you are either Adam or Eve in the aftermath of sinning, or caught up in the Apocalypse and about to be judged. Such judgment is the theme of the decoration of many a Christian *tympanum* (the area directly above a door). In Autun, at the

Figure 5.13 Isaiah, Saint Pierre at Moissac (c. 1120)

Figure 5.14 Isaiah, detail

Figure 5.15 Gislebertus, Last Judgement, Saint Lazare (c. 1120)

church of Saint Lazare, a vision at once concise and explosive conveys to all comers a reminder of the inevitable end of time.

This lavish tympanum, signed by Gislebertus and datable to around 1120, comprises numerous vignettes revolving around a central, splayed Christ who stares impassively without acknowledging them or us. The composition is teeming with figures, most of whom are moving frenetically, in joy at their salvation, in fear of their coming assessment, or in despair at their condemnation.

Enthroned on a heavenly city, like the Christ at St. Sernin, the Jesus at Autun directs our attention to either side and, by implication, to the choices all human beings are constantly called upon to make. In keeping with Catholic eschatology, the disentombed dead line up along the lintel where the winnowing has already begun; one unfortunate, and clearly unhappy, soul is being hauled upward—delivered, in what is an obvious birth image, into the weighing station where angels and demons preside. The blest on the left begin to enjoy the benefits of heaven beneath the Virgin's gaze, while on the right, a nude pair (of fornicators?) enjoy their last ride together—directly into one of the mouths of hell—while other sinners, freshly tried, are pulled aside by a hook-wielding devil, all accompanied

Figure 5.16 Detail, Last Judgement

by the sound of heavenly trumpets. The great variety of poses, some reminiscent of that of the illogically angled *Isaiah* from St. Pierre, are a visual translation of the variety of experiences and emotions of the subjects, who themselves are the representatives of all people of all time.

Sainte Foy at Conques has another memorable version of the Last Judgment, the theme remaining popular, especially for decoration of the end walls of churches, well into the Renaissance. The great sculptural programs of Sainte Foy and Saint Pierre and Saint Lazare extend beyond the church portals into cloisters and church interiors. Reliquaries, too, often provide the opportunity for rich and complex sculptural interpretations of religious doctrines and narratives; many of these reliquaries, in fact, reflect the architectural structures of the period in their forms. One such, the largest of all Medieval reliquaries and a work central to the canon of Western sculpture, is the Shrine of the Three Kings in the cathedral of Cologne, Germany. Basically a two-story, apse-less basilica, this shrine houses the bones believed to be those of the Magi from the story of Christ's infancy. Considered the masterpiece of Mosan metalworking, it is attributed to the goldsmith, Nicholas of Verdun (Verdun being a city on the River Meuse, in Northeastern France, hence *Mosan*).

Figure 5.17 Nicholas of Verdun, Shrine of the Three Kings, Cologne (c. 1200)

On the top tier of the decoration, highly individualized Apostles are seated in a simple Romanesque arcade, while below, equally distinctive Old Testament prophets occupy more elaborate, tri-lobed spaces. On the ends, Christ and the Virgin appear among scenes of the Adoration, Baptism, and Passion. Decorated with hundreds of enamels and jewels, including even pre-Christian cameos, the shrine is also a gilded catalogue of credible human portraits and postures. Joachim, for instance, emerges almost completely from his allotted niche, looking quizzically behind, perhaps to engage his neighbor. Naturalistic in both form and attitude, he gathers his garments around him as he turns; the result is a tightened knot of potential energy. Presumably created over a number of years at the very end of the twelfth century, the Shrine of the Three Kings displays a figural natural-ism at odds with the overwhelming spiritual and even anti-figural priorities of the sculptors working at such sites as Moissac, Autun, and Vezelay during the 1120s and 1130s.

It is in the 1140s that a new style, the Gothic, is born. It is rare to be able to pinpoint so precisely the moment when any widespread cultural shift occurs, but in the case of the appearance of the Gothic at the Abbey Church of Saint Denis, that is exactly what we can do. Founded in the third century to mark the final

Figure 5.18 Saint Denis Choir (dedicated 1144)

resting place of the patron saint of France,[1] St. Denis became, in the early Middle Ages, the burial place of French monarchs. A number of buildings occupied the site, and in the year 1140, the Abbot, a man named Suger, began construction of a new building in a new style. Based on innovative technologies and evolving aesthetic concerns—most notable among the latter being the constant challenge, especially in Northern Europe, to bring more light into buildings—the new style replaces the old Roman arch form with a pointed arch, and divides the weight-bearing vaults into a webbed network of ribs. The result, as seen for the first time in Europe at the unveiling of the choir of Suger's church in 1144, is a light and flexible treatment of space; that is, instead of being channeled through the ambulatory beneath a tunnel-like Romanesque vault, the visitor at Saint Denis has a freedom of movement through lighter, interconnected spaces beneath ribbed vaults of

---

1 Following his decapitation, Denis walked a considerable distance with his head in his hands; where he stopped, the church was built.

Figure 5.19 Saint Denis Vault

varying shape arranged in an open and dynamic pattern. Stone had never looked so malleable.

Where did these ribs and pointed arches come from? In fact, at Durham Cathedral in the North of England and at Sant'Ambrogio in Milan, both under way in the first decades of the twelfth century, ribs had been used to accentuate and fortify the lines of intersection in the groin vaults, and the pointed arch was already familiar to Cistercian builders in France and England. But it is at Saint Denis that these features are brought together and refined—their union is effectively consummated—for the first time.

We can characterize succinctly, if not without argument, the dual ideal of Gothic architecture as "height and light:" height being an apt metaphor for human striving after the highest knowledge, which in Christian belief is the love of God, and light being the favorite Medieval analogy for the source of and response to that love, God's love of humankind. As with the revival of ancient Roman forms during the eleventh and

Figure 5.20 Durham Cathedral (early twelfth century)

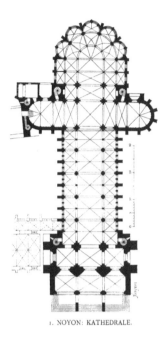

ı. NOYON: KATHEDRALE.

Figure 5.21 St. Remy, Reims (late twelfth century)

Figure 5.22 Noyon Cathedral, plan
(begun 1145)

twelfth centuries, there will be local variations and outright contradictions of this binary tendency, but proof of its enduring power can be found in every corner of Europe.

There is, of course, an organic relationship between Romanesque and Gothic architecture, and we often see, quite literally, the latter growing out of the former. Thus, many churches, built of necessity over long periods of time, illustrate the transition. And many characteristics of Romanesque architecture continued to appear in their Gothic guise. One carryover from the Romanesque church was the formal mirroring of interior and exterior. That is, we can read the interior plan from the exterior elevation, and similarly, from the plan and from the exterior, we can read much of the function, at least, of the interior spaces. This is less often the case with other types of architecture, or the architecture of other periods, domestic or public; it is more often than not impossible to identify the division of rooms in a modern house, for example, from outside it. Whereas, if we look at a Romanesque church such as Sainte Foy at Conques or Saint Sernin at Toulouse, or a Gothic cathedral such as that of Paris or Chartres, we can easily make out the various internal spaces—narthex, nave, aisles, crossing, choir, transepts, ambulatory, radiating chapels—from the exterior. Another constant that links Romanesque and Gothic church architecture is the popularity of a modular approach to the division of space. Or, to put it more organically, the "generation" of interior spaces, as is obvious from most Medieval ground plans, where the module of the aisle bay is doubled to produce the nave bay, and the nave bay is doubled to determine the proportions of the crossing. Regularity, in its special sense of following and repeating a rule, results in the clarity and accessibility of the church plan in both the Romanesque and Gothic periods.

The choir of St. Denis had an immediate impact on the architecture of Northern France and, ultimately, throughout all of Europe. In any city or town with a claim to modernity, Gothic structures appeared, and among the episcopal cities (cities with a bishop and, hence, a cathedral), a veritable, often bitter, rivalry emerged, motivated by the goal of creating the most perfect earthly house of God.

Figure 5.23 Notre Dame de Laon (begun 1160)

Figure 5.24 Notre Dame de Laon, Nave

If St. Denis is the epicenter of the earth-shaking new style, it follows that the aftershocks are felt first in and near the Ile de France. Thus, within twenty years, Gothic cathedrals were begun in Noyon (1145), Senlis (1150), Laon (1160), and Paris (1163). Notre Dame de Laon—the vast majority of Medieval cathedrals are dedicated to the Virgin Mary—provides an excellent exemplar of the Early Gothic cathedral. It has two enormous towers at the west entrance end[2] which, along with the three deeply-hewn portals and the central rose window, constitute the classic Gothic façade. Inside, the elevation of the nave, supporting *sexpartite* (six-part) ribbed vaults, is divided into four sections: the nave arcade surmounted by a gallery topped by

Figure 5.25 Notre Dame de Laon

2   It has other towers, too, including a massive one over the crossing. This multiplication of towers, which as we have seen has precedents especially among German Romanesque churches, will be significantly toned down in the Gothic period, such that, in the cathedrals at Paris and Reims and Amiens, the crossing is marked by little more than a *flèche*, or dart. It is the great western towers that become the most prominent vertical features of the exterior of a Gothic church. And these, too, have precedents, most famously in the church of St. Etienne at Caen, in Normandy, begun in 1067 by William the Conqueror.

Figure 5.26 St. Etienne at Caen
(begun 1067)

Figure 5.27 Notre Dame de Paris
(begun 1163)

Figure 5.28 Laon

Figure 5.29 Laon, Detail

a nearly blind triforium, the whole crowned by a somewhat diminutive clerestory. The alternate support system beloved of Romanesque builders has dwindled here to a simpler alternation of three or five engaged cluster colonettes rising from the more autonomous supporting piers to the springing of the vaults. This decorative motif, which provides variety but also breaks the eye's path toward the sanctuary, disappeared almost entirely in the High Gothic phase; its vestigial presence here is in keeping with the overriding sculptural priorities of the local builders. In fact, from outside, the cathedral of Laon, with its lavish pierced towers and its richly excavated surfaces, is reminiscent of Greek religious architecture in one particular sense—that it functions sculpturally in the landscape—a similarity enhanced by the fact that Gothic cathedrals, like Greek temples, tend to be built on high ground. How did the builders get their materials to these elevated sites? They used carts drawn by bulls. Thus, in

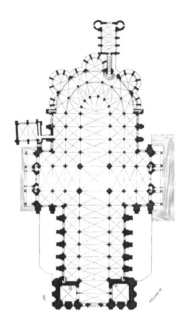

Figure 5.30 Chartres Cathedral (finished 1220, towers completed later)

Figure 5.31 Chartres Cathedral, plan

what we might almost call a recurrence of the Minoan feeling for nature and respect for the codependence of man and beast, several of the towers at Laon have, in addition to the usual gargoyles, great staring figures of the oxen who collaborated on the sacred commission.

Whether or not it is, as most scholars declare, the supreme monument of French Gothic architecture, there can be no question that the Cathedral of Our Lady of Chartres is an extraordinary building in every sense. It is also a great rarity, in that the Chartres we know today, which replaced an earlier church almost completely destroyed by fire in 1194, was built at record speed—for the most part completed in a single generation—and, equally rare, most of the early thirteenth-century ensemble, including stained glass and elaborate sculptural decorations, remains intact.[3]

---

3 The central part of the façade predates the fire, as does the south tower. The north tower was completed in the sixteenth century.

Figure 5.32 Chartres Cathedral, Interior

Famously rising above the wheat fields of the Eure-et-Loir in North-Central France, Chartres Cathedral marks the consolidation and culmination of Gothic church design. In plan and interior, we see that streamlining and simplification have been the order of the day. The usual six ribs of the Early Gothic nave bay have been reduced to four. The alternate support system has disappeared; what remains is a rigidly repeating series of clustering columns that sends the eye straight from the entrance to the sanctuary. The gallery, too, has been eliminated, leaving us with a steep nave arcade surmounted by a clerestory of the same impressive height, the upward movement broken only momentarily by a thin triforium. Though the overwhelming effect of the interior is of soaring height—at 121 feet (the nave vaults were the highest in Europe to date) it is the dynamic play of this vertical orientation with the horizontals (the nave is also the widest in France, at 52 feet, and the distance from doorway to apse is an astonishing 427 feet) that results in the remarkable, seeming perfection of this sacred place.

If we are dazzled by the scale and proportions of Chartres, we are further indulged by the panoply of interior and exterior decoration. The interior is in fact completely subject to—quite literally, under the control of—the light that penetrates so much of the surface via the stained glass windows. When we are directed to appreciate the "light-filled" interiors of Gothic buildings fortunate enough to have retained much of their original glass, as at Chartres or King Louis IX's exquisite reliquary-cum-chapel, the *Sainte-Chapelle* in Paris, we must remember that the light that fills the spaces is not the bright light of day, but a rich light in a range of colors, often a "dark" light, volatile and unreliable as the weather, changing, and consequently calling into question the solidity and reliability—the reality—of stone floors, columns, walls, and even the people upon whom it falls. At Chartres, it is no exaggeration to say that the lights produced by the windows, with their highly saturated chromaticism—heavy on the deep blues and scarlets—trump the stone architecture, humbling it as the human body is humbled in this age, and creating an otherworldly atmosphere that is the prefiguration of a world to come.

Figure 5.33 Sainte-Chapelle Apse (1242-48)

What is surely the best-loved window at Chartres actually predates the present building, having been rescued from the great fire, restored, and reset into an aisle in the choir. Known as *Notre Dame de la Belle Verrière* (Our Lady of the Beautiful Stained-Glass Window), this great lancet represents the Virgin Mary in her ancient rôle as the Throne of Wisdom, the seat from which the infant Jesus rules. Architectonic, hieratic, but not aggressively or overbearingly so, the flattened, symmetrical image is easily related to contemporary (the window dates to around 1150) Romanesque figural sculpture, such as the examples we have seen; the style traces its ultimate, if distant, roots in Early Christian and Byzantine

Figure 5.34 Chartres Cathedral, Notre Dame de la Belle Verrière (c. 1150)

Figure 5.35 Chartres Cathedral, South Portal (1210-35)

traditions. The iconography of the enthroned Virgin and Child surrounded and presented by angels was one of the most popular in the Middle Ages, an epoch in which most people looked to the Virgin as mother and queen, and it remained so well into the Renaissance.

As the interior of Chartres Cathedral is transformed if not dematerialized by the gorgeous windows, the exterior is divided and subdivided into a veritable showcase of High Gothic stone carving. The progress of these sculptures illustrates an increasing tendency toward naturalism in large scale, three-dimensional representations of the human form,[4] a tendency confirmed by contemporary and

---

4   In the smaller scale decoration of each of the portals at Chartres, the figures are more identified with and subservient to the shape of the individual *voussoirs* that make up the roughly concentric archivolts surrounding the tympanum. Even the postures of earlier jamb figures, the so-called "statue columns," bodies set onto pedestals and inseparable from their architectural ground, are dictated by the main axis of the stone they are carved from. The voussoirs and the lintel figures appear almost as brush strokes in an extended halo for the main characters or actions of the tympanum; they orbit the principal scenes. A supporting

later works at the cathedrals of Reims (the coronation church of French kings, begun 1211) and Amiens (begun 1220), among others. The left portal of the south transept at Chartres includes a row of jamb figures portraying, from left to right, Saints Theodore, Stephen, Clement, and Lawrence. Of these four men, carved between 1210 and 1235, three are content to be jambs; like most of the saints that decorate these doors, they are cylindrical, even tubular, and seem quietly conscious and respectful of their architectural boundaries. But Theodore, with his slanted belt and his spear at the ready, celebrates his ability to move. His posture, tending to the left as though disassociating himself from those sticks-in-the-mud, is a model of contrapposto and potential energy. The vigor and naturalism of the Chartres Theodore, and the fact that these qualities can assume a variety of forms, is demonstrated in a famous figure group on the central Royal Portal at Reims (early 1230s). Here, the figures of Gabriel and Mary in the *Annunciation* at left and of Mary and her cousin, Elizabeth, in the *Visitation* at right, seem altogether independent of their architectural background. The archangel, swathed in abundant, naturalistically rendered draperies, with a sweet and inviting smile that would put anyone at ease, greets a very demure, simply robed, and still rather columnar Virgin. But, having accepted the divine proposal, what the Virgin becomes! Shown next to her former self, the Virgin of the *Visitation* is grand and noble; she is no longer passively draped, but controls her multi-fold garments, gathering them at her outthrust hip, a hip that is destined before long to support

---

cast, these lesser figures are the building blocks of the church, and in this they are analogous to and models for the faithful who make up the congregation.

Figure 5.36 North Porch Center

Figure 5.37 Royal Portal at Reims (1230's)

Figure 5.38 Amiens (begun 1220)

her holy child. The great serpentine of her body suggests something of the monumental rhythms of ancient sculpture, and if that s-curve becomes formulaic throughout the thirteenth and fourteenth centuries, it remains a powerful vehicle of figurative movement—the movement of a real body reflecting the movement of the even more real soul inside.

Generally speaking, the evolution of French Gothic style, whether in sculpture or in architecture, follows a trajectory toward ever greater dynamism and elaboration. The simple *Rayonnant* (radiating) style of tracery, exemplified by the spoked wheels of the rose windows at Notre Dame in Paris, gives way to the foliate refinement of the Flamboyant style, such as we see in the western rose at the cathedral in Amiens, the interior height of which ascends to an unprecedented (and, among French Gothic churches, unsurpassed) 139 feet. And as the Gothic is disseminated throughout Europe, rich local and national variations arise. Fan vaulting, for example, appears in England in the mid-fourteenth century, and it, too, spreads throughout Europe; an exquisite—perhaps the earliest—example is to be found in the cloisters of Gloucester Cathedral, where the heaven-pointing arches seem drizzled with an icing of tracery. Another ingenious exploitation and elaboration of the malleable web of ribs first perfected at St. Denis, fan vaults often display the subtlest balancing of upward and downward forces, which was a preoccupation especially among later Gothic builders.

Whether the Gothic style ever really went out of fashion is an open question. Purveyors of the so-called "Gothic Revival" of the nineteenth century, especially in Northern Europe and America, seem at times to have overlooked the continuous recurrence in those territories of Gothic architectural motifs. But it is fair to say that in Italy, despite wonderful, monumental examples of Gothic architecture—for example, the church of San Lorenzo in Naples, or most famous of all, the still unfinished cathedral of Milan—the style was never embraced as wholeheartedly as it was in the North, or even in Spain. It was almost as though Italy could not forget its classical past, and was holding out for … something. By the time the cloisters at Gloucester Cathedral were finished, in 1412, the Tuscan artist Giotto had already been dead for decades. In his architectural ideas, Giotto seems to have understood and even practiced the Gothic style. But Giotto was first and foremost a painter, and in his approach to the human figure, he was exactly what Italy had been waiting for.

Figure 5.39 Amiens, Rose Window

Figure 5.40 Gloucester Cathedral (completed 1412)

six

The Renaissance

"Renaissance" is the French word for "rebirth." Rebirth or renewal seems to be a universal human objective akin to food and shelter. What is reborn in the Renaissance? Cultural ideals and practices associated with an ancient and mythically glorious past, specifically that of Classical Greece, as those ideals and practices were imported, interpreted, imitated, perpetuated, transformed, and disseminated by the ancient Romans during their own golden age. In history as in life, things recur, and the places we are going to are, as often as not, places we are *returning to*. The Renaissance is, in a nutshell, a conscious and contagious—that is, increasingly widespread—return to the cultural models of the ancient Greeks and Romans, a revival of their shared artistic ideals derived, above all, from first-hand examination of nature, and the endeavor to reconcile the classical past with the Judeo-Christian world view in order to conceive and construct a new and greater age.

As we know, such a revival was consciously attempted several times before the fourteenth century by rulers with aspirations of world, or at least pan-European, domination, another Roman ideal. It is fitting that the Italian peninsula was the birthplace—or re-birthplace—for these cultural inclinations and activities, the landscape there being littered with the artifacts of Roman and Greek civilization (remember that long before their territories were assimilated by the Romans, the Greeks had colonized much of the southern half of the Italian peninsula). The eighteenth-century German writer, Goethe, in Part II of his *Faust*, likened the Renaissance to a sunrise from the south.

It is most interesting, however, that it was not in Rome itself, but in the wealthy city of Florence, in the heart of the old Etruscan territory now known as Tuscany, that the Renaissance was born.[1] While all scholars agree that Florence was the birthplace of the Renaissance, they do not agree as to when it began. Any discussion of the Renaissance, however, must commence with the monumental personality of Giotto di Bondone (1266 to 1337).

Trained in the seemingly indestructible traditions of Byzantine art by its last great practitioner in Italy, Cenni di Pepi, known to history by his nickname, Cimabue,[2] Giotto came to revolutionize

Figure 6.1 Cimabue's Madonna Enthroned with Saints (c. 1280)

---

1   In fact, the closest to a world ruler in the Middle Ages was the pope; though his was ostensibly a spiritual empire, it was no less territorial or dictatorial for that, and consequently, Rome was a city of great political strife and chaos, even more so than most medieval cities. This extreme volatility may help to explain why the Renaissance did not originate there. Florence is close, but not too close.

2   "Dehorner of oxen." The man apparently had quite a temper.

image-making and profoundly influenced all subsequent generations of artists on the peninsula and beyond. In other words, between Cimabue and Giotto, a great cataclysm occurs. A *Madonna Enthroned with Saints* (c. 1280) by Cimabue gives us the flat, hieratic frontality and rigid symmetry of Romanesque sculpture and stained glass (for example, the *Belle Verrière* at Chartres), as well as the hyper-linear treatment of drapery folds in the Romanesque and Gothic work we have seen (the *Isaiah* from Moissac, for instance). Forty years later, the same iconic subject was treated by Cimabue's former pupil, Giotto. Despite relatively superficial similarities—the gold background suggesting heaven, ultimately derived from the Byzantine mosaic tradition; the attending saints and angels, arranged symmetrically around the central group shown on a larger scale—Giotto's work is light years away from his teacher's. The most

Figure 6.2 Giotto's Ognissanti Madonna (1310-20)

significant difference is easily summarized: Cimabue's picture is a plane, Giotto's is a space. And Giotto fills his newly invented, and still far-from-mathematically-consistent, space with figures that have weight and volume and, like us, are all subject to gravity. Folds of cloth, which in Cimabue's vision are peripatetic and dominate especially the figure of the Virgin as they did the figures of Christ in the Romanesque *Maestàs*, in Giotto's vision are subject to and reveal the living forms beneath. Giotto's earthbound saints and angels are a figurative restatement of the space; they also pay attention to the Virgin and Child and leave room in the foreground for us to do the same.

Giotto's little barrel-shaped Jesus may not be everybody's idea of a baby, but He is unquestionably physically present. Creating the illusion of physical reality is perhaps the greatest of Giotto's fundamental achievements; the Renaissance in painting will be built upon it. Giving flesh to form—literally, *incarnating* the human subjects of art—is a revolutionary concern for painters, and it is overwhelmingly manifest in Giotto's largest surviving commission, the Scrovegni, or Arena,[3] Chapel in Padua, which fittingly has as its subject the story of the Incarnation. In over thirty frescoed scenes, beginning with the infancy narrative of the Virgin Mary and ending with the Last Judgment, Giotto brings Christ, His family, and His contemporaries, both good and less so, down to earth. The very trajectory of the narrative sequence, which begins at the upper right of the altar and spirals downward through three rungs of dramatic events, provides the overriding analogy for this achievement.

Figure 6.3 Giotto, Scrovegni Chapel. Detail. (completed 1305)

---

3 "Arena," because the palace and adjacent chapel were built along the rim of an old Roman arena. The palace has not survived.

Figure 6.4 Meeting at the Golden Gate (Scrovegni Chapel detail)

But Giotto doesn't stop with the body. The human beings who crowd into the various scenes—the joyous meetings; the panicked journeys; the banquets; the heavenly interventions; the physical interactions, both loving and violent; the deaths and resurrections—express real emotions and are subject to the indignities and ecstasies inherent in every human narrative. They express these emotions both gesturally and in their faces, above all in their eyes.

Though Giotto had numerous competent, and even gifted, pupils and many more followers and imitators, such that it is fair to refer to the entire fourteenth century as the Age of Giotto, none of his disciples completely absorbed the truly revolutionary lesson inherent in his work, namely, that nature takes precedence over artistic formula and is the true source of creative achievement. Not that dependence upon artistic models is to be avoided; one of the most impressive motifs in the Arena Chapel, for example, is Giotto's revival of Roman *trompe-l'oeil* (literally, "eye-fooling") representation of expensive marbles and sculptures in stone. Of course, Classical artists themselves turned constantly to nature for the information necessary to carry out their work. In reviving their practice, and throwing himself into the dialogue across the centuries, Giotto proved to be the master of nature and first artist of the Renaissance.

It was not until the earliest years of the fifteenth century, the *Quattrocento*, that artists began to seriously understand and explore the convergence of nature and classicism in the art of Giotto. And it was not, in fact, in painting, but in sculpture, that the first fruits of the investigation appeared. Some scholars choose, as the official herald of the Renaissance, the announcement of a competition in Florence—the wealthiest city in Europe at this time, thanks to the enterprising banking families led by the Medici—for a second pair of doors for the Baptistery of the Cathedral.[4] The finalists were two young sculptors, Filippo Brunelleschi and Lorenzo Ghiberti. Having been set the task of representing, in a quatrefoil format, the story of the Sacrifice of Isaac from the Book of Genesis, Ghiberti and Brunelleschi each produced true Renaissance works of art. Each evinces an understanding of human anatomy, more than a slight familiarity with ancient sculpture, and, above all, a mastery of the language of narrative as translated by Giotto.

Figure 6.5 Brunelleschi's Sacrifice of Isaac (1401)

Though, during the competition and ever since, both panels were recognized as successful and beautiful works, the winner was Lorenzo Ghiberti. Why did he win? Or, to put it another way, is the triumphant panel by Ghiberti more exemplary of Renaissance ideals than that by Brunelleschi? Certainly Ghiberti's Isaac is radically different from his rival's gawky but plausible adolescent, and in fact reveals an overriding determination to revive classical idealism—overriding in the sense that this Isaac is no mere boy, but a perfect male nude at the peak of

---

4   The Florentine baptistery was a separate building in front of the cathedral. It already had one set of doors, executed by Andrea Pisano, a pupil of Giotto, in the 1330s.

his form, and as such, the focus of all interest. From the angel soaring through the plane at the upper right, to the almost unnoticeable ram opposite, to the overlapping figures of attendants and beast at lower left, Ghiberti has shown a willingness to risk legibility for the sake of the drama. Brunelleschi's figures are, throughout, more autonomous; consequently, the action is clearer. Ghiberti, in a winning move, conveys more credibly the chaos attendant upon actual tragic climax.

The retardataire set of doors that Ghiberti executed after his victory did not fulfill the promise of his competition panel, but they were sufficiently prized to obtain for him a commission for yet another set of doors for the same building. These are Ghiberti's claim to fame. Celebrated as the *Gates of Paradise*, the ten Old Testament scenes decorating the doors bring to belated fruition the true classical vision foretold by the earlier *Sacrifice of Isaac*. The decades between the two commissions saw the emergence of the monumental figure of Donatello, whose groundbreaking advances in sculpture provided inspiration and challenges, not only to Ghiberti, but to all contemporary and later sculptors.

Figure 6.6 Ghiberti's Sacrifice of Isaac (1401)

Figure 6.7 Florence Baptistry Doors (1425-52)

Figure 6.8 Donatello's Gattamelata (c. 1450)

At the pinnacle of his career, Donatello's fame brought him from his native Florence to Venice. In Padua, a Venetian dependency, the sculptor created a larger-than-life equestrian bronze monument—the first such work since the Roman *Marcus Aurelius*, which Donatello knew well—depicting a successful *condottiere* (mercenary warlord), Erasmo da Narni, known to history as *Gattamelata*. Our description of the work, especially of the great and noble horse, will necessarily echo what has already been said about its Roman predecessor: an immensely powerful animal presents himself under the seemingly effortless control of a relaxed and confident rider. Nature is as much the model as the ancient prototype, just as nature under control is the true classical subject here. But nature is also transcended; this horse is a tank. No less imposing is the man astride the animal, together they are bigger than nature, larger than life, and represent a true renaissance of the fifth-century Greek practice of creating, from observed facts, an edited version, an ideal.

At the beginning of his career, after visiting Rome in the company of the despondent Brunelleschi and after returning home and working for a time under Ghiberti, Donatello entered into a multi-commission relationship with the *Orsanmichele*—the Guildhall of Florence. His first triumph there was for the linen merchants guild, a statue of Saint Mark represented appropriately under a superabundance of fabric. This was followed by a youthful and defiant *Saint George*, on the base of which is a delicately carved scene of the warrior saint rescuing a princess from a dragon. Long before the *Gattamelata*, this horse and rider came together as a dynamic unit, a vortex of energy right in the middle of a beautifully balanced composition. The actual technique here—a technique known as *rilievo schiacciato*, "squashed relief"—demonstrates one of Donatello's greatest contributions to the history of sculpture. With this innovation, he created the impression of distance and depth in a paradoxically shallow relief of finely drawn lines (which read as more or less distant, depending on their fineness) and

Figure 6.9 Donatello, Saint George, detail (c. 1415)

palpable forms (which read as immediate and concrete). The manipulation of line and form results, miraculously, in atmospheric perspective. True linear perspective is also at work here, visible mainly in the arcade at the far right and even the rough-hewn cave at left. The *Saint George* relief is one of the first manifestations of this great invention by Brunelleschi, a mathematical and visually consistent system of perspective, a system that Lorenzo Ghiberti will also exploit, but only later, in his second set of Baptistery doors.

It is inevitable that an artist of Donatello's ingenuity and range should have come to the attention of the most powerful family in Florence, and it is for them that he executed the first large-scale, free-standing nude since Roman times. For some time situated in the courtyard of Michelozzo's vast new Medici Palace, the bronze *David* was most likely commissioned in the late 1430s or early 1440s to celebrate a wedding. It is a shocking portrayal of the adolescent hero whose personality dominates much of the Old Testament. Wielding a sword too heavy for him to lift, twiddling his toes in the beard of his superhuman foe, Goliath, this is a David with no precedent, and no clothes! Boots and a party hat only emphasize the fact.

Figure 6.10 Donatello's David (c. 1435)

Figure 6.11 Masaccio's Pisa Polyptych Madonna and Child (c. 1426)

The young David's body is unlike any of the excavated ancient works to which the artist might have been exposed in Rome. The contrapposto is doubtless classically inspired—his earlier works, including the *Saint Mark* for the Orsanmichele and a stone *David* for the exterior of the Duomo, all reveal this inspiration—as is the attention to anatomical detail. But Donatello has softened the anatomy of the torso, and this treatment elides with the slim elegance of the limbs and the slight suggestion of youthful indulgence to create an androgynous and even anti-heroic figure who is still an ideal, but an ideal of lassitude and sensuality.

The revolutions and innovations that characterized Donatello's long and brilliant career clearly had a profound effect on his contemporaries, not least in the realm of painting. A good friend of Donatello's, whose own promising career was not to last so long, was the painter Masaccio, and it is in his work that we find the torch of Giotto relighted. In what was originally the central panel of a large *polyptych*, or many-paneled altarpiece, painted for the Duomo of Pisa, Masaccio rendered a Madonna and Child seated in a true Renaissance throne, the sides embellished with Corinthian supports, the base etched with the strigil form from many a Roman sarcophagus. Compare this *Pisa Polyptych Madonna* of c. 1426 to Giotto's *All Saints Madonna* of almost a century earlier. In the work by Giotto, the light is evenly dispersed, and there is no mathematically consistent perspective system. Masaccio has gathered that light into a single source from the upper left, as he has gathered the multiple points of view into a single vanishing point in a logical perspective grid, a grid the artist most likely learned first-hand from its inventor, Brunelleschi. The result is a more convincing three-dimensional image, the figure of the Virgin is in high relief (reminding us that, in the first decades of the Renaissance, sculpture led the way), and the beautifully foreshortened details of musical instruments and the baby's halo—a very special, dinner-plate sort of halo, the only one subject to the laws of perspective—are all imbued with a new and tangible reality. If the concentrated light and the logical perspective make possible this new reality, the mother and child take us further into the particular reality of motherhood and babyhood. Masaccio's Madonna is truly human, unidealized, showing signs of the fatigue any parent of a young child knows. And the baby—bottom-heavy, teething, and temperamental—represents a distinct veering from the man-child type seen in most earlier versions of the subject, toward the believable and normal.

As in the *Pisa Polyptych Madonna*, the vanishing point in Masaccio's *Tribute Money* is Jesus. The *Tribute Money* is a large scene from a cycle of frescoes in the Brancacci family chapel in the Florentine church of Santa Maria del Carmine. On the same stage created in stone by Donatello in his *Saint George* relief ten years earlier, Masaccio presents several moments from the Gospels, all revolving around the theme of money, and making the point that Florentines, like Christ, should pay their taxes. Monumental figures, the kindred of the *Pisa Polyptych Madonna* and heirs to the inhabitants of the Arena Chapel, surround and react to their master. They are individualized

Figure 6.12 Masaccio, Expulsion from Eden (1425-6)

and expressive, and above all, they fill the space. Among them, the barelegged tax collector flits like a page among judges. To the left of this pageant of ponderous human characters is the smaller scene of *The Expulsion of Adam and Eve*, perhaps the most succinct representation of human despair ever painted.

As we have seen, Donatello and Masaccio both owed a great deal to their older friend, Filippo Brunelleschi. We last glimpsed Brunelleschi stomping off to Rome in high dudgeon after his defeat in the competition for the Baptistery doors. It was by all accounts in Rome that Brunelleschi transformed himself into the first and greatest architect of the Renaissance. Returning to Florence, he put to use his

Figure 6.13 Masaccio, The Tribute Money

detailed study of old buildings to create such masterpieces of classical proportion as the arcade of the *Ospedale degli Innocenti*—an orphanage built to his design— and the sacristy—now called the Old Sacristy, since Michelangelo created the New Sacristy in the following century—of his church of San Lorenzo, sponsored by the Medici family. For the crowning achievement of his career, the dome of Santa Maria del Fiore—the Duomo of Florence—Brunelleschi revived neither the time-honored 1:2 and 1:3 proportions, nor the coffered vaults preferred by the ancient Romans. Instead, he created what we might call a cumulative, completely original version of classicism which is a watershed in the history of design.

The Gothic cathedral of Florence, under construction throughout most of the fourteenth century, had been left with no covering over the crossing, and no architect capable of bridging the vast octagonal space. Numerous more or less absurd solutions were proposed to the Duomo authorities, but only Brunelleschi understood the engineering problems involved. It would take a separate volume to enumerate the ingenious machines and devices invented by the architect for transporting and raising the men and materials to the springing of the projected dome, 177 feet above the paving. The final achievement of Brunelleschi's design is that it distributes the enormous weight of the dome without immensely thick walls (such as the drum of the Pantheon) or buttresses (such as we find in most Gothic cathedrals). He accomplishes this by means of a double shell. The dome of the

Cathedral of Florence is actually two domes, an inner, stronger and heavier, shell and an outer, thinner and lighter, one. Even more interesting, the outer shell was constructed from the inner one, which supports it. The result is a monumental hollow structure, swelling and magnificent but also light and attenuated. Aesthetically, we are presented with another surprising paradox: a great classical architect gives us a ribbed

Figure 6.14 Florence Duomo (fourteenth and fifteenth centuries)

and pointed dome unlike anything in the ancient world. But this is a tribute to Brunelleschi's prodigious sensitivity to context—the context here being the pre-existing Gothic building by Arnolfo di Cambio. Brunelleschi's dome remains the focal determining feature of the perfect and proverbial Renaissance skyline.

Brunelleschi's classicism is both historical and personal. The un-Roman ribs of his vaults are, in fact, mere tools in the construction of his truly Pythogorean heavens, as we see in the Old Sacristy of San Lorenzo and the interior of his late masterpiece, the Pazzi Chapel adjacent to the church of Santa Croce. In the Pazzi Chapel, perfectly calibrated arcs and gears wheel majestically overhead; these are carved from the same local warm gray stone, *pietra serena*, with which Brunelleschi characteristically outlines his interiors. The gray stone against the white stucco is like a three

Figure 6.15 Brunelleschi, Pazzi Chapel, cupola (begun 1429)

dimensional design drawn in air. When you enter a space by Brunelleschi, you are entering the artist's mind.

Brunelleschi's architectural aesthetic as well as his invention of linear perspective can indeed be traced to his knowledge and mastery of line. The far-reaching network of Italian commerce meant that the perspective grid was widely disseminated throughout the cosmopolitan centers of Europe during a period in which the predominant pictorial style has been characterized as the International Style. A Netherlandish artist who was supremely aware of Italian innovations in spatial illusionism was Jan van Eyck, who, with his brother Hubert, painted a monumental altarpiece for the church of Saint Bavo in Ghent.[5] Dedicated in 1432, it is one of the first large masterpieces in the new oil-based medium—formerly, most portable paintings, including the Madonnas of Cimabue, Giotto, and Masaccio, were done in egg tempera. The Northern invention[6] of the oil technique had an enormous impact on the history of Western art. Because linseed oil is slow to dry, the new medium allows (and demands) more time for execution. Furthermore, varying the proportion of pigment to oil creates a range of optical effects from opaque to transparent; layering these presents infinite possibilities.

Figure 6.16 Hubert and Jan van Eyck, Ghent Altarpiece, closed (dedicated 1432)

Closed, the *Ghent Altarpiece* confronts us with twelve panels. In the lower corners are the *donors*—the people who paid for the work—Jodocus Vijd and his wife, Elizabeth Borluut, flanking the *grisaille* figures of the two Saint Johns beloved of Christ, the Baptist and the Evangelist. The four panels above represent a single, continuous space, a tour de force of the new Italian perspective. Within the softly lighted interior, the Angel Gabriel hails the Virgin, while above, sibyls and prophets look down on the holy meeting they foretold, reminding

---

5   An inscription on the frame of the polyptych proclaims that the work was a collaboration between the brothers, but their actual professional relationship and respective contributions to individual works remain unclear and controversial. In any case, Hubert was dead by 1426.

6   "Invention" may be too strong a word, as the actual origins of mixing oil and pigment remain obscure. But there is no question that the van Eycks' particular recipes and techniques were tantamount to the production (and even perfection) of something new.

Figure 6.17 Ghent Altarpiece, open

us that one goal of the Renaissance was to reconcile pagan and Judeo-Christian versions of history.

Open, the *Ghent Altarpiece* gives us the world when the world becomes heaven—that is to say, at the end of the world. The lower zone, comprising five separate panels, represents one continuous scene, the *Adoration of the Lamb*, as envisioned by the Evangelist John in the Book of Revelations, which completes the Christian Bible. The story of this sacrificial lamb, the allegorical Christ, whose earthly existence begins with *The Annunciation* on the reverse, is also completed here, in His drawing to Himself the redeemed of the world. Artistically, the perspective grid, applied here not to architecture but to the infinite landscape, is brought alive and personified by the vast crowds of gorgeously attired worshippers; the point of the perspective grid coincides with the point of human existence. Invented by Brunelleschi, utilized by his friends Donatello and Masaccio and others, perspective finds here its most ambitious and meaningful realization: the literal convergence of the three-dimensional figures upon the lamb is the allegory of all human movement in a New Testament view of time.

Adam and Eve, shown above in the outermost panels and separated by a heaven presided over by a crowned Christ flanked by His mother, His cousin John the Baptist, and a well-dressed celestial choir, also have an important place in the wide-ranging narrative of the *Ghent Altarpiece*. In fact, by sinning, they set in motion the story of redemption so gloriously concluded in the lower zone. If Van Eyck embraced and expanded the new Italian perspectival system, he similarly embraced the new Italian naturalism of figural representation and, with the new medium of oil paint, he has taken that naturalism to new heights. Unlike the Adam and Eve of Masaccio's *Expulsion*, Van Eyck's original sinners are detached, literally and otherwise; they seem divorced from their larger narrative, and devoid of dramatic emotion. Instead of casting Adam and Eve as believable actors in the first human tragedy, as Masaccio has done in his fresco, the Northern artist concentrates on the minute recreation of their physical bodies, each unruly hair of Adam's beard, the rising flush of Eve's cheek, contributing to the overwhelming illusion of actual presence.

The evocation of individual physical being is nowhere more startling than in Van Eyck's portraits and portrait groups, including the so-called *Arnolfini Wedding* and the presumed self-portrait known as the *Man in a Red Turban*. In *The Madonna with Chancellor Rolin*, the painter combines portraiture with the most popular of all religious iconographies. Nicolas Rolin was the chancellor of the duchy of Burgundy, and a patron of Van Eyck. Here he is shown kneeling in a private audience with the Virgin Mary. The tiled floor is a tour de force of perspectival illusionism. Similarly, and to the same end, every surface texture

Figure 6.18 Jan van Eyck, Rolin Madonna (1430-4)

is convincing, even breathtakingly so. So we have great range in the treatment of, for example, human hair, from the fine spun corn silk of the baby and the waving gold of His mother to the cheek stubble and highly questionable "bowl" cut of the praying Chancellor. The composition—basically a two-shot of richly dressed adults in an arcaded chamber overlooking an eventful townscape divided by a river—is mirrored in a slightly later work by another Netherlandish artist who may have studied with Van Eyck, Rogier van der Weyden. His *Virgin and Child with Saint Luke* reverses the positions of the Holy Family and their guest. Saint Luke, probably a self-portrait of Van der Weyden, is shown in the act of sketching the Virgin as she offers her breast to a baby who splays his fingers with delight. This picture may have been exhibited in a chapel in the Saint Catherine's Church in Brussels, in which case it would have been seen regularly by members of the guild of painters.

Figure 6.19 Rogier van der Weyden, Madonna with Saint Luke (1435-40)

Whereas many of the goals of the original Italian Renaissance—the new naturalism, the revival of interest in the human nude, etc.—were swiftly assimilated by Northern artists, and whereas Italian collectors showed an early interest in Northern Renaissance works of art, the current of influence from North to South was slower and, at first, less noticeable. Masaccio remained the great source and model for all Florentine artists trained in the fifteenth century, and the Brancacci Chapel became the unofficial school of Florentine painting. Painters of the generations following Masaccio explored and expanded upon particular innovations made or implied by the work of the prematurely deceased master, according to their particular interests and talents. So, for example, Filippo Lippi, the renegade friar and protégé of the Medici family, investigated, to great effect, the human character of his subjects and, in the meantime, developed an increasingly lyrical use of line, while another, considerably more devout, monk, Fra Angelico, helped to create a new genre of painting, the *sacra conversazione*, or sacred conversation, basically the Virgin and Child holding a salon of heavenly personages drawn from various periods of history. Andrea del Castagno and Antonio del Pollaiuolo experimented with dramatic narrative, while Andrea Mantegna and Piero della Francesca delved deep into the mysteries and refinements of perspective.

Filippo Lippi's most famous and successful pupil was Alessandro di Mariano di Filipepi, known to us by his nickname, Botticelli. Botticelli's reputation has proved to be something of a roller coaster: he outlived his fame, was virtually forgotten in the seventeenth and eighteenth centuries, and later became the genius darling of those connoisseurs who, in the nineteenth century, rediscovered the "Italian primitives," as the painters of the fourteenth and fifteenth centuries were known.

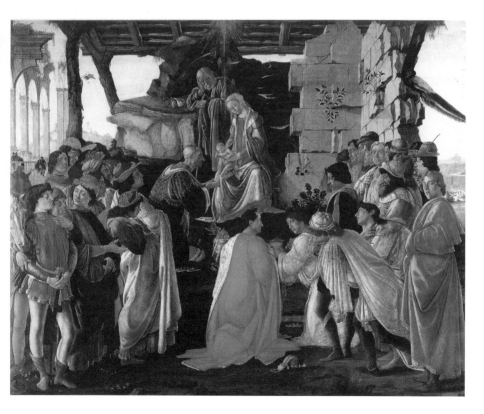

Figure 6.20 Botticelli's Adoration of the Three Kings (1474-5)

A picture that coincides with and proves Botticelli's rise to stardom is the Uffizi *Adoration of the Kings* of 1474–75. This work, a virtual poster for the Medici regime, introduces an important device. By setting the sacred story against a backdrop of classical ruins, Botticelli reconciles the pagan and Christian worlds in a new way. Furthermore, he illustrates an organic relationship between the two: the birth of Christianity occurs in the context of the crumbling Roman world, literally in the cella of a Roman temple. Another feature of the *Adoration*, which has a future in Italian painting, is the inclusion of the artist himself at far right. There is nothing novel about an artist painting himself, even in the presence of the Virgin and Child—remember the Van der Weyden of forty years earlier. But here, Botticelli occupies a position in the very inner circle of Florentine power, as the three kings themselves are portraits of the late Cosimo de Medici and his sons, Piero and Giovanni; directly across from the artist, on the same level, is Cosimo's grandson, Lorenzo the Magnificent. The reference to levels is apt here, as Botticelli most often constructs his pictures as series of shallow spaces rising and receding into the picture plane. As a great, voluminous, Masaccesque form, Botticelli is a cornerstone of both the early Christian and contemporary subjects; his bold and prideful stare in our direction indicates a clear recognition of his place among the great and, by implication, the status of the artist in history and in the world.

At about the same time that Botticelli was called to Rome to collaborate on the decoration of the walls of Pope Sixtus IV's newly-constructed chapel, he was working as well on several mythological pictures for the Medici family.

Figure 6.21 Leonardo's Adoration of the Magi (1481-2)

Figure 6.22 Botticelli's Birth of Venus (c. 1484)

One, which has assumed a mythic stature in the modern world—reproduced and referenced and mocked and manipulated and made into an ever-regenerating commodity—is the *Birth of Venus*, a large painting on fabric of around 1484. The story represented here can be found in numerous ancient and contemporary sources, including works by the Roman writer Ovid and the neo-Platonic Florentine Agnolo Poliziano. The goddess of love and beauty rises from the foam generated when Saturn cuts off the sexual organs of his father, Uranus, and tosses them into the sea. Venus is shown arriving at her sacred island of Cyprus, blown there by the winds and greeted by an attendant with a flower-embroidered mantle to cover her. In pose, specifically in the dual gesture of indicating and concealing her breasts and genitals, this Venus ultimately derives from Praxiteles' famous *Aphrodite of Knidos*, one of the most frequently copied, and, thus, eminently available, sculptures of the ancient world.

With its rich borrowing from both written and visual sources, it is hardly surprising to find, in Botticelli's *Venus*, a very complex icon of female beauty. The artist foregrounds this beauty; there is no real middle- or back-ground, the goddess and her retinue exist in the same frontal plane, giving the picture the appearance of a frieze. The figures seem weightless, the feet of the newly born daughter of heaven barely rest on the shell beneath her. Botticelli's *Venus*, which revives the monumental female nude in the same way that Donatello's *David* revived the male, displays a beauty at once believably physical and suggestively divine.[7]

Despite its statuesque leading lady, *The Birth of Venus* is a paean to line. Each figure is crisply defined and divided from its after-all cursory environment. In this respect, the picture—in fact most of the artist's work—is noticeably unlike that of his younger contemporaries, a group that includes Leonardo da Vinci, who worked beside Botticelli in the workshop of Andrea del Verrocchio. It is tempting to say that Botticelli straddles the Early and High Renaissance, but that is merely to avoid the fact that he is, finally, an uncategorizable artist, and in this sense, a true modern—only, always, and above all himself.

A prodigy in so many spheres of activity, whose life and career remain a source of fascination, not to say outlandish, obsessive speculation and misinterpretation, is Leonardo da Vinci. The illegitimate son of a provincial notary and a peasant woman, Leonardo rose to become the first great personification of the Renaissance at its zenith. He possessed the most famously wide-ranging intellect of anyone, perhaps in the history of the world. Though his young admirer, Raphael, would portray Leonardo as Plato in the center of his *School of Athens*, he was really more like Aristotle—he was the ancient philosopher *redivivus*, Aristotle reborn. Like the protagonist in Robert Browning's "My Last Duchess," Leonardo liked whatever he looked on, and his looks went everywhere. Everything, everything

---

7   In 1453 AD, Constantinople finally fell to the Muslims. Greek scholars flooded out from the old Byzantine capital into the West, and many found their way to Florence, where Lorenzo de' Medici welcomed them into his home. These scholars brought with them the works of Plato, who, unlike Aristotle, had been relatively unknown to Medieval Europe. One of the greatest of twentieth-century art historians, Erwin Panofsky, wrote a very influential article on the Botticelli *Venus*, arguing convincingly that it is, in fact, Botticelli's own neo-Platonic commentary on Plato's *Symposium*, the dialogue in which Socrates and his disciples discourse on the nature of love. So, Botticelli's Venus is, according to Panofsky, both *Aphrodite Pandemos*—the goddess of earthly love—and *Aphrodite Urania*, the goddess of divine love. See E. Panofsky, *Studies in Iconology: Humanistic Themes in the Art of the Renaissance*, Oxford University Press, 1939.

accessible to the human senses, was his subject matter and subject to investigation, commentary, and remaking in his art.

From his early days in the workshop of Verrocchio, Leonardo exemplified new artistic ideals. The naturalism that prevailed throughout all of Europe in the middle decades of the fifteenth century was not good enough for Leonardo. Collaborating with the master under the eyes of older pupils like Botticelli, the young painter created figures whose divinity was not dependent on anything but the manner in which he portrayed them. It is very fruitful to compare one of his earliest autonomous commissions, an *Adoration of the Magi* for the monks of San Donato a Scopeto near Florence, with Botticelli's celebrated representation of the same theme. As in the earlier work, we find a self-portrait of the artist in the lower right corner, but the similarity ends there. Botticelli, as we have seen, composes with line in shallow planes. Leonardo works from the outset in the round; his grouping of highly animated figures is a whirlpool or solar system orbiting a calm center, the demure young Virgin and her engaging but dignified baby boy.

Leonardo never came close to finishing his *Adoration of the Magi*,[8] thereby establishing a pattern for himself that was a problem for a number of actual and potential patrons. In the early 1480s, not long after many of Verrocchio's assistants were invited to paint the walls of the Sistine Chapel in Rome, Leonardo headed off in the opposite direction, abandoning the *Adoration* and accepting a position at the court of Milan.[9] There, he produced what is arguably the most reproduced picture in the history of art, *The Last Supper*. Christ, now an adult on the brink of crisis, is once again the calm center of a storm. Flanking rather than surrounding Him, the Apostles gesticulate, exhibiting the same intensity

---

8   But somebody else did paint over the picture, and long after Leonardo's time, according to the celebrated art diagnostician, Maurizio Seracini, whose meticulous study of the work led to the conclusion that only the drawing is from the hand of Leonardo. Thus we have limited our remarks here to the composition, and to those drawn elements that are still visible. It is worth pausing to consider that, just as many ancient Greek bronzes are known only from later Roman copies in stone, a number—perhaps the majority—of paintings produced in the late Middle Ages and Renaissance have been retouched and restored and repainted, such that they are truly palimpsests through which, if we are lucky, we can still make out the original artist's work.

9   Why wasn't Leonardo—the handsome, clever prodigy—among the artists who went to work for the Pope? Was he already known for his seeming inability to complete projects on time? Was his illegitimacy an issue, or the anonymous charges of homosexual behavior? These are open questions.

Figure 6.23 Leonardo, The Last Supper (c. 1495-8)

of emotion found among the worshippers in the *Adoration*. Their psychological turmoil is nevertheless subsumed by their careful, symmetrical, even musical arrangement; in keeping with the ancient Greek ideal, they are ordered in their chaos. The long, linen-covered table is perpendicular to the axis of the room, a tunnel or vacuum made real by the perspective. With Jesus as the vanishing point, we are taken back to the *Tribute Money* of Masaccio, but Leonardo gives us not a story or two from the Gospels, but rather, the whole history of the world. That is, Christ in this picture isn't merely the Christian savior prophesying His death on the following day. He also radiates, along the orthogonals, all things, including all people throughout all time—including you, looking at the picture today. And that same eternal creation inversely bears down upon Him, transfixing Him in the center. *The Last Supper*, then, is also the Crucifixion, and the creation and end of the world.

Back in Florence after the fall of Milan to the French, Leonardo found himself a celebrity. He began a number of projects, including a portrait he would carry with him and continue to work on for the rest of his life. Mona—meaning "Lady"—Lisa

Figure 6.24 Leonardo, La Gioconda (Mona Lisa) (begun c. 1503)

di Antonio Maria Gherardini was the wife of a well-heeled Florentine, Francesco del Giocondo. In Leonardo's portrait she is the first, if not the only, subject of art who possesses and projects a profound awareness of her own invulnerability to time. Time is, in fact and to some extent, the subject; behind her, in the furthest distance, ice-capped mountains melt into a primal sea, giving way to a landscape shaped partly by man, those man-made elements leading to the present moment, the lady herself. She is literally woven into or out of the background; the light traces paths on her sleeves that rhyme with the distant paths; the uppermost folds of her mantle continue unbroken the contours of the rock formation and the bridge at right. The picture is a graphic realization of a universal idea, specifically, that myriad forces and all of time move forward and give rise to the individual.

Leonardo's stay in Florence was relatively brief. The tireless genius was also a restless one; having spent almost two decades in Milan, worked in Cesena for Cesare Borgia, and visited Venice, he went on to Rome before returning to Milan and, finally, moving, at the invitation of King Francis I, to France, where he died at the age of 67. It is fascinating, if moot, to wonder what his death meant to his young compatriot and rival, Michelangelo Buonarroti.

Twenty-three years younger than Leonardo, Michelangelo was the son of an impoverished member of the lesser nobility. Like Leonardo, he was a prodigy. In his early teens he was apprenticed to Verrocchio's great rival in Florence, Domenico Ghirlandaio. While still an adolescent, he became one of a select group of artists to study sculpture in the Medici gardens, with access not only to their extensive collection of antique and contemporary art, but also to the ideas and philosophies of prominent Florentine intellectuals. Both challenged and admired, it was in the Medici circle that the precocious young sculptor first demonstrated his ability to imitate the ancients and, like them, to transform marble into flesh. Classical sculpture may have been the standard by which early Renaissance artists were judged, but Michelangelo strove to surpass the ancients, as well as the late, but still looming, figure of the great Donatello.

While the unearthing of Roman and Hellenistic statues and marble fragments increased in frequency during the fifteenth and sixteenth centuries and major discoveries (the *Laocoön* among them) occurred during his lifetime, Michelangelo's relentless pursuit of perfect form was driven by a personal image of the ideal and a deep belief in, first of all, the primacy of sculpture among the arts and, secondly but no less importantly, his own supremacy as a sculptor. These convictions, as well as his complex character—he was by turns shy and boastful, confident and jealous, tender and wrathful—meant that he was also, for much of his life, alone and on the move. So, when the Dominican monk, Savonarola, succeeded in taking over Florence and ousting, if only temporarily, the Medici family, Michelangelo left the city, going, in a roundabout way via Venice, to Rome. There, at the age of twenty-three, he signed a contract promising a sculpture that would be more beautiful than any work in marble seen in the city. "In marble" is an important phrase here, since Michelangelo identified himself as, first, last, and always, a carver in stone. During his career, he painted the most famous frescoed ceiling in the world; he designed spectacular buildings and public spaces, including the Piazza del Campidoglio, with new façades for the Capitoline palaces, and—long after his rivals, Raphael and Bramante, were dead—the dome of the new Saint Peter's Basilica. But his art is inevitably that of the subtractive sculptor, freeing living, three-dimensional forms

Figure 6.25 Michelangelo's Rome Pietà (1498-9)

from primal stone. The forms he freed in his *Pietà* certainly fulfilled his side of the contract.

Created for a French cardinal and occupying the first chapel to the right in the new Saint Peter's basilica, the *Pietà* represents, in keeping with an iconographical tradition especially popular in Northern Europe, the Virgin Mary supporting her dead son. Michelangelo's surprisingly youthful Mary holds the lifeless body of her adult son across her lap, her head the pinnacle of a stable triangular composition, the deeply cut, cascading folds of her drapery contrasting with the smooth clarity of His perfectly rendered, nearly naked form. Rather than open grief, her face demonstrates timeless patience and dignified restraint, and the subtle gesture of her left hand is an acknowledgement of our presence, inviting us to witness the tragedy and the triumph of her son's death. And Michelangelo's triumph, too; the *Pietà* made the young artist's name, not only in Rome, but back in his beloved home town of Florence, to which he was recalled by the new, idealistic but ill-fated republican government. To symbolize the new republic, Michelangelo was entrusted with an enormous block of battered marble, out of which he carved his seventeen-foot-high Old Testament hero,

David, a figure that ever since has dominated Florence and the history of Western art. Like the Virgin in the *Pietà* and, for that matter, like the *Mona Lisa* of Leonardo currently being painted close by, Michelangelo's *David* is a complex psychological study, as haunted as he is haunting, troubled and capable of causing trouble, at rest but ready for action. In a pose that cannot help but recall the ideal of Polykleitos's *Spearbearer*, with a faultless, almost transparent modeling of human anatomy such as we see occasionally in the best Hellenistic work, Michelangelo's *David* is a bold new entry in the endless pageant of Western figurative sculpture, one which clearly redefines the genre and makes not only his enemies—the Philistines, the enemies of the Florentine Republic—but his artistic predecessors—Donatello's *David*, the

Figure 6.26 Michelangelo's David (1501-4)

male nudes of classical Greece—take notice

and, at least momentarily, tremble. This figure has a new tension, in the hand clutching the stone, in the sinews of the arms and neck, in the ominously lowered shoulder, in the furrowing of the brows. He is a colossal embodiment of super-human energies, emotional as well as physical, and as such, he also personifies Michelangelo's *terribilitá*, the awesome power that characterizes most of the artist's monumental work from this point on.

The projects, ill-fated and not, that occupied Michelangelo during the next decades of his life were monumental indeed. Leaving the David in Florence to proclaim and protect the Republic, Michelangelo was summoned to Rome to execute a tomb for Pope Julius II, who was still very much alive.

This tomb project was epic in scale, and was to include forty or so life-size and larger-than-life-size figures, with two of the Pope himself. And then, the Pope changed his mind. He decided instead to have Michelangelo fresco the broad barrel vault of the chapel built by his uncle, Pope Sixtus IV. Crestfallen at the abandonment of the tomb, relatively inexperienced—and certainly less interested—in the art of painting, Michelangelo nevertheless climbed the scaffolding and began the

Figure 6.27 Michelangelo, Sistine Chapel Ceiling (1508-12)

Figure 6.28 Sistine Chapel

Figure 6.29 Sistine Chapel Last Judgment (1536-41)

five-year task of covering over five thousand square feet of ceiling, in the process teaching himself, and ultimately transcending all standards for, the art of large-scale figural decoration. The spine of the finished work is nine Old Testament scenes divided into groups of three: the creation of the universe, the creation and fall of Adam and Eve, and stories of Noah and the flood. Enthroned in elaborate fictive architecture enclosing these scenes, Prophets and Sibyls read, write, and twist in their towering niches; the adjacent triangles and lunettes contain the ancestors of Christ, going back to Abraham. Illusionistic representations of nudes in flesh, bronze, and marble reiterate and activate the frames out of which many of the larger figures seem to explode.[10]

Since its unveiling in 1512, the Sistine Ceiling has provided the standard, Judeo-Christian vision of the creator god and the beginning of history, especially human history. Michelangelo's primal pantheon is one of willful, powerful, dynamic male forms—that is what you see when you look up at the Sistine Ceiling. Stone is Michelangelo's medium, even when he is painting, and the three dimensional male nude is his inspiration, his model, and his goal, even when he is representing a clothed female, such as the sibyls seen here.

This constant and intense focus on the monumentalized, idealized male body is even more pronounced, and more accessible, in the *Last Judgment* that Michelangelo painted on the altar wall of the Sistine Chapel more than twenty years after completing the ceiling. The center of an all-encompassing, cataclysmic meteorological event, Christ is born out of oblivion into our space, in order to moderate the end of the world. With arm upraised, He conducts the vast symphony or march of heroic nudes—the revivified bodies of the martyrs and the blest, but also the damned who fill the lower right quadrant, all variations of the masculine ideal—while His mother contracts herself at His side. In Michelangelo's last work, the so-called *Rondanini Pietà*, which the master was literally hammering away at days before his death in the eighty-ninth year of his life, the relative placement of mother and son are meaningfully reversed. Now the grown child shrinks beside the mother, who seems barely able to support Him. Michelangelo's longstanding ideal, passionately pursued throughout an awe-inspiring, almost mythic career, is the male body as

---

10 This projection of the figures out of the space is something Michelangelo developed as he worked. So, the prophet Zechariah, painted over the doorway in 1508, sits placidly, in profile, well within the confines of his niche. More than four years later, Michelangelo painted Jonah over the altar wall; Jonah bursts forward and outward, kicking up his legs and twisting his torso backward to look at the finished ceiling.

Figure 6.30 Michelangelo, Rondanini Pietà (1556-64)

Figure 6.31 Alberti, Basilica of Sant'Andrea, Mantova (1470's)

tangible proof of divine being. Here, in the end, is the abnegation of that ideal. The Virgin who, in the artist's first great success, the Saint Peter's *Pietà*, presented her son to the world, in the last *Pietà* takes Him back again, into herself, as both of them are borne backward and upward, into nothingness.

Younger than both Leonardo and Michelangelo, Raffaello Sanzio was also, if only unofficially and without their full approval, their greatest pupil. In fact, his tragically brief career exemplified perfectly the conception of the artist as pupil, since Raphael never stopped absorbing and learning and borrowing from his worthy contemporaries. But he is also the model of the artist as transmogrifier and perfecter; the lessons and inspiration Raphael took from others he transformed into a new and sublime art that was entirely his own.

Born in Urbino in 1483, Raphael spent time in Perugia and Florence before finally coming to Rome at the end of the first decade

Figure 6.32 Raphael, The School of Athens (1509-11)

of the sixteenth century. Though we all know that the Renaissance was originally a Florentine phenomenon, it reached new heights with the convergence of
the three masters—Raphael, Michelangelo, and Leonardo—on the Eternal City.
Already working for Pope Julius II when Raphael arrived was his fellow Urbinate,
another giant who had known Leonardo in Milan, Donato Bramante. Bramante
was in charge of the construction of the new Saint Peter's basilica, to replace the
ancient—but by this point utterly unstable and hazardous—church originally
built by Constantine. It was presumably as the protégé of Bramante that Raphael
received his first great commission, the fresco decoration of several papal apart-
ments, or *Stanze* (*stanza* means "room" in Italian), in the Vatican palace. The *Stanza
della Segnatura* was the room used to store the papal seal; inside, on walls facing
each other, Raphael represented the *Disputa* and the *Philosophy*, the latter more
commonly known as *The School of Athens*. The former shows a convocation of great
prophets and Christian thinkers discoursing on the nature of the Eucharist, the
wafer of bread transubstantiated into the body of Christ at the high point of the
Catholic mass. The round wafer, shown in a golden monstrance on the altar, is the
focal point of the gathering, which includes the Trinity and the Virgin Mary above

and, seated on a bank of clouds, several of the best known saints. The entire composition is divided into smaller and larger circular and semi-circular groups, the rayed wheels of the heavenly nimbuses suggesting that, while he was in Florence, Raphael spent some time studying and admiring the Pythagorean machinery of Brunelleschi's vaults.

The pagan counterpart to the *Disputa*, *The School of Athens* brings together the great minds of the pagan worlds. In the center, Plato—a presumed portrait of the aging Leonardo—points heavenward, while his pupil, Aristotle, indicates that his is the empirical sphere, the world of tangible, measurable, classifiable things. Another portrait is that of Michelangelo, represented here as an afterthought (he does not appear in the still extant finished cartoon for the work) in the guise of the be-smocked and leather-booted Heraclitus, leaning pensively, in a pose like those of the prophets he was painting down the hall, against a great block of stone. At the far right, modestly peeking out from a crowd, is Raphael himself, the well-spoken, affable, courtly lover of women and friend to great men. The architecture here is decidedly not Brunelleschian and certainly not Athenian; rather, with its lofty, barrel-vaulted, truly Roman spaces, it reflects Bramante's vision for the new Saint

Figure 6.33 Raphael, Portrait of Baldassare Castiglione (c. 1515)

Peter's basilica, a vision inspired by buildings such as the *Baths of Diocletian* and the *Basilica of Maxentius and Constantine* and informed by the work and ideas of the great Leon Battista Alberti, who was responsible for a more purist renaissance of Roman architecture in the middle of the fifteenth century. The frescoes of the Stanza della Segnatura, by convening the great thinkers of the classical and Christian worlds in a single room, are yet another manifestation of quintessentially Renaissance optimism. It is fascinating to consider that, in 1511, at the very moment when Michelangelo was entering the home stretch on his ceiling project and Raphael was daubing away in the *Stanze*, a German monk named Martin Luther was paying his first and only visit to the Eternal City.

A faster worker than Leonardo, and a more amenable artist than Michelangelo, Raphael produced the most famous series of Madonnas in the history of art. He was also a prolific and enthusiastically patronized portraitist. Among his canonical works in the genre is one of the great writer and diplomat, Baldassare Castiglione, who, like the painter himself, hailed from Urbino. In pose—sitting at an angle to the picture plane but facing frontally with hands together—as well as in the tension between the accessibility and inscrutability of the character, Raphael's *Castiglione* is clearly derived from and a great tribute to Leonardo's *Mona Lisa*. In the beloved Madonnas and in these great likenesses, physical textures are refined, and so is the subtle use of all outward details, in order to convey psychological complexity. These qualities also feature prominently in the work of Raphael's great contemporary in the North, Albrecht Dürer.

Dürer, born in Nuremburg in 1471, was originally trained by his father, a prominent goldsmith, and then apprenticed with the painter, Michael Wolgemut, whose workshop also produced woodcut prints. The artist continued his education in Italy. There, he found a greater emphasis on human form, a strong connection to the classical past (a classical past that was not available in Germany), and a continuing exaltation of the role of the artist. The influence of these ideas is evident in his *Self Portrait at 26*, painted only a few years after his first trip over the Alps, visible through the open window behind him. Dürer portrays himself not as a craftsman but as a gentleman, expensively and even fussily dressed, gazing self-confidently at the viewer. The image combines Italian

Figure 6.34 Dürer's Self Portrait at 26 (1498)

design with a Northern Renaissance attention to precise detail and subtle differences in surface texture.

Dürer's early exposure to printmaking was formative. Woodcut is one of the oldest forms of printmaking, used for text as well as images before the advent of movable type. Removing wood from the surface of a block results in light areas, wood left behind bears ink. The difficulty of preserving thin lines of wood while carving, and the fact that such a line could be easily damaged or more quickly worn down while making successive prints, often meant thicker, clunkier marks. Throughout a prodigious number of woodcuts that included an *Apocalypse* series and the collections known as the *Small* and *Large Passions*, Dürer's ability to create fine graceful lines allowed him to portray subtle gradations in light and texture and helped to elevate printmaking from the subsidiary illustration of books and publications to an independent art form. Dürer also explored iron engraving and became a prolific master of engraving on copper; producing multiple copies of a work made it possible for Dürer to sell, give away and trade them for prints by other artists, thereby bolstering his income, increasing his fame, and spreading the influence of the Italian Renaissance throughout Europe.

A woodcut of *The Last Supper*, published after a second trip to Northern Italy (1505 to 1507), is part of the *Large Passion* series. Dürer gives us the same moment portrayed in Leonardo's

Figure 6.35 Dürer's The Last Supper (1510)

Milan mural of ten years earlier, but employs a very different geometry. Christ, with the remains of the meal (a sacrificial lamb) on the table before Him and Saint John collapsed in His arms, has just spoken the words, "One of you will betray me." The Apostles react with a degree of agitation and an assortment of gestures comparable to those in Leonardo's work, which Dürer presumably never saw. In place of a halo, we find a burst of light, roughly cruciform, which blends with the fine lines of the background value on the wall behind Him, all of which are radii emanating from His head—they turn onto the side walls and move toward us. The shorter table means that the apostles are arranged around it in a half circle, and the scene takes place beneath an old groin-vaulted ceiling which is beginning to show signs of wear.

In spirit as in detail, Dürer's *Last Supper* shares much with Leonardo's legendary version. But the twisting pose of Christ and the closer conglomeration of Apostles in Dürer's image mean that it also has much in common with a stylistic movement that emerged in Rome during the second decade of the sixteenth century and is particularly visible in the late work of the short-lived Raphael, to which the movement is sometimes traced. Raphael's *Transfiguration*, now in the Vatican picture gallery, was begun in 1518 and completed by assistants after his death in 1520. Complex and multifarious in theme (the miracle of Christ's mid-air meeting with Moses and Elijah is shown simultaneously with the unsuccessful attempt by several Apostles to heal a demonically possessed boy), the *Transfiguration* is

Figure 6.36 Raphael, The Transfiguration (1518–20)

equally dense in terms of its tight overlapping of figures, many of whose movements and expressions are theatrical in the extreme. The picture is also packed with formal quotations, the most obvious being that of the woman in pink and blue at lower right, whose costume and pose derive from Michelangelo's *Doni Tondo*, a rare, round (*tondo*) panel painting of the Holy Family executed for Agnolo Doni in 1503. These characteristics—overlapping, often attenuated forms; complex and erudite, if not recondite, intellectual themes; dramatic and often melodramatic postures; quotations and variations of the work of other artists—combine to create the hybrid phenomenon, which itself varies from artist to artist and is very hard to define definitively, known as Mannerism.

If, as is traditional and perfectly justifiable, we think of Leonardo, Michelangelo, and Raphael as embodying the essence of the High Renaissance in Florence and Rome, we might consider what the three of them, despite their unique artistic personalities and achievements, shared or had in common. The most obvious and important overlap was that each of them was interested, above all, in investigating—that is, studying in detail and in depth[11]—the human body and, in representing and idealizing it, inevitably magnifying the role of the human organism in the larger universe. This is perhaps the most accessible connotation of the term "humanism," so often identified as a dominant characteristic of the Italian Renaissance. Northern European artists adopted a variety of different attitudes to this particular aspect of the new culture. Overall, Dürer's work evinces a whole-hearted embrace of Italian humanism. Others, working further from the classical epicenter, adopted a bemused or satirical stance toward the revived classical traditions, including the prioritization and glorification of the human form. Still others, affected alike by the secularism inherent in much of the Reformation message and the pessimism to be extrapolated from particular versions of Protestantism, evolved what we may call a more modern perspective on our place in the world.

And so, for example, we have the evolution of landscape painting, in which the human element, if present at all, is significantly diminished. One of the best and earliest examples of true landscape was painted by the artist considered by many to be the "father" of the genre, Albrecht Altdorfer. Like Dürer a German, Altdorfer executed *The Battle of Issus* for the Duke of Bavaria in 1529. In it, the painter shows the army of Alexander the Great at the moment he puts to flight his

---

11   At least in the case of both Leonardo and Michelangelo, "studying in depth" included dissecting the human body.

Figure 6.37 Altdorfer, The Battle of Issus (1529)

nemesis, Darius III of Persia. The lower section of the picture teems with soldiers on both sides of the battle, shown in such numbers and on so small a scale that, were it not for their flags and the nearness of a few figures in the foreground, they would hardly be distinguishable from the rocky terrain. The upper half presents an unprecedented vista, a dizzying landscape of mountains and islands and rivers and seas, all under a roiling sky that encompasses both sun and moon and renders negligible the power of the individual human being.

We also have the fantastic, often allegorical but not always decipherable, visions of the Netherlandish painter, Hieronymous Bosch. Like his Italian contemporary,

Figure 6.38 Bosch, The Garden of Earthly Delights (c. 1505)

Botticelli, Bosch is a *sui generis* artist, difficult to pin down. His best known work is a secular commission, a triptych that is, despite its *being* a triptych and its profusion of allusions to Christian themes, a riot of incongruous characters and clearly un-religious vignettes centered upon the largest panel, from which the work takes its title, *The Garden of Earthly Delights*. The landscape of the smaller panel at left, depicting Adam and Eve, blends into that of the central image, while the panel at right represents a dark and disaster-riddled inferno worthy of Dante. And in the central panel we are engulfed in an orgy of unexpected and—if not impossible, still—far from advisable activities. In all three scenes, we find large vessels or machines, like futuristic fountains or abstract sculptures, which some scholars have taken for references to alchemical equipment. Despite an at-times nightmarish distortion of scale, such that a strawberry is as large as the naked man misusing it, the human figures are all dwarfed by their strange environment; their diminutive, doll-like bodies, nude and anemic, are inevitably reminiscent of the figures from Last Judgment scenes over Medieval church doors—whether an allegory of life on earth, a critique of or warning against indulgence, a highly imaginative prophecy of oblivion, or the pleasures of the afterlife, there is certainly something very pre- or post-Apocalyptic about this Garden. The work is among the most popular and the most closely scrutinized in the canon of Western art.

It is interesting to consider the strong probability that, during his lifetime, Bosch's work was especially prized in one of the great capitals of Renaissance culture, Venice. We know that in the Middle Ages Venice was a melting pot of Byzantine and Gothic influences, making it one of the proverbial places where "East meets West."[12] Now, in the Renaissance, it is also the place where North meets South. For instance, Venetian artists were among the first in Italy to adopt the Northern technique of painting in oil. Remembering that there was no Venice in the ancient period when the Romans dominated the continent, it is not surprising to find the city turning southward in the fifteenth century to fulfill its classical needs, importing the Florentine Renaissance in the form of actual artists, among them Donatello, Andrea del Castagno, and Andrea del Verrocchio. But the rich and thriving Venetian republic proved a quick study and soon developed its own variations on Central Italian artistic innovations and practices, such that, by the end of the Quattrocento, Venetian masters came to rival their Florence- and Rome-based colleagues. We have in this rivalry the beginnings of the great dichotomy—at once theoretical and practical, useful and misleading—between two approaches to artistic creation, one based on the primacy of drawing, and the other on painterliness in the broadest sense. Thus, Central Italian artists advocated *disegno* or draughtsmanship as the foundation of art, while the Venetians came to represent the school of *colorito*, coloring. As we will see, the rivalry spread far beyond Italy and lasted far longer than the Renaissance.

Any account of the Venetian Renaissance begins with the name "Bellini." Jacopo Bellini was the patriarch of an august family of artists. His prolific sons, Gentile and Giovanni, stood for the two overlapping styles of Venetian late Quattrocento painting: Gentile for the straightforward, naturalistic—more often than not, journalistic—style that prevailed throughout much of Italy in the latter decades of the century, and Giovanni for the softer, more sympathetic and penetrating, yet at the same time more imaginative, treatment of nature and its human representatives. Their brother-in-law was Andrea Mantegna. No wonder that the workshop of Giovanni Bellini came to be the largest in all of Europe.

Giovanni Bellini had a long and successful career, and he seems always to have been open to new influences, without abandoning his inherited cultural loyalties and proclivities. His ability to combine, with unparalleled grace, this Venetian,

---

12 Consider that, in the period of a decade or so between 1495 AD and 1505 AD, Leonardo, Michelangelo, and Dürer were all in Venice, though their visits did not overlap.

Figure 6.39 Giovanni Bellini, San Giobbe (Saint Job) Altarpiece (c. 1488)

and ultimately Byzantine, heritage with a Northern mastery of surface texture and a Southern instinct for capturing the human form and character, is nowhere more apparent than in his *San Giobbe* (Saint Job) *Altarpiece*, of c. 1488. A true and stable triangular High Renaissance composition, the colors and textures—the *cangiantismo* of Job's loincloth, the tender modeling of Saint Sebastian's youthful body, the glow of the gold ground Byzantine mosaic that crowns the apse, which is the setting for this sacred conversation—are all recreated with a uniquely Venetian conviction, which is also unique to Bellini. Unique except that the softness and the warmth—of gold and flesh and tempered light—are also characteristics of the work of Giovanni's great but short-lived pupil, Giorgio da Castelfranco, known as Giorgione. Though no more than six or eight works survive that are indisputably from the hand of Giorgione, these nevertheless document the preoccupations and talents of one of the great poets of Western visual art. And, like the best poetry, works such as his celebrated *Tempest* seem immutably condensed and untranslatable; scholars continue to rack their brains as to what is really going on in this dreamy landscape, where an elegantly dressed young man stands among ruins on one side of a river while, on the opposite bank, a nearly nude young woman nurses her baby below a sky rent by the lightning of an approaching storm. And in the very center is the suggestive bridge, which we want, perhaps, to be a symbol of compatibility or reconciliation.

Another of Bellini's pupils, and the most famous exemplar of the High Renaissance in Venice, was Tiziano Vecellio da Cadore: Titian. After the death of Giorgione, Titian assumed the latter's commissions and his place as the up-and-coming artist in the Republic. His first monumen-

Figure 6.40 Giorgione, The Tempest (c. 1508)

tal masterpiece, *The Assumption of the Virgin*, was painted between 1516 and 1518 for the high altar of the Franciscan basilica in Venice, Santa Maria Gloriosa dei Frari. Entering the church at any time of day, under any lighting conditions, one is immediately riveted by and drawn to this three-story painting that dominates the choir of the great Gothic church. Studying it is like watching open heart surgery—it is a hot, pulsating scene in which reds and golds predominate, and movement abounds. The recently deceased and revivified Virgin, still following the dictates of classical composition re-established by the Florentines, is the apex of a great triangle; she also rides the rim of a wheel of light, a circle tangential to the square or cube comprising the Apostles who marvel at her assumption from below. The astonishing new element is the suggestion that, however dependable the underlying classical armature, the figures here move, and the Virgin herself seems conscious of the miracle of her balance and rising,, and capable of tottering even now.

Figure 6.41 Titian's Assumption of the Virgin (1516–18)

Titian had an extraordinarily long and successful career, and his stylistic evolution is fascinating to follow. After the remarkable decade of the Frari *Assumption*, the artist gravitated increasingly to imbalanced compositions, simultaneously developing a loose, painterly manner. No doubt it was this manner that Michelangelo was adverting to when he met Titian in Rome in 1545; the sculptor of the *David* and the painter of the *Sistine Ceiling* said he found the Venetian and his work likable, but lacking in draughtsmanship.

It was probably in the early 1560s that Titian painted his *Rape of Europa* for King Philip II of Spain. Zeus, in order to avoid recognition by his wife, Hera—theirs had been a troubled, non-traditional marriage from the start—disguised himself as an irresistibly handsome bull, and when the latest object of his lust, the virgin Europa, came close enough, he carried her off. Titian represents the abduction as one of earth-shaking drama; the whole world seems literally to respond. The heavens are torched by the evening light, the mountains strain forward and back like the poor princess's frantic attendants, the air erupts with Cupids while Zeus

Figure 6.42 Titian, The Rape of Europa (c. 1562)

plows headstrong through the waves, diagonally from the left distance, roughly toward—and watching—us. Europa herself is another great dynamic diagonal, insecurely mounted on the god, her legs and arms thrashing wildly, her eyes rolling back in her head. The palette, like the passions that motivate the characters— whether the ardor of Zeus or the more complex combination of terror, worry, and wonder of his victim—is very warm, reds, golds, and flesh tones predominating. Emotions burst forth frankly as action; the volatility and violence, both formal and psychological, of Titian's *Rape of Europa* make it one of the first masterpieces of baroque style.

seven

Barococo

If you ever find yourself on a quiz show and the big challenge is to define "baroque," the quickest path to the prize money will be to say simply, "Baroque means seventeenth century." Like "Renaissance," "Baroque" is a convenient term referring to a specific period of European history, in this case, the 1600s. But "baroque" is also a stylistic term with far-flung, often surprising and unfounded connotations. The true characteristics of baroque style—dynamism, asymmetry, immediacy—can be found in art long before the seventeenth century, in ancient Roman architecture for example, or in the paintings of artists working in the Renaissance, notable among them being Antonio Allegri of Parma, known as Correggio, and, most influentially of all, the dominant figure of the sixteenth century in Venice, Titian. Similarly, baroque style does not disappear at the end of the Baroque century; in painting and sculpture, many of those same characteristics—diagonal compositions, a heightened suggestion of movement, extreme naturalism—continue to animate the work of artists whose

Figure 7.1 Caravaggio, The Crucifixion of Saint Peter (1601)

Figure 7.2 Boucher, Madame de Pompadour (1756)

preference for lighter subjects and handling and coloring makes them proponents of the quintessentially French offshoot of the Baroque known as the Rococo. Finally, and somewhat confusingly, even throughout the entire Baroque century, there remains a strong, often reactionary but equally often open and syncretic, classical tradition. This point is vividly made by Annibale Carracci's ceiling fresco, *The Loves of the Gods*, in the great *salone* of the Palazzo Farnese in Rome, painted on the cusp of the sixteenth and seventeenth centuries. While filled with allusions to ancient sculpture, and especially to Michelangelo's *Sistine Ceiling*, Carracci's work is never merely imitative—he builds on, and thereby perpetuates, the Renaissance. And so we have the ironic but serviceable distinction between "Baroque classicism" and "baroque Baroque".

The most famous—and, for many, the first, greatest, and most baroque— artist of the Baroque is Michelangelo Merisi da Caravaggio. Born in or near Milan in 1571, Caravaggio was apprenticed to a painter, Simone Peterzano, who was himself a pupil of Titian. By the early 1590s, Caravaggio had traveled south- ward, possibly via the Carraccis' hometown of Bologna, and was living, probably

Figure 7.3 Annibale Carracci, The Loves of the Gods (unveiled 1600)

hand-to-mouth, in Rome. By the end of the decade, his shockingly naturalistic narrative scenes, painted directly on canvas without recourse to preliminary drawings, made him the rising star among fellow artists and an elite, aristocratic clientele. His heyday was brief: in 1606 he killed a man, and by 1610 he, too, was dead.

Passion and violence—physical and spiritual—we find in both his life and his art, and although it is always dangerous to equate artistic style with personal character, it is never more tempting than when our subject is Caravaggio. A textbook example of his baroque style is the *Crucifixion of Saint Peter*, painted and paired with his *Conversion of Saul* for the Cerasi Chapel in the Roman church of Santa Maria del Popolo in 1601. In both works, light slashes across the space, shaping the forms and cinematically revealing details. In the *Crucifixion*, light is as harsh and unforgiving as the dreadful activity it exposes, Saint Peter being crucified, with his head down at his own request out of respect for Christ. Along with the stark chiaroscuro,[1] gravity is a major player in the drama, as the three faceless men struggle to raise the cross bearing the living "rock" who is the foundation of the church. Caravaggio does not pull any punches; he shows us the old saint's wrinkled face and straining torso, the furrowed red brow of the man at left, the filthy feet and rearing backside of his weight-bearing colleague. All the elements of Caravaggio's naturalism serve to annihilate the traditional separation between real and painted worlds.

A summary of many of Caravaggio's artistic preoccupations can be found, of all places, in a basket of fruit he painted around the same time that he was working on a trio of scenes from the life of Saint Matthew for San Luigi dei Francesi and the pair of works for Santa Maria del Popolo. The *Ambrosiana Still Life*—so-called because it was in the first batch of gifts made by Cardinal Federigo Borromeo, Archbishop of Milan, to the Ambrosiana library and art gallery he founded in that city in 1607—seems a relatively sedate affair, but it is filled with incident. Its outstanding feature is its unflinching naturalism; the slight fog on the grapes, the worm hole in the apple, the weave of the basket and the way it seems to sag with its burden, overlapping—only slightly, but tantalizingly—the painted sill, together present a *tour de force* of illusionism. The brush strokes disappear entirely into the eye-fooling surfaces. The composition of the elements is also distinctly aligned along the diagonal. And most fascinating of all, if we read the picture as is natural, from left to right, following the compositional slope, we find a narrative that begins with ripe fruits and green leaves, and ends with withered black leaves, with rot and decay. So the naturalism

Figure 7.4 Caravaggio, Basket of Fruit (Ambrosiana Still Life) (c. 1599)

---

1 *Chiaroscuro* means simply light and dark; nearly all pictures have it. Caravaggio and his many followers often go to extremes in contrasting the two.

includes the passage of time, and the result is a true and original *nature morte* or still life—life in the process of being stilled.

The themes of time stopped and time passing are constants in the work of Caravaggio, to the point almost of obsession. In the early painting, *Ecstasy of Saint Francis*, now in Hartford, Connecticut, Saint Francis is shown as a haggard, middle-aged man supported by a youthful male angel, and their bodies are physically conflated: the saint becomes the angel where and when the wound in the former's side is opened. In numerous representations of violent dramas, including *The Sacrifice of Isaac* and the career-making *Judith Beheading Holofernes*, youth and age are juxtaposed, or overlap, or coalesce in this manner. In the latter work,

Figure 7.5 Caravaggio's Judith Beheading Holofernes (c. 1597)

depicting the climactic moment of the story of the Old Testament heroine, we are in the tent with Judith and her maid, who, in their placement, not only remind us of the passage of time from youth to old age, but also, in the transparency of their expressions, convey depths of their distinct characters. Killing the Philistine warlord, Holofernes, is presumably not, from the look on her face, Judith's idea of the perfect ending to the perfect date. But she is young and beautiful enough to seduce her enemy, and strong enough, despite her squeamishness, to do the job. And backing her up, her faithful servant provides a closing parenthesis to the gory scene; neither young nor beautiful, rather withered and frail, she nevertheless supplies the resolution that may be lacking in her mistress. In any case, she makes it clear that nobody is leaving the tent until she has the head in the bag. Exploring the interrelationships of the accessories to violence is another of Caravaggio's recurring themes, seen again, for example, near the end of his life, in the *Salome with the Head of Saint John the Baptist,* in which Salome and her mother are shown as two heads sharing a single body, and sharing as well, but with very different reactions, the head of their victim.

That he became identified with climactic scenes of revelation and conversion and violence—graphic violence, in which sexual overtones often abound—helps to explain Caravaggio's soaring reputation in our time, and the admiration and aversion he elicited in his own. But it is important not to overlook the consummate clarity with which, in his maturity, he communicated his human narratives. Compared to the Mannerism that prevailed among the artistic elites of the later Renaissance, Caravaggio speaks a singularly comprehensible language. His pictures answer the Catholic Counter-Reformation call to make religious art that is accessible to all people. Caravaggio's characters and their actions are invariably accessible—sometimes they seem inescapable. His originality gained him a large number of followers, and his fame and his style spread far beyond his lifetime and his adopted home. One of the greatest of the so-called Caravaggisti must have known him personally, as her father was, at least for a time, on friendly terms with him. In a world with few opportunities for aspiring female artists, the painter Orazio Gentileschi trained his precocious daughter, Artemisia, in the new style. In 1611, when she was seventeen, Artemisia was raped by one of her father's artistic collaborators, the painter Agostino Tassi, which undoubtedly colored her interpretation of the traditional themes she depicted. But neither the assault nor the subsequent prolonged, and very public, trial (during the proceedings, she was tortured in order to ensure her honesty) prevented her from becoming one of the most celebrated and sought-after artists of her time. She was patronized by the Medici in Florence, painted pictures for King Philip IV of Spain, traveled to England (where many of her works made their way into the royal collection) and Venice, and died, probably of the plague, in Naples, in 1652 or 1653.

The Biblical heroine Judith was a subject Artemisia visited repeatedly during her career. Her first version of *Judith Beheading Holofernes* was probably painted within a year or two of the assault. Comparison with the famous version by Caravaggio is inevitable and fruitful. Created in the shadow of her personal disaster, and under the spell of the recently deceased master, Artemisia's picture demonstrates a devastating instinct for sexually-charged

Figure 7.6 Artemisia Gentileschi's Judith Beheading Holofernes (c. 1612)

violence and a complete understanding of the voyeuristic appeal of revealing with light acts often carried out in darkness. But while Caravaggio's Judith is young and uncertain, Artemisia's is a strong adult woman who undertakes her gruesome task with grim determination and more than a hint of satisfaction. Undeterred by the blood and the struggle, she forces the weapon through her enemy's throat without regret, putting her whole body into the effort. Her maidservant here provides practical assistance, using her weight to pin one of the arms of the drunken Holofernes. The two women will often be reunited in Artemisia's later paintings representing both the violent act in progress and the immediate aftermath, when they listen in suspense for the enemy soldiers as they make their escape.

Though, as was the case with that of another great revolutionary naturalist, Giotto, Caravaggio's influence waxed and waned and remained a vital strain in painting throughout the subsequent century, his truest heir was in fact the first and greatest sculptor of the Baroque, Gianlorenzo Bernini. A celebrated prodigy, Bernini was born in Naples to a Florentine father and a Neapolitan mother. Brought to

Figure 7.7 Bernini, Apollo and Daphne (1622-24)

Rome when his parents recognized their son's potential, little Gianlorenzo soon found himself in the highest circles of aristocratic patronage. Still in his teens, he was taken up by the nephew of Pope Paul V, Cardinal Scipione Borghese, who was in the process of building and furnishing the most fantastic villa in Rome. There, among masterpieces by Caravaggio and his contemporaries, Bernini's *Apollo and Daphne* still startles visitors in the same location for which it was made.

You can tell upon first glance at this sculpture that something strange is occurring. Daphne, her lower body partially concealed, races in your direction. Then, as you walk clockwise around the group, the story made famous by Ovid and other ancient writers unfolds: the sun god pursues the beautiful nymph, whose father, in answer to her prayers, transforms her into the laurel tree, which is all that you can decipher when you have completed your circumnavigation—her hands and feet and hair have become branches and roots and leaves. When late Renaissance and Mannerist sculptors represented such themes in the round, they treated the figures as locked into a specific point in time; for example, when you walk around another abduction scene, Giambologna's 1580 *Rape of the Sabines* in the Loggia dei Lanzi in Florence, you are treated to a variety of views of the same climactic moment in that particular drama. Bernini breaks with this tradition in a way which is revolutionary in sculpture, but which is anticipated by such paintings as Caravaggio's *Ambrosiana Still Life*. In Bernini's *Apollo and Daphne*, and in his other large scale statues for Cardinal Borghese, the *Pluto and Persephone* and the *David*, time and the narrative depend on the active participation of the viewer.

It is not only in the treatment of narrative, but also in more specific and formal ways, that Bernini extends the baroque repertory of his artistic mentor. For example, in each of his Borghese works, the angle of the cuts as well as the depth of the carving results in a chiaroscuro worthy of Caravaggio. With regard to the overriding concern of all baroque artists for textural naturalism, the polished marble of the *Apollo and Daphne* has the reflective quality, if not the color, of flesh, and some leaves are so thin that light passes through the stone. This technical virtuosity set him on the fast track to become the virtual arbiter of art in Rome under a succession of popes, most notably Urban VIII Barberini, who bankrupted the city in order to have Bernini transform it. In fact, Rome *is* Bernini's city, its avenues like its galleries and church interiors seeming inevitably to lead us to the artist's major works, from the *Baldacchino* over the high altar of Saint Peter's basilica to the *Constantine* at the end of the narthex, from the *Triton Fountain* in Piazza Barberini to the *Fountain of the Four Rivers* in Piazza Navona, from the façade of Santa Bibiana to the little elephant topped by an obelisk in front of Santa Maria sopra Minerva.

In an obscure little church dedicated to the Virgin of Victory, the artist executed his most powerfully charged religious monument, for a Venetian cardinal, Federico Cornaro, in the transept to the left of the high altar. Bernini has transformed the Cornaro Chapel into a sort of theater. Prominent, mainly deceased, members of the Cornaro family flank, in a brace of loges or boxes, the main event,

Figure 7.8 Bernini, The Ecstasy of Saint Theresa (1647-52)

which is a representation of the Spanish mystic Saint Theresa of Avila swooning as a bare-shouldered, beaming, distinctly Caravaggesque angel prepares to pierce her lower abdomen with a fire-tipped golden arrow. Again, our appreciation of the work of art—which brings together a wide range of materials, from the mosaic skeletons illusionistically drawn upward from the floor before the altar through the dappled and expensive marble surfaces of the chapel interior, to the light pouring in from a hidden window above, to the stucco clouds and angels and the scroll of text[2] in the frescoed ceiling—depends upon an investment of time and movement. We are drawn from the dark doorway into the church by the gaze of one of the marble witnesses; handed off at the crossing, we are then granted access to the divine narrative. Thus, manipulated by Bernini, our visionary experience simulates that granted to the saint herself. More blatantly, what the angel is to Saint Theresa, Bernini's creation is to us: a shocking, penetrating, transforming visitation in which we are no longer the visitor, but the visited.

The interaction of work with viewer that occurs in Caravaggio's paintings and Bernini's sculptures, we find as well in baroque architecture. As we have seen, the great architects of the Renaissance studied the proportions and decorative motifs of the ancient Romans. No architect better exemplifies the widespread sixteenth-century devotion to and ingenious reinterpretation of classical forms and geometries than Andrea Palladio. From his birthplace in Vicenza in the north of Italy, Palladio came to Rome, and then returned to transform his hometown

Figure 7.9 Palladio, Church of the Redeemer (begun 1577)

---

2   The text represented comes from the writings of the recently canonized saint. During one visitation, Christ addressed to Theresa the line, "Nisi coelum creassem ob te solam crearem," "If I had not created heaven I would create it for you alone."

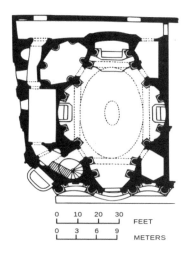

0 10 20 30
FEET
0 3 6 9
METERS

Figure 7.10 Borromini, San Carlino alle Quattro Fontane (c. 1633)

Figure 7.11 San Carlino, plan

and the entire Veneto (the territories—including such cities as Vicenza, Padua, and Verona—under Venetian control) with an impressive series of urban palaces and suburban villas, the most famous being the centralized Villa Rotonda for the Capra family. In Venice itself, Palladio designed three great churches facing the wide Giudecca canal; each of these reaffirms the Renaissance commitment to classical models, though Palladio transposes and remixes them in innovative and ingenious ways. So, the Church of the Redeemer, begun in 1577, presents a façade comprising three superimposed pagan temple fronts. For all the play between these overlapping surfaces, however, Palladio still maintained the conception of the church façade as primarily composed of flat planes.

Like Palladio, the first great architect of the Baroque, Francesco Borromini, was from the North, though from even further away, in what is now Switzerland. In Rome, he was trained by and collaborated with his kinsman, Carlo Maderno, who was in charge of completing the new basilica of Saint Peter's in the first decades of the seventeenth century. Around 1633, Borromini began building the little Roman church of Saint Charles, *San Carlino alle Quattro Fontane*, and his design included the first curvilinear church facade of the Baroque. No longer a simple skin or system of planar surfaces marking the spatial boundaries of the church, the front of San Carlino moves into and out of the street in a great double serpentine; it breaks through its presumptive plane as surely and compellingly as Caravaggio's fruit basket overlaps its sill, and with the same result, namely, that our space interpenetrates—is the same as—that of the work of art. A masterpiece of baroque energy and movement, the church of *San Carlino* comes out to meet you, even to get you.

Inside, too, *San Carlino* represents new inclinations. Though, like his early and high Renaissance predecessors, Borromini was deeply engaged with ancient Roman culture throughout his ca-

Figure 7.12 Borromini, Sant'Ivo alla Sapienza (begun 1642)

reer, the sources and motifs he was most attracted to were not the standard, best known, officially sanctioned ones. The ground plan of *San Carlino*, for example, is neither a traditional basilica plan, nor centralized in the circular manner of the Pantheon or Santa Costanza, but instead attempts a synthesis of the two, and is ultimately derived from the oval. And what an oval! A busy concatenation of curved and straight lines, of deep concavities and shallow convexities, all of which are resolved in the heavenly zone, the simple straightforward oval of the cupola or dome. Fifteen years later, living and working the whole time in the shadow of the always-popular and ubiquitous Bernini, Francesco Borromini created the even more dramatically animated little church of Sant'Ivo alla Sapienza, the interior of which is like a great tent with pleats of stucco and stone, the exterior of which is crowned by an enigmatic spiral lantern.

Dramatic chiaroscuro and dramatic, sometimes violent, dynamism are qualities that we find in architecture as well as sculpture and painting in the Baroque era and in the baroque style. The dissemination of baroque ideas throughout the rest of Europe was begun on a grand scale by the Flemish artist, Peter Paul Rubens, who, like the German Dürer a hundred years earlier, spent a formative period in Italy, drawing constantly and, in so doing, creating for himself an extensive catalogue of Italian masterpieces that would serve as source and inspiration for the rest of his life. One of the most prolific artists of his, or any, time—nobody painted faster better—Rubens also worked in Spain, England, and France. Personifying what used to be praised or derided as the inherent eclecticism of Baroque art, Rubens incorporated into an unprecedentedly broad repertoire techniques and motifs culled from artists as diverse as Leonardo, Michelangelo, Titian, Veronese, Tintoretto, the Carracci (Annibale was only the most famous of many), and Caravaggio. His work reconciles seemingly divergent styles. For example, his *Prometheus* of c. 1611 combines the painterliness of the Venetians with a body seemingly borrowed from Michelangelo's *Last Judgment*, all arranged along an unstable diagonal straight out of Caravaggio's baroque.

The lighting in the *Prometheus*, like the graphic representation of violence, also betrays an affinity with Caravaggesque chiaroscuro, but that is not typical of Rubens. It is, however, a recurring feature

Figure 7.13 Rubens, Prometheus Bound (1611)

Figure 7.14 Rembrandt, The Blinding of Samson (1636)

in the work of another Netherlandish artist, Rembrandt van Rijn. Painted when Rembrandt was in his late twenties, *The Blinding of Samson* illustrates the three c's of the Caravaggesque baroque: chiaroscuro (dramatic), climax (violent), composition (diagonal). Given that the artist was never in Italy, the picture also testifies to the reach and currency of the style.

One of the most ambitious and original interpreters of religious history—he created definitive versions of countless Biblical stories—and of human character—he redefined the function of portraiture—Rembrandt undertook pictorial experiments in a range of media and techniques, and paradoxically (many would say miraculously, despite, for example, the thick impasto of his later paintings or the build up of ever deeper blacks in successive states of his prints) pierced, and made visible, the interior lives of the figures he represented. His career was a famously up-and-down one, though his talents were by no means tied to his fortune. After a relatively inauspicious apprenticeship in his native Leiden and then in Amsterdam, he enjoyed youthful success as a portraitist and history painter and also as a painter in several more recently established genres, such as comfortable domestic interiors with figures, and heads typifying particular states of emotion. One of his favorite themes is the scholar, or artist, or philosopher shown at work in a room, usually lighted—following a tradition that goes back to the age of van Eyck—from the left, but shrouded in darkness on the right.

Throughout the vicissitudes of his later life, Rembrandt's investigation of the human psyche intensified; his self portraits, among the most courageous and convincing records of artistic self-examination in the history of art, provide ever subtler nuances of light and shade suggesting equally complex and profound movements of soul. In a 1648 print that combines etching, engraving, and drypoint techniques, the master glances moodily towards us as though we have interrupted him in the act of drawing on a cloth-banked metal plate, the same sort

Figure 7.15 Rembrandt's Self Portrait at a Window (1648)

of plate that produced this very image.[3] What we might call the relief of the face—the minute accretion and consequent irregularity of flesh that denotes experience and endurance—is handled with unparalleled sensitivity by Rembrandt, and is virtually synonymous with his style. In the painting *Bathsheba*, of 1654, for example, the ill-fated object of King David's desire has just received his ardent summons. Her beautiful, soft and lived-in body is prepared for the royal rendezvous, and her face is grave with

Figure 7.16 Rembrandt, Bathsheba (1654)

a foreknowledge of the tragic consequences. We see her, and, through her, what she sees: the adultery, the murder of her husband, the death of her child.

Though it is often reductive to refer to one artist as the counterpart of another, it is fair and a compliment to both when we say that Rembrandt finds one in his Spanish contemporary, Diego Velasquez. Equals in their ability to convey human character, they are also peers when it comes to their expert manipulation of the medium of oil paint to serve that end. Each is justifiably famous for his particular suggestive impastos and for the "spontaneous" and evocative brushwork of his mature style.

Like Rembrandt, Velasquez was trained in the Caravaggesque baroque of extreme naturalism and artful chiaroscuro. The debt is clear in works such as *The Water Seller of Seville* and *Los Borrachos* (*The Drunks*), painted by Velasquez even

3   Of course, in the *process*, Rembrandt is most likely looking at himself in a mirror. In the *product*, as the artist is well aware, he is looking at us.

before he made his first of two trips to Italy with the friendly encouragement of Rubens, who was visiting Spain at the time (1629). Velasquez's maturity provides a dazzling template of baroque artistic practice: nature, and Renaissance and contemporary painting, are the mines from which he selectively draws the raw materials of his art, forging out of them something completely new and original and transcendent.

Transcendent and original on every level is the artist's most celebrated work, a group portrait of members of the family and court of King Philip IV of Spain. *Las Meninas* is to the Spanish what Rembrandt's *Night Watch* is to the Dutch, and what the Lincoln Memorial is to us.[4] In a room hung with paintings which themselves represent other worlds, the little *infanta*, Margarita, is surrounded by, among others, two handmaidens (the *meninas*), two dwarves, a dog, and the painter himself. Showing himself in the very act of painting, Velasquez clearly takes artistic creation as one of his themes, and also reminds us that what we are looking at is a construction.[5]

The painting is a place of myriad conversations—within the work, and with the viewer, though our input must always devolve into inquiry. Abandoning any hope of extorting from the picture anything like a comprehensive, much less definitive, translation or explanation of its meaning, we can nevertheless find in *Las Meninas* a trove of unprecedented motifs and techniques.

The most startling technical feature is the loose brushwork, a far cry from the invisible strokes of Caravaggio's *Ambrosiana Still Life*, and, given that this is a royal commission on a grand scale, more daring than anything to be found in the work of Rubens or Rembrandt. There is in fact no precedent in Western art for the sheer laying on of paint, the loose strokes defying any expectation of traditional finish, in details such as the frills on the dresses, the body of the mastiff, and, most tellingly of all, the artist's hands blending into his brush and palette. What is even more surprising, this generous and evocative handling only furthers the naturalist agenda. And so the light, moving as a slow wave from the window at right, recognizes and describes the living figures; it blurs the little Nicolosito with his foot on the dog, and hums in the hair and face of the older dwarf, Maribarbola

---

4   Just to be clear, the similarities are limited. Philip IV was no Abraham Lincoln.
5   Among the staggering number of speculative notions about *Las Meninas* is the recurring one that the artist is in fact shown painting the picture we are looking at. The authors consider this both attractive and plausible.

Figure 7.17 Velasquez, Las Meninas (1656)

(such an impression of the quavering of all organic things will not reappear in static images until the earliest days of photography). Here is a naturalism that was not part of the language of painting before now. But there is also a hole in

Figure 7.18 Poussin, Saint John on Patmos (1640's)

the naturalism—obvious, deliberate: the mirror in the center of the image. If it is a mirror. And if it is a mirror, does it reflect us? Are we Queen Mariana and her uncle-husband, King Philip, to whom most faces turn? Are *they* both subject and exclusive object—the viewers, for all time—of the picture? Or does the mirror simply reflect one more picture, of them?

We have implied that during the Baroque century many genres attained independence and came to be codified. Before this period, artists hardly ever painted autonomous still lives, for example, or landscapes, or domestic genre scenes—Van Eyck never painted an independent seascape, Botticelli never painted just a bouquet. But in the Baroque, a hierarchy developed which maintained as its highest category the painting of religious and historical subjects on a large scale. Landscape, especially, came into its own at this time. In early Baroque landscapes, as in the seminal forays of Altdorfer, there is usually an ostensible or nominal subject drawn from the canon of Western history and myth. So the landscapes of Annibale Carracci and his followers, Domenichino and Albani, as well as those of the great

French expatriates in Rome, Nicolas Poussin and Claude Lorraine, invariably include figures and classical buildings, but those figures rarely do little more than ornament or accessorize the larger world, which is well ordered, clear, and rational in Carracci and Poussin, suffused with the first or fading light of day in Claude. Velasquez, too, painted landscapes, and is in fact credited with being among the very first artists to paint *en plein air*—outdoors, on the spot. Rembrandt's contemporary in Holland, Johannes

Figure 7.19 Vermeer, The Concert (c. 1665)

Vermeer, painted a cityscape of his native Delft, but he was more active in establishing another genre, that of the well-appointed, middle-class domestic interior with figures. Vermeer could in fact be said to treat the room like landscape, a landscape as accessible to us as the fruit in a still life is accessible. In these "roomscapes" are any number of objects and other images— landscapes, too—representing avenues of contemplation and meaning. But it is the figures that dominate these hushed scenes; in their expensive clothes, they are like the fine things surrounding them, but their situations are pregnant with the potential for intimacy or disjunction. In Vermeer's *Concert*,[6] a paradox similar to

---

6 This masterpiece, formerly in the Isabella Stewart Gardner Museum in Boston, Massachusetts, was stolen, along with works by Rembrandt, Manet, Degas and others,

that found in Velasquez' *Las Meninas* arises; in spite of the heightened naturalism of texture and perspective and detail in both works, in spite of our consequent sensation of being there, the conversations are blocked from us. In *The Concert*, it is as though the music not only accompanies what is being said by the couple on the right, but also covers it up.

Recording land- or townscapes is one relatively new or newly-respected genre of image-making, but making and remaking the actual environment continues to occupy some of the greatest artists and patrons of the period. So the plans of Popes Sixtus V (1585–90), Urban VIII (1623–44), Innocent X (1644–55), and Alexander VII (1655–67) transformed Rome into the city we know today. The last-named commissioned from Bernini his largest undertaking in terms of scale, the great colonnade in front of Saint Peter's. In keeping with baroque architectural practice, at least one *concetto*—literally "conceit," in the sense of a symbolic allusion—underlies the plan of the colonnade. Drawings made by the artist reveal that the arms of the great structure are indeed the arms of Christ drawing in the faithful and, in the largest such demonstration of Counter Reformation ideals, welcoming back those whose protestant beliefs have led them astray. The shape of the great colonnade also resembles a keyhole, keys being the primary attribute of Saint Peter, whose basilica this is. [7]

No welcoming gesture underlies the evolving plans of another great architectural project on an even larger scale than the Colonnade. With one eye always on the scenographic achievements of Italian baroque designers, including Bernini, whom he hosted in Paris in 1665, the Bourbon king, Louis XIV, created the palace to end all palaces, not far from the French capital, in the forest of Versailles. Just as, under Louis, the balance of political and military power in Europe shifted from the South (Spain, Italy) to the North (France, Holland), so French artists and intellectuals challenged Italian cultural supremacy. The building of the palace at Versailles is a microcosm (however strange it seems to use such a term with regard to such a thing) of Louis's establishment of the modern nation of France. Its *concetto* is order, plain and simple, and the king, as the most ambitious and successful of absolute monarchs, is the source and personification of that order. Thus the

---

in 1990. If you recognize *The Concert* and have information as to its whereabouts, please notify the Boston Police.

7   Similarly, Borromini gives us two *concetti* in the plan of his Sant'Ivo: one, the Barberini bee, and two, the star of David or wisdom—which makes sense for the chapel of a university nicknamed "La Sapienza", "The Wisdom".

Figure 7.20 Bernini, St Peter's Square (1656-67)

gardens surrounding the palace—awesome in scale, staggering in effect, but rigid in their geometry—are a visual translation of the new order superimposed onto the landscape. In previous epochs, all roads led to Rome; now they lead to Louis. Quite literally, in the sense that, at the center of the complex of royal edifices and courtyards which will continue to arise for decades, in the very space formerly used by his father as a hunting lodge (but now enveloped in finer stone), is Louis's bedroom. What more natural choice than for the king to take as his personal device or emblem, the sun?

Louis XIV's favorite word was *"gloire"*—glory—and he managed to sustain his own glory for a daunting sixty-two years, though by the end of his reign, his military program had suffered enormous setbacks. Most of the artists Louis employed at Versailles, including his court painter, Charles le Brun, had visited Italy, and their decoration of the interiors of Versailles perpetuated and expanded upon what we call the High Baroque. This quintessentially Italian style of operatic narrative painting and grandiose illusionism continued to thrive throughout the eighteenth century—for example, in ceiling after ceiling by the Venetian painter Giambattista Tiepolo, and in the work of a host of Italian and French artists who,

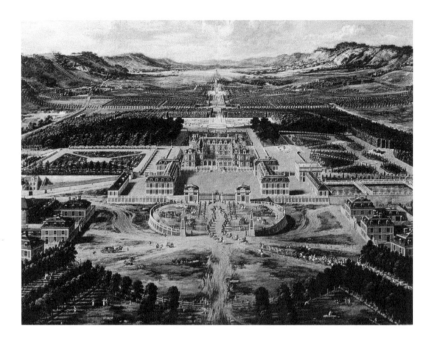

Figure 7.21 Versailles (1665)

like Rubens at the beginning of the previous century, thought big and tended to be itinerant, thus transforming the churches and palaces of Europe into theaters of ritual and event. By the early 1700s, however, an alternative to baroque grandiloquence had emerged, especially in France, where in any case the new style seemed most at home. The rococo derives from the baroque and, more often than not, shares its dedication to naturalism and compositional dynamism, and its preoccupation with human character and narrative. But, generally speaking, rococo artists prioritized a sensual over a strict or "scientific" naturalism[8], toned down the bombast of baroque drama implicit in the great diagonal compositions of the previous century by breaking down those overriding armatures into subsidiary motives, and accentuated the lighter and more intimate aspects of their subjects and stories, simultaneously lightening their palettes and their brushwork.

---

8   Sensual in the sense of softer and more suggestive, scientific in the sense of wholehearted fidelity to observed detail. The point is made when we compare Caravaggio's Ambrosiana fruit basket with any still life by Jean-Baptiste-Siméon Chardin.

A case in point is François Boucher's *Portrait of Madame de Pompadour*, painted in 1756 and now in the Wallace Collection in London. Mademoiselle Poisson ("Miss Fish) was a famously charming and intelligent woman who rose (or fell, or moved sideways) to become the most enduring mistress among thousands claiming the favors of Louis XIV's great-grandson and successor, Louis XV. Muse of the French rococo, Madame de Pompadour leans elegantly, but comfortably and above all thoughtfully, against the cushions of her bed, the gold curtains of which seem to have been parted for us. Her boudoir is strewn (in the intimate theater of the rococo setting, we say "strewn" rather than "littered") with flowers, books, and papers. The place is frankly a mess, but an inviting one. The rich stuffs, the marquetry and ormolu, together with the writing materials—not to mention the woman herself, her blushing cheek and her gorgeous blue-green dress—evince luxury and pleasure and ease, but also education and taste. Mimicked in the pose of the carved cherub above her head, the great diagonal of the sitter dissolves in a plethora of silk ribbons and roses and frills. These are the same motifs—cupids and flowers and curvilinear patterns—that characterize so much of rococo decoration, from that of the porcelain produced at the royal

Figure 7.22 Boucher's The Rape of Europa (c. 1734)

factory at Sèvres (of which Madame de Pompadour was a great patron) to silver and furniture and the elaborate *boiseries* that covered the walls of the homes of the wealthy in France and, increasingly, elsewhere. The nonchalance of the picture, its avoidance of rhetoric, in conjunction with what we might call its ambition to be unostentatiously "pretty" (that matches so well its subject), removes it from most portraiture, and indeed most painting, of the previous century. The same is true of more overtly narrative imagery produced during the rococo; compare, for example, Boucher's c. 1734 *Rape of Europa* with the proto-baroque treatment of the theme by Titian. The Titian is a tragedy on an epic scale. The Boucher is a pajama party.

An English artist with a keen understanding of the French rococo style—and a love-hate relationship with that and most Continental culture, which he felt was unfairly preferred by the patrons in his native land—was William Hogarth. Born in 1697, Hogarth was trained as an engraver in the new mode, and included among the drinking companions of his early maturity the French engraver Hubert Gravelot, a former pupil of Boucher. It is easy to identify the superficial similarities between Hogarth's version of the rococo and that of his French contemporaries: the choice of lighter themes, including current customs and manners; the lightness of handling, which often takes the figures to the brink of caricature; the animation, and integration along ebullient rhythmic patterns, of all the elements of a scene—human beings, but also decorative objects, furniture and sculpture, trees and clouds, garden ornaments and lapdogs and doo-dads of every sort. For Hogarth these rhythmic patterns were intimately related to and derived from what he considered the source of all natural beauty, the serpentine line. In fact, the artist wrote a treatise, *The Analysis of Beauty* (1753), about, among other things, the ideal line as it is found or applied, serpentining through the world of three dimensions—in petals and fronds, in the legs of chairs, in the corseted backs of young females. The line appears prominently in Hogarth's playful self-portrait, truly a portrait *of* his portrait, with his pug dog, Trump.

But there is something different about Hogarth's rococo. The charm and humor of his portrait are constants throughout his work, but the tongue in his cheek is often a sharp one, and he uses it to comment critically, sometimes scathingly, on fellow members of his species. Like other artists we have encountered, Hogarth divided his talents between painting and engraving. Engraving was particularly useful when it came to popularizing and profiting from his paintings, which were often produced in series. *Marriage à la Mode*, *The Rake's Progress*, *The Harlot's Progress*—these are pictorial equivalents of the novel, itself a novel form of literature enjoying a prodigious success in eighteenth-century England and France. As his satires play an important role in the history of the political cartoon, so Hogarth's serial work is among the important prototypes for the comic strip and the cinematic franchise; think *Star Wars* or *Saw* (if you must). The artist was also instrumental in securing the rights of artists to own their images or designs—in other words, copyrighting their work.

Hogarth is often considered the first great painter of the British School. His successors went on to develop a grand manner, especially in history painting and portraiture; they painted bigger pictures, they painted prettier subjects, they painted more heroic scenes, but none of them eclipsed the nobility and wit of their forbear. Unlike Hogarth, many of them

Figure 7.23 William Hogarth, The Painter and His Pug (1745)

wholeheartedly embraced a cosmopolitan view, which looked to the Continent to bestow seriousness on an increasingly ambitious national school. Following the French example of the previous century, a Royal Academy was founded in England in 1768. The first president was Sir Joshua Reynolds, whose annual lectures to the Academy, subsequently published as the *Discourses*, articulated the tastes and artistic policies of his age; in them, more than in his own paintings, Reynolds championed the cause of ancient and Renaissance classicism, leading to the veritable equation of "academic" with "classical". It was into the hands of Reynolds (at the time, he was merely Mr. Reynolds) that a picture by a young American painter, John Singleton Copley, found its way in 1766.

A portrait of Copley's half-brother, Henry Pelham, *Boy with a Squirrel* is a charming and memorable reminder of the recurrent universality—again, the "reach"—of European artistic tastes and practices, tastes and practices which flourished in the later eighteenth century independent of declared ideals. The picture is decidedly not in the grand manner, but comes close to some of the

Figure 7.24 Copley, A Boy with a Flying Squirrel (Henry Pelham, 1765)

quieter, more intimate images produced by Reynolds and his contemporaries throughout the West, from the Swiss-born Jean-Étienne Liotard to the Frenchman Jean Honoré Fragonard, from the Venetian Giandomenico (son of Giambattista) Tiepolo to the Scottish Allan Ramsay. Its subject—youth—is one that became especially popular during the eighteenth century. Its palette and accessories, from the boy's pink lapel and yellow waistcoat to the little gold tether and the tiny, soft-brown squirrel, are pure rococo. The naturalism of surfaces—that of the reflective mahogany tabletop is particularly impressive—is matched by a naturalism of expression or attitude. The red curtain, so dramatic and meaningful when Caravaggio introduced it into the background of his *Judith Beheading Holofernes*, has been cut down to size, and is now a pretty stage prop setting off the subject, which is, specifically, the boy and, by analogy, human character—or if you prefer, a slice of life.

In a nutshell, the eighteenth century was one of myriad revivals and expansive repertoires. So, for example, in England, the Gothic style, which had never been abandoned altogether in the North, re-emerged, if at first only superficially, as a decorative option. The growing antiquarian movement, as well as aristocratic itineracy, the most obvious manifestation of which was the Grand Tour (artists often accompanied their wealthy patrons on these transcontinental trips), heightened interest in and increased exposure to great stores of ancient and more recent artistic models. Classical imagery and motifs—the focus, as we have seen, of perennial, more or less widespread revivals throughout the history of art—were all the rage again after the rediscovery, in the first decades of the eighteenth century, of Herculaneum and Pompeii, Roman towns which had been buried (and thus preserved) by an eruption of Mount Vesuvius in 79 A.D. Perhaps the most fascinating subject in the history of eighteenth-century design—illustrated by works of art in every medium, from silver, china, and textiles to wall painting, interior decoration, and architecture—is the rocky courtship between classicism—a multifarious classicism, viewed, catalogued, and interpreted with increasing seriousness, according to increasingly stringent historical methods—and the rococo style—really a repertory of styles linked by lightness in every sense, the indulged and indulgent offspring of a baroque which was, and continues to be, defined, if incompletely, as a forceful reaction to classicism. To understand, and even to participate in, this aesthetic dialogue, to contribute something original that could be said to expand the variety of the tasteful or beautiful, was a primary goal of educated individuals in this enlightened age.

In Jean-Antoine Houdon's *Thomas Jefferson*, we find a portrait of just such an individual. Houdon's bust is an excellent example of a style of sculptural portraiture going back to Bernini, whose sitters were often shown in a moment of spontaneous alertness, as if flinching mildly at a sound or call.

Like Copley in his portrait of Henry Pelham, Houdon renders details of dress and flesh in a convincing, naturalistic manner. There is a nonchalance in the pose as in the clothes that seems the essence, the expression, of candor. And again, it is the gesture that brings the figure to life, and brings us into that life.

In 1789, when Houdon carved his portrait, Jefferson was forty-six, serving his final year as American Minister to France. The Declaration of

Figure 7.25 Houdon, Thomas Jefferson (1789)

Figure 7.26 Jefferson, Monticello (1770-1826)

Figure 7.27 Palladio, Villa Capra (1556-71)

Independence was in his past, the presidency in his future. He had traveled a long way from his native Virginia, and farther still from his inherited, circumscribed position in life as a colonial planter, to become one of the best educated, most free-thinking public men of his time. Among his interests and occupations was architecture; his country must be grateful that it was also one of his talents. He spent much of his adult life planning, building, and altering his home, Monticello, which is a fitting monument to his wide-ranging intellect, his versatility, and his taste. Ultimately based on the centralized plan of Palladio's venerated Villa Rotonda, Monticello is a new American version of the classical ideal, one which transplants something of the longer standing European traditions onto American soil. In spite of its overt dependence on Renaissance and ancient forms and motifs, it is a highly original *tour de force* of lightness—not in the sense of lack of seriousness, but rather, in terms of the lightness of touch and the play of its references to earlier models. It is lighter, too, in scale, and in its primary materials, locally produced brick and wood. It is less grand than its European ancestors, and more human.

Humanity, domesticity, the responsibilities and comforts of home and family—these were clearly the themes that the French court painter, Louise Elisabeth

Vigée-Lebrun, intended to emphasize in her *Portrait of Marie Antoinette with her Children*, meant for display at the annual *Salon* exhibition in the Louvre in 1787. The unpopular wife of King Louis XVI of France is shown surrounded by her children, each sensitively and convincingly portrayed; the little Dauphin pointing to the empty cradle of his recently deceased infant sister is a particularly poignant detail. But the picture as a whole falters before the daunting—perhaps impossible—challenge to reconcile the grand manner aristocratic portrait with the intimate and immediate—what might almost be called the "anti-aristocratic"—approach so clearly and desperately required by this particular family at this particular time. The image, still to be seen at Versailles, survives, in light of subsequent events, as

Figure 7.28 Vigée-Lebrun, Marie Antoinette and her Children (1787)

an icon of the irreconcilability of the *ancien regime* with something decidedly more democratic and modern. It is counterintuitive to speculate, but perhaps if the Queen had been painted in the true rococo style advocated by, and so thoroughly identified with, the aristocracy, the result would, at least from an artistic point of view, have been a happier one. Charm can be a tool of propaganda in art, but timing is inevitably of the essence. Thomas Jefferson might well have seen this picture in 1787. Two years later, he left France and its Revolution behind.

eight

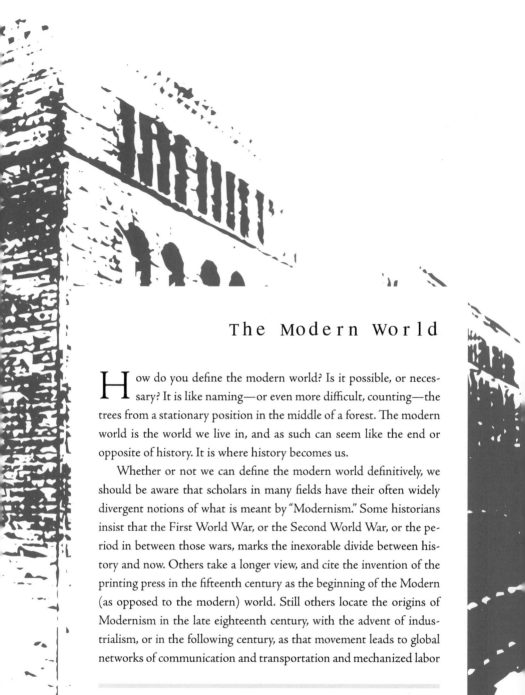

The Modern World

How do you define the modern world? Is it possible, or necessary? It is like naming—or even more difficult, counting—the trees from a stationary position in the middle of a forest. The modern world is the world we live in, and as such can seem like the end or opposite of history. It is where history becomes us.

Whether or not we can define the modern world definitively, we should be aware that scholars in many fields have their often widely divergent notions of what is meant by "Modernism." Some historians insist that the First World War, or the Second World War, or the period in between those wars, marks the inexorable divide between history and now. Others take a longer view, and cite the invention of the printing press in the fifteenth century as the beginning of the Modern (as opposed to the modern) world. Still others locate the origins of Modernism in the late eighteenth century, with the advent of industrialism, or in the following century, as that movement leads to global networks of communication and transportation and mechanized labor

Figure 8.1 David, Oath of the Horatii (1784)

on an enormous scale. Traditionally, cultural historians have tended to identify Modernism as the child—perhaps the rebellious child—of the Enlightenment, and to date its birth to the Age of Revolution.

The end of the reign of rococo style coincides with the first violent political upheavals in Europe and America in the late eighteenth and early nineteenth centuries. While far from new or revolutionary, classicism came to dominate European and American culture during and after the various political crises and (to put it mildly) political and sociological reconfigurations that created the Modern world. In fact, the rejection of tradition and the increasingly rapid succession of stylistic movements that will characterize nineteenth and twentieth century Western art can inevitably be traced to the acceptance or rejection—but in any case, the recognition of the authority—of the "new" neoclassicism established in Europe by the end of the eighteenth century.

For artists it was neither the best of times (academicians everywhere pined for the great days of ancient Greece and Renaissance Rome) nor the worst of times (the fact that there *were* academies was a hopeful sign, and everybody *was*, after all, talking about art; it was taken seriously, it was a subject of public discourse, and artists maintained a role in society that they had not always enjoyed). There were ever more opportunities for artists to produce and purvey their works, and, consequently, ever more variations of prevailing styles and ever greater possibilities for the expression of individual talents and interests.[1] Democracy, then, became the ideal and, eventually, the rule in art as well as government, leaving behind the *ancien regime* and the rococo style recently and popularly identified with it.

For French painter Jacques Louis David, it was as though there had never been a rococo. He reached directly back to the Italian Renaissance and, more surprisingly perhaps, to the Italian Baroque for his inspiration and models. His best known work, *The Oath of the Horatii*, was painted in 1784, and was soon embraced—but to what extent was it intended?—as a banner of Revolution. It was certainly, in terms of content and forms, a direct challenge to the rococo style of light and "feminine" imagery associated with a decadent, oppressive, and increasingly oblivious aristocratic regime. In this particular respect, in combining, actively and consciously, the roles of artist and politician (he was a vigorous member of various Revolutionary committees and tribunals, and voted for the execution of King Louis XVI, ironically, the original purchaser of the *Oath*), David truly served as one of the founding fathers of Modernism. After David, the politics of all artists—even of those who declare their political stance to be a-political—must be integrated into any comprehensive understanding of their work.

A starkly lit stage set of three spare Tuscan arches dominated by an equal number of Roman men pledging their lives to their father and their tribe, the *Oath* contains a clear message of patriotic duty applicable to all people of all times, regardless of their specific political situation. As such, this picture prefigured David's role, not only as political force, but as the arbiter of art and as the primary propagandist of Napoleon Bonaparte, the brilliant and energetic protector of France and its Revolution who, paradoxically, proved to be an even more absolute monarch than any previous occupant of the throne. As we all know, Napoleon's military ambitions led him into wars against most of the European nations, among them Spain, where David's contemporary, Francisco José de Goya y Lucientes, was a pillar of Modernism in his own right, if for

---

1   A situation that has expanded, such that we are all enjoying and suffering from its consequences today.

very different reasons. Though born into a culture still under the domination of Caravaggio and Velasquez, and trained in the ways of the rococo—he was the royal tapestry designer for many years, and excelled at the light imagery associated primarily with the work of French artists such as Watteau, Boucher, and Fragonard[2]—Goya was actually the sophisticated master of many artistic styles, genres, and media, and overall his art is the most Modern of any of his contemporaries—it is the most like what art would become.

Numerous original strains combine to produce the unique chords of Goya's Modernism. What is most obviously Modern in his mysterious and compelling

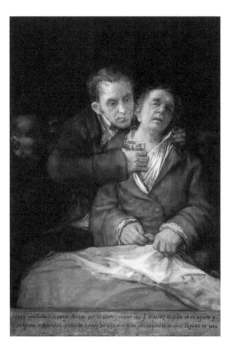

Figure 8.2 Goya, Of What Ill Will He Die? (1799)

Figure 8.3 Goya's Self Portrait with Dr. Arrieta (1820)

---

2 Though, like Hogarth, but again in different ways, Goya's tapestry designs, along with many of his portraits and genre scenes, almost always leave open the possibility that the artist is not wholeheartedly, for all the lightness of subject and palette and approach, embracing the party line. This is the very ambiguity which is at the core of Goya's Modernism.

Self Portrait with Dr. Arrieta (1820) is that it represents science in a very positive light; the picture was in fact a gift and tribute from the artist to the physician who saved his life, as Goya explicitly states at the bottom. Doctors had traditionally been viewed by society, and represented by artists—including Goya himself—as dangerous objects of disdain, ridicule, and fear. But Dr. Arrieta is the hero here, cradling, *à la Pietà*, the exhausted, delirious, malleable invalid, who is as close to being merely matter as a living body can be. Arrieta raises the restorative glass; a row of faces, barely discernible in the darkness, looks on. Who are these shadowy figures? Are they, as some scholars have suggested, friends or family members, or sickbed attendants? Or are they hallucinatory visions from a fever dream, the contents of the patient's distempered mind? The possibility that Goya is graphically depicting the aberrant concoctions of the invisible psyche, and the ambiguity of the resultant image, constitutes another of the primary Modernist features of the artist's work. And finally, speaking of ambiguity, there is the larger indefinite situation exposed by the picture: we see in this work an Enlightenment celebration of, and homage to, science, but it also inevitably raises the question of the power—of the control over others—that science has. Goya drinks the medicine that saves him, but he is not the one deciding.

In so many paintings, and in many of the prints he produced throughout his long career, including *Los Caprichos* (*The Caprices*) and *Los Desastres de la Guerra* (*The Disasters of War*[3]), Goya presents a darkly personal, often pessimistic view of a world inhabited by witches, demons, monsters, and sadistic criminals, devoid of virtue as of sense and far from the Enlightenment ideal of human society guided by rational thought. The exploration, in art, of the irrational, and of the sway of natural forces, particularly human emotions, over the lives of individuals and communities, is a primary characteristic of Romanticism.

A cross-cultural, interdisciplinary phenomenon, Romanticism was to a large extent a reaction against Neoclassicism at a time when the latter was at the zenith of its popularity and authority. In France, pitted against the establishment, against the all powerful David and his numerous disciples, the young artists of the Romantic Movement were necessarily the underdogs in what was to prove a long and often ugly conflict. The first great proponent of the movement was Théodore Géricault, a painter who was dissatisfied with his brief training under a pupil of

---

3   The latter series, among the most graphic and unforgettable images of atrocities ever produced, was not published till some time after the artist's death in 1828.

David, and who consequently followed his own syllabus, which included a period of self-directed study in Italy. An outsider from the outset, Géricault created a stir, and elicited above all stupefaction, when he exhibited his vast painting, *A Shipwreck*, at the Paris Salon in 1819.

Known today as *The Raft of The Medusa*, this icon of Romanticism represents a moment in a very real—at the time, very recent—tragedy, the blame for which lay primarily with the newly restored Bourbon monarchy. In 1816, the French Frigate *Medusa* ran aground in shallow water miles from the shore of Senegal in North Africa. The captain, a political appointee, and other high ranking officials and their families made it to land in lifeboats, abandoning more than 150 passengers, crew members, and soldiers, most of whom had been directed to board a makeshift raft that was towed briefly before being cut loose. When the raft was found thirteen days later only fifteen survivors remained, and their blood curdling account of drunken violence, mental derangement, suicide, starvation, and cannibalism horrified and fascinated France.

Géricault's *Raft of the Medusa*, painted after more than a year of careful research, appears to illustrate a moment of hope. In the face of a ferocious sea and threatening sky, a handful of figures, some already dead, form a ragged pyramid, at the peak of which the lone surviving African crew member waves a red flag in the direction of a tiny speck of a ship on the horizon. Much more than an illustration of the actual event, Géricault's work invites interpretation as an allegory of universal struggle, in which hope and death are among the forces facing off. These forces are present in the picture as two great diagonals that cross in the center. One of these rises from the nude corpse at lower right through the ropes and mast to the wind-filled sail; the other begins at the lower left and moves from the nude body of the dead youth (whose aged father refuses to surrender him to the sea) through the rising cluster of figures peaking in the dark head and upraised arm of the man waving the cloth.

If the *Raft of the Medusa* is a poster for Romanticism in the same way that David's *Oath of the Horatii* advertises his Neoclassical agenda, the two pictures—and by extension, the "schools" they represent—draw upon compatible sources, specifically from ancient figurative art (David from Greek vase paintings and Roman sarcophagi, Géricault from Hellenistic sculpture) and from more recent models (David employs a dramatic baroque chiaroscuro, while Géricault arranges his figures according to baroque compositional formulae). Similarly, both pictures encourage political readings. Nor does the novelty of the *Raft* derive from the fact

Figure 8.4 Gericault's Raft of the Medusa (1819)

that it records a current event; in 1793, David had begun his painting of the death of fellow revolutionary Jean-Paul Marat when the body was still warm. No, what renders the *Raft* a new and Romantic icon, and brings it closer to the thematic interests of Goya, is the way in which it unflinchingly foregrounds the destructive effects of nature, above all human nature. It doesn't celebrate hope so much as bring physically home to the viewer the overwhelming odds against him. What better metaphor for human vulnerability to human inhumanity than a raft of the rejected? What better metaphor for the plight of the outcast than a sea-bound band of self-devouring castaways?

The first great standard-bearer of Romanticism, Géricault died in 1824 at the age of 32, when the movement was just gaining momentum. His successor had already made himself known at the Salon of 1822 with a painting, *Dante and Virgil in Hell*, which clearly owes a great deal to the older artist's controversial shipwreck scene. Also influenced by Hellenistic sculpture, Eugène Delacroix depicts a churning river Styx filled with anguished figures through which Charon the boatman ferries the Medieval poet and his Roman guide. The source, Dante's *Inferno*, is a literary but not a classical one. Literature had a special importance

Figure 8.5 Delacroix, Dante and Virgil in Hell (1822)

for Delacroix, who, throughout his career, was inspired by and illustrated some of the best-known works of contemporary Romantic writers, including Goethe's *Faust* and the poetry of Lord Byron. Delacroix's restless romanticism led him to Morocco in 1832, and there the decidedly un-European landscape and Arab culture nourished the artist's imagination, making him an early and influential participant in the growing dialogue with Eastern cultures known as Orientalism.[4]

His earliest works already reveal Delacroix's attraction to more spontaneous pictorial effects than we ever find in the polished surfaces of Neoclassical paintings. There are passages in *Dante and Virgil in Hell* where separate strokes of pigment are applied very freely, in a manner which cannot but recall Titian and, even more obviously, Rubens and Velasquez; contiguous daubs of primary color also famously foreshadow the Impressionist technique. Painterliness, especially

---

4   For non-Westerners—self-identifying or objectified as such by Western intellectuals and governments—Orientalism was, speaking generally and considering its evolution over the past two centuries, not a dialogue but a Western-based monologue, not a discourse but a cultural annexation or appropriation. The topic is most brilliantly and revealingly addressed in Edward Said's landmark *Orientalism*, published in 1978.

as it serves as a visual translation of unrestrained emotion, became a staple of Romanticism.

One other source of inspiration for the dynamic brushwork that was so important a component of Delacroix's Romanticism was the work of the English painter, John Constable. In fact, many English artists enthusiastically embraced the new movement, no one more wholeheartedly than Joseph Mallord William Turner, whose *Rain, Steam, and Speed–The Great Western Railway*, exhibited at the Royal Academy in London in 1844, was a lesson in the potential of loosely applied paint to evoke sensation, not to mention, in its subject matter—a

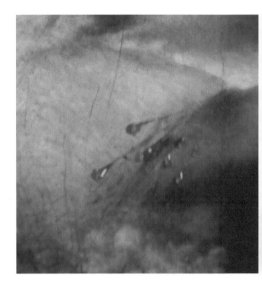

Figure 8.6 Dante and Virgil in Hell, detail

train speeding over a rail bridge—a Romantic commentary on the convergence of overwhelming forces, the natural and the man made, the timeless and the Modern.

Timelessness was clearly at the heart of the Neoclassical mission, and nobody personified that mission better than Jacques Louis David's best pupil, Jean Auguste Dominique Ingres. Throughout a career that spanned seventy years, Ingres produced some of the most earnest, if at times pedantic, classical images of the nineteenth century, tributes all to his ancient and Renaissance forebears, especially to his great hero, Raphael. Like the Romantics, Ingres occasionally introduced Orientalizing motifs into his oeuvre, and painted some of the most memorable nudes in Western art in this mode. But today he is remembered and respected primarily for a staggering series of portraits through which he interpreted a privileged world of old and new nobility, and the growing *haute bourgeoisie*.

Precision and polish are constants in the portraiture of Ingres. It is the invisible brushwork and breathtaking illusionism of Caravaggio's *Ambrosiana Still Life* brought to bear on aristocratic surfaces, beginning with the aristocrats' own surfaces, their flesh. But whereas Caravaggio's fruit basket is shown at once in isolation and flux, Ingres' sitters are more naturally integrated into environments

Figure 8.7 Turner, Rain, Steam and Speed (1844)

that receive the same meticulous *trompe l'oeil* treatment; the results are dazzling, but invariably still. In portraits like the pair of *Monsieur Rivière* and *Madame Rivière* (both 1805), *Monsieur Bertin* (1832), the *Comtesse d'Haussonville* (completed 1845), and the *Princesse de Broglie* (1853), Neoclassical clarity supplies the iconography of power and wealth with a stability and even a serenity that was more often than not lacking in French life, and certainly in French political affairs, beginning with the French Revolution—which was, remember, only the first of many revolutions in France between 1789 and 1870. Ingres maintains the supremacy of textural illusionism and the veneration of line as a vehicle of reason in the face of great challenges, among them, the emotive colorism and dynamic

Figure 8.9 Matthew Brady, Mary Todd Lincoln (1861 or 1862)

Figure 8.8 Ingres, Princesse de Broglie (1853)

painterly effects developed by Romantic artists like Delacroix (whom Ingres detested) and a very new, mechanical (and, as such, potentially more precise and comprehensive) method of capturing optical information.

In the 1830s, a truly major breakthrough occurred in the longstanding attempt to take images projected through a hole in a box or chamber (a "camera") and to fix them permanently on materials treated with light-sensitive compounds. Henry Fox Talbot in England and Louis-Jacques-Mandé Daguerre in France simultaneously developed processes—the talbotype (or calotype) and the daguerreotype—of recording visual phenomena with scientific fidelity to optical fact. In short, they invented photography, and the effect of the invention on innumerable aspects of human life was instant and profound. For visual artists, the new pictorial method was inevitably a challenge and a tool.

You would think that the invention of the photographic camera, with its potential to produce and proliferate imagery and its swift refinement into a practical and widely accessible instrument, would redefine and establish new standards for naturalism in art—in short, that photography would give rise to an absolutist

Figure 8.10 Daguerre, Shells and Fossils (1839)

form of realism. But that is not the case. In fact, from the first, photographers aspiring to exploit the new medium for artistic ends—looking to the genres and various styles associated with the "fine art" of painting as their models—sought to explore its non-objective possibilities, while artists working in more traditional media (painting, printmaking, even sculpture), whatever their relationship with the new art form, simultaneously developed an entirely new definition of realism, having above all to do with the artist's relationship with the *subject* of art. Photography is always to some extent a record of the real, but Realism, with a capital R, as characterized by its first great proponent, Gustave Courbet, proceeded from a reassessment of the artist's reason for creating art, as well as the artist's response to the question of what is to be recorded.

Born at Ornans in the province of Franche-Comté, Courbet came to Paris in 1839 as an aspiring student with a brash determination to "take on," in a very Modern sense, the artistic establishment and to be recognized by the world. After a brief, useful flirtation with Romanticism, and after some success with the public, Courbet gained sudden notoriety when he exhibited a picture that revealed mature and revolutionary inclinations—specifically, to level the field of subject matter, and to paint only what he saw: the modern, visible world. The *Burial at Ornans* is a vast canvas, almost 22 feet long, representing the funeral of the artist's great uncle, which took place, significantly, in the new, secularly sanctioned cemetery just outside the artist's hometown. The problems that the painting raised for visitors to the Salon of 1850 began with its size; it was unheard of to adopt such a scale for so ordinary (and, more problematic still, so provincial) a scene. The *Burial* contains no allusion, much less homage, to canonical art, and likewise it avoids any affirmation of the supernatural or the afterlife. Instead, it offers a somewhat shabby group of mourners milling about an open grave, to which the central figures, especially the priest and the gravedigger, rather pointedly, and again problematically, direct the viewer's attention. The community of mourners forms a thick, dark band, echoing the rise and fall of the lighter contours of the landscape and the softly painted striations of cloud and sky; the living seem merely one more layer in a physiological system or record. Jesus is present, but only as a wooden figure on a cross. In exhibiting, on a scale normally reserved for great scenes of history and religion, the simple facts of a provincial funeral, Courbet has deliberately thwarted the viewer's traditional expectations, and chosen instead to shock via the mundane. Everyday life, and death, too, *is* history, and it is democratic; it is something all people know and participate in.

The *Burial* was only the first of many works by Courbet that provoked the public by their seemingly blatant egocentrism (for example, *The Meeting, or Bonjour, Monsieur Courbet*, 1854; *The Artist's Studio*, 1855) or their portrayal of subjects traditionally thought unworthy of artistic representation (manual laborers, for example, in *The Stonebreakers*, 1849, exhibited the same year as the *Burial*; working girls in *The Young Ladies on the Banks of the Seine*, 1857). Of course, neither Courbet nor his new realism appeared out of nowhere. Géricault, for example, had stupefied viewers with the immediacy and verisimilitude of his translation of a contemporary, real-life drama in *The Raft of the Medusa*, and both Caravaggio and Giotto had proved revolutionary in their times for insisting that art begins with, and is responsible to, observable reality. Furthermore, Courbet's realistic approach was not always problematic or controversial; his landscapes and

Figure 8.11 Courbet, Burial at Ornans (1850)

hunt scenes, for example, kept him steadily employed, and in these he displayed an extraordinary range of surface treatment and effects. But they were consistent with the artist's unflinching mission to recreate the actual, the *seen*. Ostensibly noncommittal, Courbet's artistic realism nevertheless coalesced unmistakably with his political socialism, and the result was Realism, and the establishment of a strong Realist tradition, with its connotation of representing contemporary life—especially of the poor or the typically under-represented—that continues into our own time.[5]

If Courbet preached the painting of modern life, Edouard Manet and the Impressionists practiced what Courbet preached. Manet was a sophisticated and urbane Parisian by birth; there was nothing in his background which would have foretold an artistic career. But like Courbet, Manet had a strong vocation, and he was strongly attracted to the honesty and contemporaneity of the older artist's approach. There are few works more Modern than Manet's *Olympia*, which caused, in 1865, an uproar reminiscent of that which attended Courbet's *Burial* over a decade earlier. A great deal has been said by subsequent scholars in an attempt to recreate the context in which the *Olympia* was found to be so subversive; though it was only the latest in a long and venerable line of reclining female nudes, it was found to be shocking in its Realism. The setting, for example, was unambiguous: the bedroom of a young woman wearing a pink bow, a little jewelry, and shoes. Not since Donatello's *David* have we been confronted by someone so nude, or, rather, naked. In such a setting, the viewer's intimacy with the woman is also beyond question, though the specific nature of the relationship—business or pleasure, or both—is left open. The direct gaze of the model, Victorine Meurent, is also open, almost blank. The black servant bearing (our?) flowers and the black cat arching at the foot of the bed complete a picture of a sexual assignation. No soft Renaissance Venus, this is an Olympia with an address down the street, and regular office hours. And, as at least one Salon critic noted, she looks a little sickly.

But though critics of Manet's early work, especially his *Olympia* and the *Déjeuner sur l'Herbe*, shown at the Salon of Rejects (*Salon des Refusés*) in 1863, were clearly discomfited by the artist's presumed reportage of modern amorality

---

5 A hundred years after Courbet, the Neo-Realist movement in European cinema, best known from the works of Roberto Rossellini, Vittorio de Sica, and others, represented a recurrence of themes and motifs perfectly in keeping with those inherent in the work of the first Realist painter.

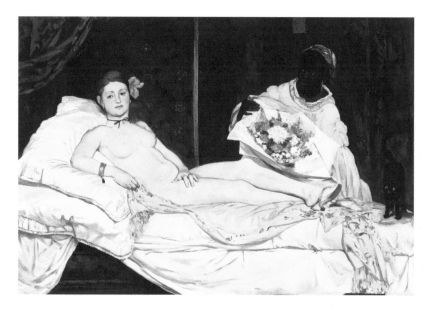

Figure 8.12 Manet, Olympia (1865)

(despite Manet's overt, formal allusions to works by respected artists such as Titian, Giorgione, and Raphael), it was the painting technique itself that seemed most scandalous. This technique began and ended with the application of oil rich medium; the finished work, then, lacked the meticulous glazes associated with the academic tradition (remember, Ingres was still alive in 1865). Painting in this way, the artist was undeniably giving up what was originally most prized in the oil medium, namely its potential, when slowly applied in increasingly transparent layers, to create a resonant depth of surface resulting in an illusion of solid forms. What Manet gained, on the other hand, was a brighter surface, and greater play between areas of color. This *peinture claire*, along with the artist's instinctively loose handling, so obviously informed by his exposure to Spanish artists from Velasquez to Goya, had a profound effect on that group of young men who gathered about Manet, whose less-than-wholehearted mentor he became.

Figure 8.13 Monet, Impression, Sunrise (1874)

The heterogeneous band of young artists known as the Impressionists, so christened by a critic who fixed on the title of a picture in an exhibition of 1874,[6] shared Courbet's commitment to painting the modern world, just as they shared a love of Manet's *peinture claire*, Delacroix's experiments with disconnected daubs of primary colors, Velasquez's broken brushwork, and Turner's diffuse, atmospheric effects. But several of them, especially Claude Monet, Camille Pissarro, Pierre-Auguste Renoir, and Alfred Sisley, shared an unorthodox appreciation of the fact that a painting, whatever it depicts, is also, always, a two dimensional surface covered with pigment. The way that surface is covered can transform the static medium into an active—and so, more real—record of observation. The sketch, with its traditional spontaneity and first-hand relation to the artist's original conception, was recognized as a possible end in its own right. And so, just as Courbet got into trouble for representing a provincial funeral on a heroic scale, the Impressionists were taken to task for displaying what appeared to be oil sketches as finished works. But for the Impressionists, the sketch was the natural way of translating the ephemerality of optical experience. The sketchiness itself suggested the changeability inherent in (and essential to any recreation of) light on an object or scene. And the human eye was left the active rôle of blending the strokes of the sketch into a whole. When Claude Monet returned to a subject—say, for instance, the façade of Rouen Cathedral, or haystacks in a field (and there is no more fitting metaphor for Monet's Impressionist technique than a haystack, a large

---

6   The critic was Louis Leroy. The exhibition was put together by a group of artists calling themselves the *Société Anonyme des Artistes, Peinteurs, Sculpteurs, Graveurs, Etc.* There were eight of these Impressionist exhibitions between 1874 and 1886.

form constructed of smaller, autonomous, elemental forms), at different
times of day or different seasons of the
year, the optical reality was different,
and to accommodate the different reali-
ties, he needed to use different palettes,
and to represent different forms.

With the Impressionists, we have
come a long way from the academic
Neoclassicism that dominated painting
throughout Europe at the turn of the
nineteenth century. For sculptors, too,
the first decades of the 1800s were
marked by a rededication to the classical
past, nowhere more striking than in the
work of Antonio Canova. Canova was
born in 1757 in the Venetian Republic
to a family of stonemasons, and trained
in the style of the late Baroque. Trips
to Rome in 1779 and 1781 set him

Figure 8.14 Canova, Perseus with the Head of Medusa (1801)

on the road to becoming the greatest of all Neoclassical sculptors. His commissioned works included papal and royal tombs, and even a portrait of the emperor
Napoleon, nude, *all'antica*. While Canova never slavishly copied from the antique,
a number of his pieces betray an ambition both to honor and to compete with
ancient art. For instance, *Perseus with the Head of Medusa* (1801) is an unequivocal
homage to the *Apollo Belvedere*, a famous Roman sculpture (probably a copy of
a Hellensitic work) revered throughout the Enlightenment and afterward as the
embodiment of ideal classical form.

Canova died in 1822, but his fame was such that his influence extended far
beyond his lifetime, and for the remainder of the century every sculptor was inevitably compared to him. As in painting, the academic authority of Neoclassicism
was challenged by artists with one foot in the Romantic camp, such as François
Rude and his multi-talented student, Jean-Baptiste Carpeaux, but it was François
Auguste René Rodin, an admirer of both of these, who definitively redirected
sculpture away from the past and into the Modern world.

Figure 8.15 Rodin, Monument to Balzac, 1891-97 (Photo by Edward Steichen, 1911)

Rodin's first efforts were in many ways comparable to Canova's; both were criticized for the naturalism of their early works, both were accused of casting from life, and both experienced a profound change, like so many artists before them, following visits to Italy. But while Canova turned to the ancients for his classicism, Rodin looked paradoxically to the Renaissance, and specifically to the mature work of Michelangelo, to free him from a rigid, academic classicism. Recurring references to the power of nature and human emotion tied him to the Romantic Movement, but his work also foreshadowed the expressionisms of the twentieth century. The ostensible subjects of his sculptures were inevitably vehicles for the artist's own internal struggles and searches. Representation became less important than the evocation of a mood. He allowed his materials (clay and plaster) and the processes that shaped them (modeling and casting) a greater voice in the expression of his ideas, in which sense he resembles the Romantic painters and his true soul mates and peers, artists working in the Impressionist style.

Rodin's *Monument to Balzac*, commissioned by the *Société des Gens des Lettres* in 1891, was not so much a likeness of the prolific author of *La Comédie Humaine* as it was an expression of the moment of creative inspiration. Identifying Balzac's enormous talents and productivity with physical, even sexual, energy and cloaking the rotund figure of the writer in a dressing gown that simplified the form into a column, Rodin created what is essentially a herm.[7] The dramatically modeled head with its explosion of hair seems to cap the upward-sweeping figure, whose backward tilt only exaggerates his looming quality, creating an impression of

---

7   A herm is a standard type of statue popular among the ancient Greeks. Often used to mark crossroads and boundaries, the herm took its name from Hermes, a divine personification of the male procreative force.

elemental force. The monument, when finally unveiled years after the original deadline, was rejected by the *Société* and the requisite public battle over artistic style ensued. Rodin had already been the subject of a number of these battles; earlier commissioned pieces (*The Burghers of Calais* and the monument to Victor Hugo) had inspired similar critical controversy.

Rodin, like a growing number of his artist compatriots, threw himself into challenging traditional academic principles and the viewing expectations of a growing middle class. Thus, the increasingly broken and pock-marked surfaces of what seemed to be damaged or unfinished sculptures baffled and angered his critics. Critics were also puzzled by the unusual poses; many of Rodin's sculptures appear to be of ordinary people caught in awkward, immodest, or unintelligible positions. This was a characteristic his work shared with that of other artists, especially Edgar Degas, who was associated with the Impressionists but is otherwise impossible to pigeonhole.

It is his extraordinary range that makes Degas difficult to illustrate in any summary way. More perhaps than any of his contemporaries in France, if not in the West, Degas pursued the new, though he was also the master of the past, and in fact in many ways can be said to bridge the wiiiide gap between Ingres and the proliferating "isms" of the late nineteenth century. If it was Courbet's ambition to shock with the real, it was Degas' impulse to expand the parameters of the real, and to experiment with medium, form, and composition with the intention always of providing novel subjects from novel points of view.

Degas often depicted his human subjects in unguarded moments—a tired ballerina adjusting her slipper, a laundress brushing back her hair, a young woman bending over to bathe or artlessly toweling herself dry. Often their faces are not visible, often their bodies are seen from unexpected angles, often they are cut off by the edge of a canvas or printing block, such that the resulting image has a hurried or unprepared look, as if the artist had accidentally stumbled upon or was surreptitiously approaching the scene.

These compositional traits are common among Japanese wood-block prints— *Japonisme* being a specialized manifestation of Orientalism in the second half of the nineteenth century, embraced by artists from Manet on. Mary Cassatt picked up on another convention of Japanese art, a preference, especially in her prints, for broad areas of flat color. Cassatt, who was close to Degas, was the only American to exhibit with the Impressionists. She represented an important link between the United States and the capital of European culture. Among other things, her

Figure 8.16 Degas, At the Louvre-The Painter (Mary Cassatt, 1879-80)

Figure 8.17 Cassatt, Maternal Caress (1890-91)

career—that of a cultivated woman from a wealthy Pennsylvania family living and working in Paris—raises the question, particularly in a survey of the longer history of Western art, "Who is an artist in the Modern world?" Or more succinctly, "Who is a Modern artist?"

In America, where artistic aspiration toward greater sophistication and a more international attitude increased considerably during the nineteenth century, the popular image of the artist was of a foreigner, or an itinerant portraitist, or a lone, wandering painter of vast, untamed landscapes. The first indigenous American artistic movement, known as the Hudson River School, was no school, really, but a loose group of artists who shared an approach to the American countryside that balanced realistic record with romantic idealization. Frederic Edwin Church was a pupil of the unofficial leader of the group, Thomas Cole, and represented the best of its tastes and talents. Though he traveled the world in search of spectacular prospects—Roman ruins at Petra; a volcano in Ecuador; a sunset in Syria; Niagara Falls—the pictures Church painted at home in the Hudson Valley are just as dramatic. The grandeur, the infinite variety, the startling visionary effects of nature are invariably his subject, as for instance in the little picture in oil and graphite on paperboard of a *Sunset across the Hudson Valley, New York* (1870). But these widely traveled

Figure 8.18 Church, Sunset Across the Hudson Valley (1870)

landscape artists exemplified only one facet of the growing cosmopolitanism of the American art world, and provided only a very limited and traditional definition of the Modern artist. Henry Ossawa Tanner is an extraordinary personification of the new democratization of that definition. The son of a free-born Episcopal minister and his escaped-slave wife, Tanner would have a successful career as an artist in Paris, proving a point of international Modernism: if any subject was worthy of representation, talent was the most important prerequisite for being the representer.

Racism was the reason for Tanner's leaving the United States to pursue his vocation as a painter after concentrated study under the great Philadelphia artist and teacher Thomas Eakins. Returning from Paris in 1893, he received some attention for genre paintings in a Realist mode; these included *The Banjo Lesson* and *The Thankful Poor*. A commission from his friend in Chicago, George Washington Gray, helped Tanner to relocate permanently to the French capital, where race played little part in his success or his subject matter. Already in *Spinning by Firelight–The Boyhood of George Washington Gray* (1894), which reimagines the early life of his patron, Tanner presents a universally accessible family group in a spartan if not impoverished

Figure 8.19 Tanner, Spinning by Firelight-The Boyhood of George Washington Gray (1894)

setting—we are familiar with the subject from French Realism. But Tanner's is a realism that more often than not embraces traditional religious narrative, his interest in the latter sending him to Africa and The Holy Land for inspiration and authenticity, timeless ideals that have never been entirely disavowed by Modernism.

The ideal *of* timelessness was as much a preoccupation of the painter Paul Cezanne as it had been for Ingres—both sought to imbue their images with a permanence beyond the actual, to create, in effect, a super-actual, as they had found in the great works of the past. But their results were almost diametrically opposed. And whereas the Impressionists (Cezanne belonged to the group originally, but was never a faithful dues-paying member) took it upon themselves to break the visible world down into elemental components, and to reproduce experience of the world using the equivalent of those components, the brushstroke, Cezanne undertook to rebuild that world. He restructured the visual environment, including the human figure, in a way that made two-dimensional sense; he was true to the two-dimensional surface on which he worked, as opposed to the old masters, who attempted to recreate the three dimensional world through textural and

Figure 8.20 Cezanne, Boy in a Red Vest (1888-90)

Figure 8.21 Titian, Portrait of Ranuccio Farnese (1542)

spatial illusionism. This does not mean that Cezanne rejected the art of the past. On the contrary, the Louvre was his school, but nature itself was the principal.

In extracting permanence from the everyday and the ephemeral, Cezanne may even recall Leonardo da Vinci. An apple, for Cezanne, is as eventful a form as the façade of a cathedral, and he revisited the former with the same constancy and sensitivity that Monet brought to the latter. As with an apple, so with Mont Sainte-Victoire in his native Provence, or the human body. In its subject, for example, Cezanne's *Boy in a Red Vest* begs to be juxtaposed with treatments of the same basic theme, the adolescent male, by the Old Masters; Titian's *Portrait of Ranuccio Farnese* seems the most obvious choice. Titian's is a *tour de force* of illusionism, impressive not only in its credible surfaces—fur, velvet, youthful skin—but in the precision with which it identifies the blend of public and personal character, impossible though that may be to translate into words. Compared to the Renaissance work, Cezanne's *Boy* is all suggestion and tentativeness, and as with so many of Cezanne's pictures, small areas of unpainted canvas show through. But adolescence is to Cezanne's technique of meaningful unfinish what a haystack is to the Impressionist technique of different, and lesser,

Figure 8.22 H.H. Richardson, Marshall Field Warehouse Store, 1885–87 (demolished 1930; 130ft high).

Figure 8.23 Michelozzo, Palazzo Medici-Riccardi begun 1445 (c. 71ft high)

unfinish. No mere illusion, the *Boy in a Red Vest* is becoming what he is, and in a way that is profoundly new.

Cezanne's fruitful relationship with the past, an essential element of his originality and his Modernism, was comparable to that of many groundbreaking artists in the late nineteenth century, regardless of medium. In architecture, for instance, the new technologies that made it possible to build with new materials—or rather, to use old materials, such as metal and glass, but to use them for the first time in large-scale construction—did not bring about an abrupt end to classicism, much less to historicism in the larger sense. One of the founding fathers of Modernist architecture, Henry Hobson Richardson constantly quoted the great urban structures of the past, perhaps most obviously and influentially in his groundbreaking Marshall Field Warehouse in Chicago, finished in 1887 and demolished in 1930. Richardson used iron and wood to support the interior floors of this structure, and most of the outer surface was glazed. With iron and glass, materials of increasing interest to architects since the outset of the Industrial Revolution,[8] Richardson helped to set the stage for the more dramatic vertical experiments of his many American and European disciples, among them Louis Sullivan and Daniel Burnham.

---

8   The best known early example of large-scale iron and glass architecture was Sir Joseph Paxton's Crystal Palace Exhibition Hall, opened in 1851. This structure hosted the first of the great "world" expositions that brought together innovations and accomplishments in everything from the fine arts and industrial machinery to domestic appliances and crafts. A first step, clearly, toward both global thinking and the shopping mall.

But nothing in the technology of treating and strengthening metal, for example, could have prepared the world for the staggering size and completely original form of Gustave Eiffel's iconic tower. Erected for the Paris *Exposition Universelle* of 1889, the Eiffel Tower remained the tallest man-made structure in the world for decades, and continues to cast its shadow over all in the Modern era who would undertake to raise an urban landmark to the level of myth. Eiffel was an engineer, a builder of bridges and supporting structures for such monuments as Fréderic Auguste Bartholdi's recently completed *Statue of Liberty* in New York, another super-scaled work of art that is synonymous with a place and a people. Thus Eiffel, too, challenges the traditional definition of the artist and the boundaries between art and science, and between one artistic medium and another. A telling American response to Eiffel's challenge was presented at the next major international fair, this time back in Chicago, where, at the World's Columbian Exposition of 1893, George Washington Gale Ferris's gigantic, kinetic wheel dominated the Midway, and literally swept visitors off their feet. The American version of monumental Modernism rolls.

Figure 8.24 Eiffel Tower (1889)

Visiting Paris or Chicago in the 1890s, it would have been hard not to feel that the world was soaring into a new age, and riding in one of the five Eiffel Tower elevators, or floating in one of the thirty-six cars of the Ferris Wheel, would not only have opened up new vistas but

Figure 8.25 Ferris Wheel (1893)

also inevitably suggested unbounded possibilities in every sphere of activity. In the visual arts, the dramatic break—with tradition; with time-honored practices and the venerated criteria for assessing results; with the notion that style choices were limited, and accessible only through the academy; and, at last, with Realism itself—was fast becoming an ideal in its own right. Painters in particular, never losing site of their debt to Géricault and Courbet and Manet, seemed at the same time to be discovering and even indulging in the most profoundly Modern "ism" of all, individualism.

And so, unlike Impressionism, Post-Impressionism was neither a style nor a sub-style, neither a temporary collective nor a technique, but a period, the period in which the most innovative and unorthodox artists, many of them raised on Realism, expanded, on the individual level and according to personal visions and motivations, the notion of style. In other words, these artists shared the fact that they shared, in fact, very little. Their originality was multifarious. For instance, for Georges-Pierre Seurat, Impressionist forms were further broken down into particles of color. For Henri de Toulouse-Lautrec colors grew more jarring. And for Dutch painter Vincent van Gogh, the separate brush strokes became more and

Figure 8.26 Vincent van Gogh, Starry Night (1889)

more distinct, took on lives of their own and flowed, like currents, through the paintings, their role in defining form now secondary to their potential as vehicles for the artist's emotional and psychological response to, for example, a vase of irises, or a starry evening sky. The tortured friendship between Van Gogh and Paul Gauguin is a succinct illustration of the new and intense individualism of painters, and the consequent, profound divergences in their approaches to art: barely able to share a house, the two men certainly did not share a style. Such could hardly have been said of any two budding or established artists at the beginning of the century.

Gauguin is especially interesting in terms of the future of Modernism, as he represents the search for an uncorrupted past, an age which might positively be described as "golden" and, more cautiously, equated with "the primitive". This search led the former stockbroker away from Paris to Brittany, then to Martinique, Tahiti, and finally the remote Marquesas, where he died in 1903. His paintings and polychrome wood carvings, whether of primly dressed Breton housewives or impassive Polynesian nudes, bring together broad color fields with bright, dynamic patterns; similarly, they bring together, sometimes in non-representational spaces and sometimes with surprising inconsistencies of scale, observed forms and details and memories and imaginings.

Gauguin was a self-styled savage, and that concept, too, infiltrates the definition of the artist at the end of the nineteenth century. At least that archetype became one option for the individual engaged in the very Modern process of inventing an artistic persona. And another option or model, at the opposite end of the spectrum, is the scientist, the investigator of untried opportunities and unexplored avenues of research. No one reconciled the two extremes more productively than Pablo Picasso, who re-enacted, in the earliest, prodigy phase of his career, most of the major stylistic movements of the nineteenth century. Afterward, in the

Figure 8.27 Paul Gauguin, Soyez Amoureuses Vous Serez Heureuses (1889)

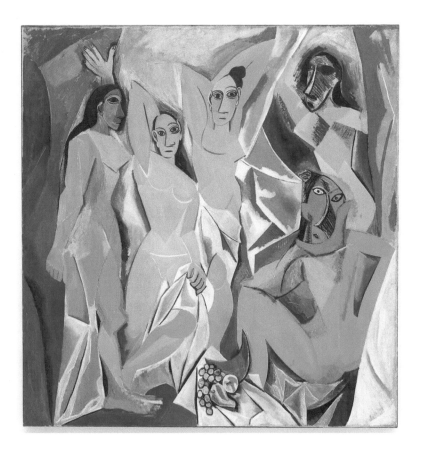

Figure 8.28 Picasso, Demoiselles d'Avignon (1907)

first decades of the twentieth, he was the most public player in a period famous for experimentation in all the arts. So public and so successful was he that experiment itself became one of the modern connotations of art. Picasso's Cubism, a misleading term for the initial, direct, "analytic" fragmentation, and the subsequent, more playful and more "synthetic" manipulation of the human figure and all subjects, combines multiple points of view in a single image, a practice as old as ancient Egypt and Mesopotamia. On the stage prepared by Cezanne, the Cubist splaying of form into time-lapse record was, among other things, a direct response to the invention of cinema—the exact same interval had existed between the invention of photography and the Realist movement. Since the Renaissance, artificial perspective required the implied or actual immobilization of the subject and the viewer (as in photography); Cubism (like film) granted movement to both. Cubism is perhaps most interesting when viewed within, rather than in opposition to, the larger tradition of representational art.

The same could be said for early twentieth-century abstract art, overlapping as it does (especially in the person of Wassily Kandinsky, whose forays into "pure abstraction" took place at the same time as the Cubist experiments) with the less easily defined Expressionism. By no means the least experimental, but not necessarily the most radical, figure at this dynamic and liberated juncture was Marcel Duchamp, from whom the modern concept of conceptual art, sometimes called Conceptualism, flowed. Downgrading the physical making of objects or images and elevating the idea which is their origin and true content or function, Duchamp was, like Brunelleschi five hundred years earlier, inventing a new perspective. The ready-made urinal that Duchamp purchased, named *Fountain*, signed and dated "R. Mutt 1917," and submitted to an exhibition at the Society of Independent Artists in New York that year, was interpreted then and now in widely divergent ways, and that was clearly the artist's intention. In teasing or taunting the viewer, in asking old questions in a new way (What is art? What is the role of the artist?), *Fountain* at once announced and summarized Conceptualism.

To recapitulate, we find at the end of the nineteenth century the rise and proliferation of the "ism" as a way of thinking about, classifying, and assimilating the innovative—or, to use the universally approved but variously interpreted term drawn

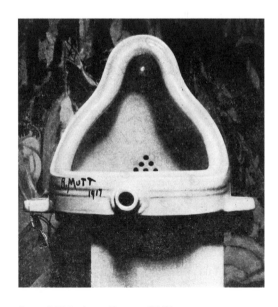

Figure 8.29 Duchamp, Fountain (1917)

suggestively from the military vocabulary, the *avant-garde*—in art and artistic movements. Classicism there had ALWAYS been; then there was the rather ostentatious alternative of Romanticism. But this dichotomy, however new it may have seemed, was to a large degree a restatement of the old debate between Athens and Pergamon, between Rome and Venice, *disegno* and *colore*, the rational and the emotional. Realism gauchely disrupted the debate, and the old timers, both Neoclassicists and Romanticists, for all their loud and ostensible differences, shared the outrage. But Realism, for all its newness, and the new technologies, was by no means entirely new. And Impressionism, for all its suspect lack of traditional finish and its apparent laziness (good artists used to finish their pictures, now we have to do that with our eyes ... and I can still see the brushstrokes ...) retained more than a strain of adherence to the representational, and in fact the Realist, agenda. Furthermore, reality itself was a moving target; in other words, as we have seen, Van Gogh's reality was not the same as Gauguin's. Symbolism, Futurism, Vorticism, Constructivism, Expressionism, Surrealism—the rapid rise and fall[9] of these movements signifies, beyond their respective intentions and effects, the complete fracturing of the authority of tradition. Art is no longer to be associated with an era or a movement, but is reinvented by the individual, and even, perhaps, in each individual work.

Which brings us from the Modern right up to the living Now.

---

9   But of course they never entirely fall, traces of these as of all widespread movements tending to survive or to be revived.

Epilogue

Individualism and Globalism (Really, Still, Romanticism)

If it is difficult to define the Modern World, that is nothing compared to characterizing concisely the art of the past hundred years. The trauma of World War I sent all the latest European "isms"—and their offshoots in the United States, which was, after all, still very much the clinging child of European culture—wobbling on their respective axes. In effect, the artists' laboratories shut down. The initial aftermath of the war saw a temporary retrenchment, and a complete rethinking of the nature and purpose of art in the face of the irreligious nothingness, personal or global, raised by, and remaining as the specter of, the first global conflict. The "look" of this period was, generally speaking, a conservative one, and as such was destined to fracture and give way, again, to even more daring experimentation which was magnified tenfold after World War Two, when New York became (thanks both to the maturing sensibilities of American intellectuals and the large-scale emigration of Europeans) the new center of culture in the West. The possibility of complete annihilation, whether through global war or global warming, brings a new urgency to the old concept of the adversarial relationship between the individual and the unknown and negative forces of nature, especially human nature. In this we recognize a restatement of the Romantic perspective.

An icon of Romanticism by the German painter, Caspar David Friedrich, represents a *Monk by the Sea* (1809). Like other Romantic images, this work allegorizes the human presence among the larger forces of an inscrutable nature;

Figure 8.30 Friedrich, Monk by the Sea (1809)

it also invites us to consider the monumentality and mystery of the external universe as metaphors for the interior self—the conjoined mind, heart, and soul of the individual. And if, as we are wont, we speculate further, we may see in this image yet another meta-commentary on artistic creation. That is, we may ask, what do we find at the shore, and what do we leave there? We can find literally anything on a beach, but there is one thing we are almost bound to leave behind: a footprint. Is a footprint art? A footprint is a record of existence, including detailed information as to its maker's size, age, and direction. It is also a record of impact, as a result of which the earth is changed, and of movement—so it's also narrative. It is self-expression in its simplest, most physical form. In which sense it is also a self-portrait. The footprint, inevitably maintaining its connection to the individual belonging to the foot, is a charged *presence*. Because a footprint implies a body, it is figurative; because it implies three-dimensional space, it evokes a context, a scape. And for these and other reasons, the footprint is like the *Monk by the Sea*.

But we must acknowledge that whereas most footprints are accidental, the painting by Friedrich is absolutely not. Our definition of art constantly brings us back to subjective questions of consciousness (the consciousness of the maker marking the boundaries of the work and its content, and the consciousness of the viewer processing and assessing it) and the complexity of decisions reflected in the result. Without evidence that these questions have been addressed, a footprint remains just that: evidence, and nothing more.

To return to our monk by the sea. Why is he there, and what is he doing? Whichever way he is looking—it is ambiguous in the image—he is confronted by the visible, if indistinctly blended, elements of a vast, an overwhelming, world, and this is a situation most of us can relate to. If there is something suggesting the primeval in this seascape, there is also, perhaps naturally, something apocalyptic, or at least suggesting an aftermath. After confusion, after the dark, after and out of the chaos that reveals itself, if only as a thought, in every human life on a daily basis, there is creation. Whichever way you look you are confronted by the speaking proofs of that; whichever direction you turn is a spirited prospect.

This epilogue, like the proudly lightweight survey it completes, is, in fact, a foreword.

Forward!

For Further Reading

I nterested students are, as always, encouraged to seek out other voices and points of view in their ongoing exploration of the history of art. The standard surveys in English, however daunting in weight and price, nevertheless provide wonderful, time-honored contributions to the introductory discussion, and we honor them, too. They are Helen Gardner's *Art through the Ages*, H. W. Janson's *History of Art*, Laurie Schneider Adams' *Art across Time*, Marilyn Stokstad's *Art History*, and Hugh Honour's and John Fleming's *The Visual Arts: A History*. Most of these are regularly revised, updated, and republished, sometimes under separate titles that reflect somewhat more selective subjects (Western as opposed to global art, for instance, or pre- or post-Renaissance as opposed to the entire history of art).

Aside from the standard surveys, a list of some of our favorite secondary (though still basic and highly accessible) resources would begin with the following, and continue ad infinitum: Jeffrey Hurwit's *The Art and Culture of Early Greece, 1100-480 B. C.*; Vincent Scully's *The Earth, the Temple, and the Gods*; George Hersey's *The Lost Meaning of Classical Architecture*; Jerome Pollitt's *Art and Experience in Classical Greece*; John Boardman's *Greek Art*; William MacDonald's *The Architecture of the Roman Empire*; Diana Kleiner's *Roman Sculpture*; Frank Brown's *Roman Architecture*; John Lowden's *Early Christian and Byzantine Art*; Whitney Stoddard's *Art and Architecture in Medieval France*; Erwin Panofsky's *Gothic Art and Scholasticism*; Emile Mâle's *The Gothic Image*; Otto von Simson's *The Gothic Cathedral*; Frederick Hartt's *Italian Renaissance Art*; James Snyder's *Northern Renaissance Art*; Michael Baxandall's *Painting and Experience in Fifteenth-Century Italy: A Primer in the Social History of Pictorial Style*; John Pope-Hennessy's

Italian Gothic Sculpture, Italian Renaissance Sculpture, and *Italian High Renaissance and Baroque Sculpture* (3); S. J. Freedberg's *Painting in Italy, 1500-1600;* Linda Murray's *High Renaissance and Mannerism;* E. Panofsky's *Studies in Iconology;* S. J. Freedberg's *Circa 1600: A Revolution of Style in Italian Painting;* R. Wittkower's *Art and Architecture in Italy, 1600-1750;* Metropolitan Museum of Art, *The Age of Caravaggio* (exhibition catalogue); Philip Conisbee's *Painting in Eighteenth-Century France;* Michael Levey's *Rococo to Revolution;* George Heard Hamilton's *19th and 20th Century Art;* Linda Nochlin's *Realism;* Vincent Scully's *Architecture* and *Modern Architecture.* Like the standard surveys, many of these works continue to be updated and revised, and each represents a supremely intelligent and engaging invitation to the larger conversation.

Image Credits

Chapter 1

Figure 1.1 Blue Bower Bird. Copyright © 2010 by User:Summ / Wikimedia Commons / CC BY-SA 3.0.

Figure 1.2 "Venus" of Willendorf. Copyright © 2008 by Don Hitchcock / CC BY-SA 3.0.

Figure 1.3 Lascaux Cave Painting. Copyright © 2005 by User:Peter80 / Wikimedia Commons / CC BY-SA 3.0.

Figure 1.4 Palette of Narmer. Copyright in the Public Domain.

Figure 1.5 Pyramids at Giza. Copyright © 2006 by Marion Golsteijn / CC BY-SA 3.0.

Figure 1.6 Menkaure and Khamerernebty. Copyright © 2010 by User:Calliopejen1 / Wikimedia Commons / CC BY-SA 3.0.

Figure 1.7 Ramses II at Abu Simbel. Copyright © 2010 by User:Asoka / Wikimedia Commons / CC BY-SA 3.0.

Figure 1.8 Mortuary Temple of Hatshepsut (fifteenth century BC). Copyright © 2011 by Dan Lundberg / CC BY-SA 2.0.

Figure 1.9 Hatshepsut. Copyright © 2006 by Keith Schengili-Roberts / CC BY-SA 3.0.

Figure 1.10 Ti Hippopotamus Hunting Copyright in the Public Domain.

Figure 1.11 Nefertiti. Copyright © 2006 by Angelo Atzei / CC BY-SA 2.5.

Figure 1.12 Akhenaten and his Family. Copyright © 2008 by User:Gerbil / Wikimedia Commons / CC BY-SA 3.0.

Figure 1.13 Ziggurat at Uruk. Copyright © 2006 by Michael Lubinski / CC BY-SA 2.0.

Figure 1.14 Alabaster Vase from Uruk (detail). Copyright © 2013 by User:Mbzt / Wikimedia Commons / CC BY 3.0.

Figure 1.15 Goddess from Uruk. Copyright in the Public Domain.

Figure 1.16 Sumerian Priest from Tel Asmar. Copyright © 2005 by Xuan Che / CC BY 2.0.

Figure 1.17 Standard of Ur. Copyright in the Public Domain.

Figure 1.18 Sounding Board of a Lyre (detail). Copyright in the Public Domain.

Figure 1.20 Victory Stele of Naram-Sin. Copyright © 2007 by User:Rama / Wikimedia Commons / CC BY-SA 2.0 FR.

Figure 1.21 Gudea of Lagash. Marie-Lan Nguyen / Wikimedia Commons / Public Domain.

Figure 1.22 Stele of Hammurabi. Copyright © 2011 by User:Mbzt / Wikimedia Commons / CC BY 3.0.

Figure 1.23 Hittite Lion Gate at Boghazkoy, Turkey. Copyright © 2001 by User:China_Crisis / Wikimedia Commons / CC BY-SA 2.0

Figure 1.24 Assyrian Lamassu. Copyright © 2005 by Xuan Che / CC BY 2.0..

Figure 1.25 Dying Lioness from Ninevah. Copyright © 2005 by Matt Neale / CC BY 2.0.

Figure 1.26 Cycladic Female. Copyright © 2008 by User:Prof_saxx / Wikimedia Commons / CC BY-SA 3.0.

Figure 1.27 Kamares Ware. Copyright © 2010 by User:Janmad / Wikimedia Commons / CC BY-SA 3.0.

Figure 1.28 Octopus Vas. Copyright © 2009 by Wolfgang Sauber / CC BY-SA 3.0.

Figure 1.29 Palace at Knossos. Copyright © 2007 by User:Yqqy / Wikimedia Commons / CC BY-SA 3.0.

Figure 1.30 "Toreador" Fresco. Copyright in the Public Domain.

Figure 1.31 Detail, Hagia Triada Sarcophagus. Copyright © 2012 by Olaf Tausch / CC BY 3.0.

Figure 1.32 Snake Goddesses. Copyright © 2010 by User:Edisonblus / Wikimedia Commons / CC BY-SA 3.0.

Figure 1.33 Lion Gate at Mycenae. Copyright © 2008 by Andreas Trepte / CC BY-SA 2.5.

Figure 1.34 "Treasury of Atreus". Copyright in the Public Domain.

Figure 1.35 Mycenaean Gold Mask. Copyright © 2010 by Xuan Che / CC BY 2.0.

Chapter 2

Figure 2.3 Peplos Kore. Copyright © 2007 by User:Marsyas / Wikimedia Commons / CC BY-SA 2.5.

Figure 2.4 Anavysos "Kroisos" Kouros. Copyright © 2012 by User:Xinstalker / Italian Wikipedia / CC BY-SA 3.0.

Figure 2.5 Kritios Youth. Copyright © 2007 by User:Marsyas / Wikimedia Commons / CC BY-SA 2.5.

Figure 2.6 Fallen Warrior from the West Pediment, Temple of Aphaia, Aegina. User:Tetraktys / Wikimedia Commons / Public Domain.

Figure 2.7 Fallen Warrior from the East Pediment, Temple of Aphaia, Aegina. Copyright © 2009 by User:Petropoxy (Lithoderm Proxy) / Wikimedia Commons / CC BY-SA 3.0.

Figure 2.8 "Hera I", Paestum. Copyright © 2013 by Norbert Nagel / Wikimedia Commons / CC BY-SA 3.0.

Figure 2.9 "Hera II", Paestum. Copyright © 2013 by Norbert Nagel / Wikimedia Commons / CC BY-SA 3.0.

Figure 2.10 Acropolis, Athens. Copyright © 2006 by User:LennieZ / Wikimedia Commons / CC BY-SA 3.0.

Figure 2.11 Centauromachy, Metope from the Parthenon. Copyright © 2012 by Adam Carr / CC BY-SA 3.0.

Figure 2.12 Centauromachy, Metope from the Parthenon. Copyright © 2007 by Marie-Lan Nguyen / CC BY 2.5.

Figure 2.13 Parthenon East Pediment: Hestia, Dione, Aphrodite(?).Copyright © 2007 by Marie-Lan Nguyen / CC BY 2.5.

Figure 2.14 Panathenaic Procession, Parthenon Frieze (detail). Copyright © 2009 by User:Tetraktys / Wikimedia Commons / CC BY-SA 3.0.

Figure 2.15a Exekias, Achilles and Ajax Gaming. Copyright © 2013 by User:Sailko / Wikimedia Commons / CC BY-SA 3.0.

Figure 2.15b Andokides Painter, Achilles and Ajax Gaming. Copyright © by Museum of Fine Arts Boston.

Figure 2.16 Doryphoros of Polykleitos. Copyright © 2012 by User:Tetraktys / Wikimedia Commons / CC BY 2.5.

Figure 2.17 Praxiteles' Hermes and the Infant Dionysus. Copyright © 2009 by User:tilo 2005 / Flickr / CC BY-SA 2.0.

Figure 2.18 Praxiteles' Aphrodite of Knidos. Marie-Lan Nguyen / Wikimedia Commons / Public Domain.

Figure 2.19 Apoxyomenos of Lysippos. Copyright © 2010 by User:Sailko / Wikimedia Commons / CC BY-SA 3.0.

Figure 2.20 Alexander Bust. Marie-Lan Nguyen / Wikimedia Commons / Public Domain.

Figure 2.21 Dying Gaul of Epigonos. Copyright © 2007 by User: Jean-Christophe Benoist / Wikimedia Commons / CC BY-SA 3.0.

Figure 2.22 Laocoon. Marie-Lan Nguyen / Wikimedia Commons / Public Domain.

Figure 2.23 Bronze Boxer. Marie-Lan Nguyen / Wikimedia Commons / Public Domain.

Figure 2.24 Polykleitos the Younger, Theater at Epidauros. Copyright © 2008 by User:Sirabder87 / Wikimedia Commons / CC BY-SA 3.0.

Figure 2.25 Theodoros of Phokaia, Tholos at Delphi. Copyright © 2007 by User:Kufoleto / Wikimedia Commons / CC BY 3.0.

Chapter 3

Figure 3.1 Etruscan Statue of Apollo from Veii. Copyright © by Araldo de Luca / Corbis.

Figure 3.2 Etruscan Tomb of the Leopards, Tarquinia. Copyright in the Public Domain.

Figure 3.4 Etruscan She-Wolf. Marie-Lan Nguyen / Wikimedia Commons / Public Domain.

Figure 3.5 Roman Patrician. Copyright in the Public Domain. Copyright in the Public Domain.

Figure 3.6 Temple of Portunus. Copyright © 2005 by Son of Groucho / Flickr / CC BY 2.0.

Figure 3.7 Augustus Pontifex Maximus. Ryan Freisling / Public Domain.

Figure 3.8 Augustus Prima Porta. Copyright © 2007 by Till Niermann / CC BY-SA 3.0.

Figure 3.9 Ara Pacis. Copyright © 2010 by User:Quinok / Wikimedia Commons / CC BY-SA 3.0.

Figure 3.10 Colosseum. Copyright © 2007 by User:Diliff / Wikimedia Commons / CC BY-SA 2.5.

Figure 3.11 Still life with glass bowl of fruit and vases. Copyright in the Public Domain.

Figure 3.12 Aquaduct, Pont-du-gard. Copyright © 2004 by User:Prioryman / Wikimedia Commons / CC BY-SA 3.0.

Figure 3.13 The Sack of Jerusalem from the Arch of Titus. Copyright © 2008 by User:Steerpike / Wikimedia Commons / CC BY 3.0.

Figure 3.14 The Pantheon, Etching by Giovanni Battista Piranesi. Francesco Piranesi / Public Domain.

Figure 3.15 Forum of Trajan. User:MM / Wikimedia Commons / Public Domain.

Figure 3.16 Bust of Antinoös. User:Bibi Saint-Pol / Wikimedia Commons / Public Domain.

Figure 3.17 Equestrian Statue of Marcus Aurileus. Ludwig Schneider / Public Domain.

Figure 3.18 Tetrarchs. User:O.Mustafin / Wikimedia Commons / Public Domain.

Figure 3.19 Arch of Constantine. Copyright © 2005 by User:Alexander Z. / Wikimedia Commons / CC BY-SA 3.0.

Figure 3.20 Colossal Constantine (detail). Copyright © 2007 by User: Jean-Christophe Benoist / Wikimedia Commons / CC BY-SA 3.0.

Figure 3.21 Christ as the Good Shepard, Catacomb of Saint Callixtus. Copyright in the Public Domain.

Figure 3.22 St. Peter's Basilica (plan). Copyright in the Public Domain.

Figure 3.23 Santa Costanza (detail). Copyright © 2003 by User:emv / Wikimedia Commons / CC BY-SA 3.0.

Figure 3.24 Sarcophagus of Junius Bassus. Copyright © 2008 by Giovanni Dall'Orto. Reprinted with permission.

Chapter 4

Figure 4.1 Barberini Diptych. Marie-Lan Nguyen / Wikimedia Commons / Public Domain.

Figure 4.2 Hagia Sophia. Wilhelm Lübke / Public Domain.

Figure 4.3 Interior, Hagia Sophia. User:MarkusMark / Wikimedia Commons / Public Domain.

Figure 4.4 Interior, Hagia Sophia Cupola. Copyright © 2011 by Guillaume Piolle / CC BY 3.0.

Figure 4.6 San Vitale. Copyright in the Public Domain.

Figure 4.7 Justinian Mosaic. Copyright in the Public Domain.

Figure 4.8 Theodora Mosaic. Copyright in the Public Domain.

Figure 4.9 Mary as Theotokos, St Catherine Monastery. Copyright in the Public Domain.

Figure 4.10 St. Catherine Monastery, Sinai. User:Egghead06 / Wikimedia Commons / Public Domain.

Figure 4.11 Theotokos, Hagia Sofia. Copyright © 2006 by Giovanni Dall'Orto / CC BY-SA 2.5 IT.

Figure 4.12 Dafni. Copyright in the Public Domain.

Figure 4.13 Pala d'Oro, San Marco. User:Aleister Crowley / Wikimedia Commons / Public Domain

Figure 4.15 Sutton Hoo Purse Cover. Copyright © 2010 by Rob Roy / CC BY-SA 2.5.

Figure 4.15a Sutton Hoo Purse Cover, with Detail. Copyright © 2010 by Rob Roy / CC BY-SA 2.5.

Figure 4.16 Head of the Tara Brooch. Copyright in the Public Domain.

Figure 4.17 Book of Kells, Chi Rho Page. Copyright in the Public Domain.

Figure 4.18 Lindisfarne Gospel, St. Matthew. Copyright in the Public Domain.

Figure 4.19 Coronation Gospel, St. Matthew. Copyright in the Public Domain.

Figure 4.20 Equestrian Portrait of Charlemagne. Copyright © 2009 by User:World Imaging / Wikimedia Commons / CC BY-SA 3.0.

Figure 4.22 Aachen. Copyright in the Public Domain.

Figure 4.23 Interior, Palatine Chapel, Aachen. User:Zairon / Wikimedia Commons / Public Domain.

Chapter 5

Figure 5.17 Nicholas of Verdun Shrine of the Three Kings, Cologne. Copyright © 2006 by User:Amoli / pl.wikipedia / CC BY-SA 3.0.

Figure 5.20 Durham Cathedral. Copyright © 2010 by User:Oliver-Bonjoch / Wikimedia Commons / CC BY-SA 3.0.

Figure 5.22 Noyon Cathedral, plan. Copyright in the Public Domain.

Figure 5.26 St. Etienne at Caen. Copyright © 2007 by Snapshots of The Past / Flickr / CC BY-SA 2.0.

Figure 5.27 Notre Dame de Paris. Copyright © 2009 by User:Zuffe / Wikimedia Commons / CC BY-SA 3.0.

Figure 5.30 Chartres Cathedral. Copyright © 2009 by User:Zuffe / Wikimedia Commons / CC BY-SA 3.0.

Figure 5.31 Chartres Cathedral, plan. Eugène Viollet-le-Duc / Public Domain.

Figure 5.32 Chartres Cathedral, Interior. Copyright © 2008 by Paul M.R. Maeyaert / CC BY-SA 3.0.

Figure 5.34 Chartres Cathedral, Notre Dame de la Belle Verrière. Guillaume Piolle / Public Domain.

Figure 5.35 Chartres Cathedral, South Portal. Copyright © 2005 by User:Ttaylor / Wikimedia Commons / CC BY-SA 3.0.

Figure 5.36 North Porch Center. Copyright © 2005 by User:Ttaylor / Wikimedia Commons / CC BY-SA 3.0.

Figure 5.40 Gloucester Cathedral. Copyright © 2006 by Rob Coldwell / CC BY-SA 2.0.

Chapter 6

Figure 6.1 Cimabue's Madonna Enthroned with Saints. Cimabue / Public Domain.

Figure 6.2 Giotto's Ognissanti Madonna. Giotto / Public Domain.

Figure 6.3 Giotto, Scrovegni Chapel (detail). Giotto / Public Domain.

Figure 6.4 Meeting at the Golden Gate (Scrovegni Chapel detail). Giotto / Public Domain.

Figure 6.5 Brunelleschi's Sacrifice of Isaac. Copyright © 2009 by User:Sailko / Wikimedia Commons / CC BY-SA 3.0.

Figure 6.6 Ghiberti's Sacrifice of Isaac. Copyright © 2005 by User:Richardfabi / Wikimedia Commons / CC BY-SA 3.0.

Figure 6.7 Florence Baptistry Doors. Copyright © 2005 by Ricardo André Frantz / CC BY-SA 3.0.

Figure 6.8 Donatello's Gattamelata. Kjetil Ree / Public Domain.

Figure 6.9 Donatello, Saint George, detail. Copyright © 2009 by User:Sailko / Wikimedia Commons / CC BY-SA 3.0.

Figure 6.10 Donatello's David. Copyright © 2007 by Patrick A. Rodgers / CC BY-SA 2.0.

Figure 6.11 Masaccio's Pisa Polyptych Madonna and Child. Masaccio / Public Domain.

Figure 6.12 Masaccio, Expulsion from Eden. Masaccio / Public Domain.

Figure 6.13 Masaccio, The Tribute Money. Masaccio / Public Domain.

Figure 6.14 Florence Duomo. Copyright © 2006 by User:Sailko / Wikimedia Commons CC BY-SA 3.0.

Figure 6.15 Brunelleschi, Pazzi Chapel, cupola. Copyright © 2007 by User:Gesu / Wikimedia Commons / CC BY-SA 3.0.

Figure 6.16 Hubert and Jan van Eyck, Ghent Altarpiece, closed. Copyright © 2013 by Paul M.R. Maeyaert / CC BY-SA 3.0.

Figure 6.17 Ghent Altarpiece, open. Jan van Eyck / Public Domain.

Figure 6.18 Jan van Eyck, Rolin Madonna. Jan van Eyck / Public Domain.

Figure 6.19 Rogier van der Weyden Madonna with Saint Luke. Rogier van der Weyden / Public Domain.

Figure 6.20 Botticelli's Adoration of the Three Kings. Sandro Botticelli / Public Domain.

Figure 6.21 Leonardo's Adoration of the Magi. Leonardo da Vinci / Public Domain.

Figure 6.22 Botticelli's Birth of Venus. Sandro Botticelli / Public Domain.

Figure 6.23 Leonardo, The Last Supper. Leonardo da Vinci / Public Domain.

Figure 6.24 Leonardo, La Gioconda (Mona Lisa). Leonardo da Vinci / Public Domain.

Figure 6.25 Michelangelo's Rome Pietà . Copyright © 2005 by User:Glimz / Wikimedia Commons / CC BY-SA 3.0.

Figure 6.26 Michelangelo's David. Copyright © 2005 by David Gaya / CC BY-SA 3.0.

Figure 6.27 Michelangelo, Sistine Chapel Ceiling. Copyright © 2008 by Patrick Landy / CC BY 3.0.

Figure 6.28 Sistine Chapel. Copyright © 2007 by Aaron Logan / CC BY 2.5.

Figure 6.29 Sistine Chapel Last Judgment. Michelangelo / Public Domain.

Figure 6.30 Michelangelo, Rondanini Pietà, Copyright © 2005 by User:Paolo da Reggio / Wikimedia Commons / CC BY-SA 3.0.

Figure 6.31 Alberti, Basilica of Sant'Andrea, Mantova. Copyright © 2007 by User:Tango7174 / Wikimedia Commons / CC BY-SA 3.0.

Figure 6.32 Raphael, The School of Athens. Raphael / Public Domain.

Figure 6.33 Raphael, Portrait of Baldassare Castiglione. Raphael / Public Domain.

Figure 6.34 Dürer's Self Portrait at 26 . Albrecht Dürer / Public Domain.

Figure 6.35 Dürer's The Last Supper. Albrecht Dürer / Public Domain.

Figure 6.36 Raphael, The Transfiguration. Raphael / Public Domain.

Figure 6.37 Altdorfer, The Battle of Issus. Albrecht Altdorfer / Public Domain.

Figure 6.38 Bosch, The Garden of Earthly Delights. Hieronymous Bosch / Public Domain.

Figure 6.39 Giovanni Bellini, San Giobbe (Saint Job) Altarpiece. Giovanni Bellini / Public Domain.

Figure 6.40 Giorgione, The Tempest. Giorgione / Public Domain.

Figure 6.41 Titian's Assumption of the Virgin. Titian / Public Domain.

Figure 6.42 Titian, The Rape of Europa. Titian / Public Domain.

Chapter 7

Figure 7.1 Caravaggio, The Crucifixion of Saint Peter. Caravaggio / Public Domain.

Figure 7.2 Boucher, Madame de Pompadour. François Boucher / Public Domain.

Figure 7.3 Annibale Carracci, The Loves of the Gods. Annibale Carracci / Public Domain.

Figure 7.4 Caravaggio, Basket of Fruit (Ambrosiana Still Life). Caravaggio / Public Domain.

Figure 7.5 Caravaggio's Judith Beheading Holofernes. Caravaggio / Public Domain.

Figure 7.6 Artemisia Gentileschi's Judith Beheading Holofernes. Artemisia Gentileschi / Public Domain.

Figure 7.7 Bernini, Apollo and Daphne. Copyright © 2007 by Jean-Pierre Dalbéra / CC BY 2.0.

Figure 7.8 Bernini, The Ecstasy of Saint Theresa. Copyright © 2009 byUser:Welleschik / Wikimedia Commons / CC BY-SA 3.0.

Figure 7.9 Palladio, Church of the Redeemer. Copyright © 2007 by Hans A. Rosbach / CC BY-SA 3.0.

Figure 7.10 Borromini, San Carlino alle Quattro Fontane. Copyright © 2009 by User:Welleschik / Wikimedia Commons / CC BY-SA 3.0.

Figure 7.11 San Carlino, plan. Copyright © 2009 by User:Afernand74 / Wikimedia Commons / CC BY-SA 3.0.

Figure 7.12 Borromini, Sant'Ivo alla Sapienza. Copyright © 2006 by User:Helix84 / Wikimedia Commons / CC BY-SA 3.0.

Figure 7.13 Rubens, Prometheus Bound. Peter Paul Rubens / Public Domain.

Figure 7.14 Rembrandt, The Blinding of Samson. Rembrandt / Public Domain.

Figure 7.15 Rembrandt's Self Portrait at a Window. Rembrandt / Public Domain.

Figure 7.16 Rembrandt, Bathsheba. Rembrandt / Public Domain.

Figure 7.17 Velasquez, Las Meninas. Diego Velázquez / Public Domain.

Figure 7.18 Poussin, Saint John on Patmos. Nicolas Poussin / Public Domain.

Figure 7.19 Vermeer, The Concert. Johannes Vermeer / Public Domain.

Figure 7.20 Bernini, St Peter's Square. Copyright © 2011 by Jean-Pol GRANDMONT / CC BY-SA 3.0.

Figure 7.21 Versailles. Pierre Patel / Public Domain.

Figure 7.22 Boucher's The Rape of Europa. François Boucher / Public Domain.

Figure 7.23 William Hogarth, The Painter and His Pug. William Hogarth / Public Domain.

Figure 7.24 Copley, A Boy with a Flying Squirrel (Henry Pelham). John Singleton Copley / Public Domain.

Figure 7.26 Jefferson, Monticello. Copyright © 2010 by User:YF12s / Wikimedia Commons / CC BY-SA 3.0.

Figure 7.27 Palladio, Villa Capra. Copyright © 2007 by Hans A. Rosbach / CC BY-SA 3.0.

Figure 7.28 Vigée-Lebrun, Marie Antoinette and Her Children. Louise Élisabeth Vigée Le Brun / Public Domain.

Chapter 8

Figure 8.1 David, Oath of the Horatii. Jacques-Louis David / Public Domain.

Figure 8.2 Goya, Of What Ill Will He Die? Francisco Goya / Public Domain.

Figure 8.3 Goya's Self Portrait with Dr. Arrieta. Francisco Goya / Public Domain.

Figure 8.4 Gericault's Raft of the Medusa. Jean-Louis André Théodore Géricault / Public Domain.

Figure 8.5 Delacroix, Dante and Virgil in Hell. Eugène Delacroix, "[image]: Dante and Virgil in Hell," http://en.wikipedia.org/wiki/File:Delacroix_barque_of_dante_1822_louvre_189cmx246cm_950px.jpg, ~1. Copyright © 1822 by . Reprinted with permission.

Figure 8.7 Turner, Rain, Steam and Speed. J. M. W. Turner / Public Domain.

Figure 8.8 Ingres, Princesse de Broglie. Jean-Auguste-Dominique Ingres / Public Domain.

Figure 8.9 Matthew Brady, Mary Todd Lincoln. Mathew Brady / Public Domain.

Figure 8.10 Daguerre, Shells and Fossils. Louis Daguerre / Public Domain.

Figure 8.11 Courbet, Burial at Ornans. Gustave Courbet / Public Domain.

Figure 8.12 Manet, Olympia. Édouard Manet / Public Domain.

Figure 8.13 Monet, Impression, Sunrise. Claude Monet / Public Domain.

Figure 8.14 Canova, Perseus with the Head of Medusa. Copyright © 2010 by Marie-Lan Nguyen / CC BY 3.0.

Figure 8.15 Rodin, Monument to Balzac. Edward Steichen / Public Domain.

Figure 8.16 Degas, At the Louvre-The Painter (Mary Cassatt). Edgar Degas / Public Domain.

Figure 8.17 Cassatt, Maternal Caress. Mary Cassatt / Public Domain.

Figure 8.18 Church, Sunset Across the Hudson Valley. Frederic Edwin Church / Public Domain.

Figure 8.19 Tanner, Spinning by Firelight-The Boyhood of George Washington Gray. Henry Ossawa Tanner / Public Domain.

Figure 8.20 Cezanne, Boy in a Red Vest. Paul Cézanne / Public Domain.

Figure 8.21 Titian, Portrait of Ranuccio Farnese. Titian / Public Domain.

Figure 8.22 H.H. Richardson, Marshall Field Warehouse Store 1885–87 (demolished 1930; 130ft high). Copyright in the Public Domain.

Figure 8.23 Michelozzo, Palazzo Medici-Riccardi begun 1445 (c. 71ft high). User:Gryffindor / Wikimedia Commons / Public Domain.

Figure 8.24 Eiffel Tower. Théophile Féau / Public Domain.

Figure 8.25 Ferris Wheel. Copyright in the Public Domain.

Figure 8.26 Vincent van Gogh, Starry Night. Vincent van Gogh / Public Domain.

Figure 8.27 Paul Gauguin, Soyez Amoureuses Vous Serez Heureuses. Paul Gauguin / Public Domain.

Figure 8.28 Picasso, Demoiselles d'Avignon. Pablo Picasso / Public Domain.

Figure 8.29 Duchamp, Fountain. Marcel Duchamp / Public Domain.

Figure 8.30 Friedrich, Monk by the Sea. Caspar David Friedrich / Public Domain.

CPSIA information can be obtained
at www.ICGtesting.com
Printed in the USA
LVHW07n2030030818
585878LV00008B/28/P

* 9 7 8 1 6 3 1 8 9 9 3 0 0 *